THE PASTOR'S
FIRST LOVE

THE PASTOR'S FIRST LOVE

And Other Essays on a High and Holy Calling

Donald N. Bastian

Toronto and New York

Copyright © 2013 by Donald N. Bastian

All rights reserved. No part of this publication may be reproduced or transmitted in any form or by any means, electronic or mechanical, including photocopying, recording, or any information storage and retrieval system, without permission in writing from the publisher.

Published in 2013 by
BPS Books
Toronto & New York
bpsbooks.com
A division of Bastian Publishing Services Ltd.

ISBN 978-1-927483-46-6

Cataloguing-in-Publication Data
available from Library and Archives Canada.

All scripture quotations, unless otherwise indicated, are taken from the Holy Bible, New International Version®, NIV®. Copyright ©1973, 1978, 1984, 2011 by Biblica, Inc.™ Used by permission of Zondervan. All rights reserved worldwide. www.zondervan.com The "NIV" and "New International Version" are trademarks registered in the United States Patent and Trademark Office by Biblica, Inc.™

Cover design: Gnibel
Text design and typesetting: Daniel Crack, Kinetics Design, kdbooks.ca

*To our dear children, Carolyn, Donald, and Robert,
and to our special needs son, John David;
and to the three married children's spouses,
Doug, June, and Jan, all fellow believers,
all active in the world and in the church,
and all having blessed us,
each in a unique way*

CONTENTS

Preface ix
Introduction 1

PART I
THE PASTOR AS SHEPHERD

1 The Pastor's First Love 5
2 What Does It Mean to Be Ordained? 16
3 A Week in the Life of Pastor John Doe 34
4 Exploring the Pastoral Task from 30,000 Feet 43
5 Seven Characteristics of Effective Pastors 57
6 Ten Tips for Young and Soon-to-Be Pastors 73
7 Your First Thirty Days at a New Church 76
8 The Blessing of Church Order 81

PART II
THE PASTOR AS PREACHER

9 What Congregations Want Most in a Pastor 87
10 How One Preacher Prepares a Sermon 92
11 Six Questions Preachers Can Ask Themselves About Their Sermons 103
12 Writing Your Way to Clearer Preaching 112
13 Advice I Have Gathered About Preaching 121

PART III
THE PASTOR AS WORSHIP LEADER

14	Leading Worship	131
15	The Elements of Worship	148
16	We Cannot Avoid Worshipping	158
17	Three Ways We Worship God	161
18	Some Pointers on Aesthetics in Worship	170
19	The Elements of a Worship Service	176
20	Serving Holy Communion	194
21	What Makes a Funeral Christian?	197
22	Weddings: A Pastor's Great Privilege	201
23	The Hallmarks of a Christian Wedding	215
24	Standing Up for Marriage	220
25	Preventing Shaky Marriages	227
26	The Case for Church Weddings	233
27	Conducting a Wedding Rehearsal	239

PART IV
THE PASTOR AS PROFESSIONAL

28	Ministerial Ethics	249
29	Honesty in the Pulpit	255
30	Sexual Integrity in the Ministry	261
31	What Do Table Manners Have to Do with It?	281

Conclusion: From a Kitchen Chair to the Pulpit		287

PREFACE

FOR more than a dozen years I've been going twice a year to Northeastern Seminary on the campus of Roberts Wesleyan College, Rochester, New York. Each time, I meet for a four-hour session with a class of seminarians. My assignment is to share pastoral insights that I've gained across a lifetime of ministry, first as a pastor and then as an overseer of pastors: we talk about such issues as what makes a pastor effective, how to conduct a wedding rehearsal, and ethics in the pastoral life.

The students represent a broad spectrum of ages and experience. Some are already ordained and are working to complete a Master of Divinity degree. Some are recent college graduates. They also represent a broad spectrum of church traditions, from Eastern Orthodox to Free Methodist to Pentecostal to Independent. Without fail, the class is always interactive and lively. The students are eager to hear what pastoral life is like from the viewpoint of a practitioner of many years. The hours we spend together fly by.

I sometimes share how my own awareness of God's call to pastoral ministry began soon after my conversion to Christ at sixteen years of age. At first it was more like a generic call: simply a sense that I should give my life to full-time ministry. Only when I attended seminary more than a decade later did that call come into focus as a clear call to pastoral ministry. Starting with those seminary years I served three churches for a total of twenty-one years. First I served a student pastorate, then a growing mid-sized church in Western Canada, and then a college church in Illinois for thirteen years. In 1974 I was elected by my denomination to the office of bishop, a role that I held for nineteen years. Two decades have followed since retirement, during which time I have continued to preach, teach, and write.

During my more mature years of ministry, I committed to writing, for a variety of uses, some of my pastoral insights. After providing a collection of some of these to the students at Northeastern Seminary, as a basis for our discussions, I was inspired to write this more comprehensive book on pastoring.

I say "I was inspired," but I must add that members of my family also encouraged me in the writing. I would like to acknowledge them here.

In the narrative portion at the close of this book I include information about the contribution of Kathleen, my wife of sixty-five years, to our pastoral ministry together. She is not ordained, nor does she fancy herself a public speaker, though when asked to speak, she comes through with flying colors. But from our first pastoral assignment to the present she has stood ready to contribute from behind the scenes.

The congregations we ministered to have loved Kathleen for her faithfulness to the Lord and his people, her special ability to put an aesthetic touch on the everyday environment wherever we have gone, her culinary and administrative contributions to kitchen ministries, and her skill in teaching children.

Our best friends know that she is my behind-the-scenes coach on everything from preaching to appropriate dress and manners. Her standards have always been high and her commitment to my labors steady and unshakeable.

I also add a hearty word of gratitude to our children, for their loyal contribution to my ministry. Carolyn is now a retired schoolteacher, Don, a publisher and editor, and Robert, a laryngologist. John David is our special needs child, who has not been with us since he was three. The three older children experienced the usual bumps and scrapes that growing up delivers, forged their way into independent and wholesome adulthood, and in it all brought blessing to our home and the churches we served.

Similar recognition goes to their spouses, Doug, June, and Jan, respectively. Their commitment to Christ and his church, and their dedication to the Christian ideals we hold dear, have meant that their fingerprints, too, are on this book.

I express special appreciation to our son Don, for his coaching as I have drawn this book together. We share the same first name and essentially the same concerns for the well being of Christ's church, particularly for the enrichment of the pastoral function of preaching.

I am fully conscious of the limitations of what I have written. But I send it forth with the confidence that pastors and laypersons alike will find something in it to point them in a clearer direction, encourage greater diligence, or prompt heartfelt gratitude to God for the honor of serving him.

DONALD N. BASTIAN

INTRODUCTION

WHAT is the cornerstone of pastors' calling and work? Is it their enjoyment of, or excellence in, preaching, or pastoral care, or giving leadership to a company of the Lord's people? As important as these basic pastoral duties are, if they come first for pastors, their ministry at best will be worthy of a glowing obituary and at worst will lead to disillusionment. The stakes are simply too high for ministry to be powered by an inordinate love of self or even of one's calling. What is it, then? The cornerstone of all effective pastoral activity is the pastor's first love, a love for the Master, Jesus Christ.

My intention in this book is to inspire pastors young and old to a life of greater pastoral effectiveness, but only insofar as the impetus of what they achieve is their love for Jesus Christ. Loving him – or loving him back, really, because he loved us first – is what carries pastors through to the end of the race.

You will find in this book a collection of thoughts and convictions gathered across the years on the exercise of the pastoral office. Some of the subjects I take up may have become eclipsed in some evangelical gatherings, for example, the meaning and use of benedictions, or preparing oneself to serve holy communion, or giving the pastoral prayer its rightful place. I even have a piece on the "Amen" in worship.

In fact, the spread of material is organized under the

topics of the pastor as shepherd, preacher, worship leader, and professional. I conclude the book with a description of my call to the ministry and the basic facts of my ministry across a lifetime with my wife, Kathleen, who also was committed to this task.

I hope this book will fall into the hands of seminary students, or first-time pastors, or even seasoned pastors who, under the pressures of modern life, have lost their relish for their calling but carry on dutifully. It may even be helpful to bright-spirited young people not yet committed to the course God may be marking out for them and who wonder about the pastoral life as a vocation – a calling.

I hope it also falls into the hands of laypersons who want to understand the church better and who would profit from a glimpse behind the scenes at what pastoring is all about.

Whoever reads it, I pray that all of us will keep Jesus, our Lord, as our first love; I pray that this love will undergird everything we attempt for him.

PART I

THE PASTOR AS SHEPHERD

CHAPTER 1

The Pastor's First Love

THE pastor's first love is not a love for preaching or pastoral visitation or the administration of the church. The pastor's first love is a love for Jesus Christ.

I see this in the story of the disciples recorded at the end of the Gospel of John. The horror of the Crucifixion, only days behind them, is still in their minds. The reality of the Resurrection is just dawning on them; they are still uncertain whether it really happened. They haven't come to that place of exultant joy. And so here are seven of them, back where they started, toiling as fishermen.

Peter says, "I'm going fishing," and the others say, "We'll go, too."

And so as the night is coming on they get in a boat, all seven of them, push off, and disappear into the dusk. In the morning, when the light is beginning to dawn, the boat glides back toward shore, and in it are men who are tired and hungry and frustrated.

They see a strange person standing on the shore, who calls out to them, "Did you catch anything?"

They reply, "Nothing."

He says, "Put your net on the other side of the boat," which they do, and, writes John, immediately the net was

---

The baccalaureate sermon preached on May 19, 1991, at Asbury Theological Seminary in Wilmore, Kentucky.

filled so full that they couldn't pull it over the sides and into the boat.

While all this is going on they're glancing toward the person who seemed to know where the fish were, and it dawns on John first.

"It's the Lord," he says quietly to Peter.

Peter quickly grabs his over-garment – he's been fishing in his underwear – goes over the side of the boat, and, thigh deep, wades ashore.

The others bring the boat in, dragging the net behind them. And when they get there they see this fire and on it some bread and fish. And this person who has called them says, "Bring some more fish," which they do, and little by little the word is passed among them: "It's the Lord."

But, as I said, they haven't come to that place of abounding joy, where they're absolutely certain, so they sit for breakfast. It's very quiet. Not much is said. They steal sideways glances at him, and little by little, one at a time, their certainty grows.

This breakfast takes place on the west side of the lake. I visualize, nearby on the beach, an old, overturned boat that is no longer seaworthy. I imagine that some are standing, some sitting as the silent breakfast comes to a close.

Then Jesus slips up to Peter and says, "Simon, come walk with me."

They start in a northerly direction along the shore, and soon, after they've put one or two hundred feet between them and the other disciples – who are looking after the boat and the fish and the fire – Jesus faces Simon, puts his right hand on Simon's left shoulder, and, leaning toward him, says, "Simon, do you really love me more than these?"

When he says "these," he nods slightly over his shoulder to indicate these other fellows. Not long before, Simon had said, "The others may forsake you; I never will," and now Jesus, in this "closed class meeting," is asking, "Do you really love me more than these?"

Simon says, "Yes, Lord, I love you. You know that."

Jesus says, "Then feed my lambs."

They walk a few paces farther. With his hand on Simon's shoulder again, Jesus leans toward him and asks, "Simon, do you love me?"

Simon is a little taken aback, but by nature he does everything quickly, so he immediately answers, "Of course I love you."

Then Jesus broadens the assignment. He says, "Tend my sheep."

Now there's a longer silence; all that can be heard as they continue their walk is the lapping of the water on the sandy shore. Eventually Jesus asks, again, "Simon, do you really love me?"

By now Simon is hurt by this repetitive question. He's got something playing in his head; it's playing in Technicolor. It takes him back to the evening of Christ's passion when he let his Master down – dismally.

He says, "Lord, let's be candid with each other. You know everything. You know that I love you."

And, for this third time, Jesus adds, "Then feed my sheep."

Three times, "Do you love me?" Three times, the assignment, "Be a shepherd. Look after my followers."

The pastor's – the shepherd's – first love is a love for Jesus Christ.

~

Let me explain what I think Jesus is getting at here. Jesus is pressing Simon Peter with one question: Do you really love me? His question should not surprise us; he knows that Peter lives his life out of a flawed humanity. Go over the list of the disciples and consider their stories. Not one of them is a perfect specimen of humanity. Timothy, one of the most prominent New Testament pastors, struggled with timidity, which perhaps fed into psychosomatic problems. Add to the New Testament list the names of the early church fathers. All flawed.

We can add our own names to the list, too. We can add Bill, George, Betty, Mary, Don.

Don? Yes. Don.

I was assigned to my first church, a student pastorate, when I was twenty-seven years old, a church in the north end of Lexington, Kentucky. The appointment enabled me to attend Asbury Theological Seminary. Before that, I had not undergone any supervised pastoral training. And I had not experienced seminary.

In my teens I had gone to a Bible college. For about seven years I'd been a freelance youth speaker traveling here and there. I had some qualifications for that role: I was young. I was trim. I had thick shocks of wavy black hair. You must take that latter information on faith.

When I started as a youth speaker, I had one sermon. Then I had two, so I could speak in two services on a Sunday. One by one I added to the repertoire. When I had three or four, I could speak for a weekend. And eventually I had enough sermons to preach for a week.

I held meetings, and I tell you – modestly, I hope – that they were adequate sermons primarily for congregations of young people. They met the expectations of my role. I was expected to preach to people and invite them to do something, and with youthful vigor and fairly pointed preaching, the sermons "worked," by God's grace. People responded. We had energized weekends.

Now, as I sized up my first stationed pastoral assignment during my first few weeks that autumn, I decided that the people lacked Christian vigor. It seemed to me that the church needed an old-fashioned revival. I thought about my sermons. I dug them out and started to preach them, but they didn't work. I had yet to discover that Sunday morning is not youth camp. The people sat and blinked at me. They didn't come to the altar. I began to feel distress, unsure of what was going on.

One Sunday morning, a few Sundays into that first year, I once again delivered a youth camp sermon to little effect. Following the service, the congregation dispersed until there were only two people left in the little foyer of the church. I was one of them, and the other was Dr. W. C. Mavis of the seminary. I was sufficiently troubled that I asked him a question that gave him an opportunity to respond to my sermon. I can see him yet. He shook his head ever so slightly, pursed his lips a little, and said, "Pretty incisive, pretty incisive." Those few words were all I needed. I believe that was the day I converted from being a revivalist to being a pastor.

I knew I had goofed. And yet what saved me was not that I loved Christ out of a perfect humanity. The best I had given him that morning was the flawed effort of a flawed young man. What saved me in that hour was Christ's love coming at me directly and that love also coming at me indirectly through his loving servant. If my memory were strong enough I could probably recount scores of such bloopers across a lifetime of ministry. It is said that, when we boast that we have a clear conscience, we should really be saying we have a bad memory.

When Jesus talked to Simon, he knew he was talking to a man working out of a flawed humanity. It wasn't so long before this that Jesus had said to the disciples in a serious moment, "You're all going to run," and Peter had come forward saying, "Not I."

Peter remembered that bold assertion when Jesus asked his question three times, and he hurt because of it. And yet here before him was this same Master, not scolding him, not casting him off, but saying to him again, "Do you love me? Really love me? Then I've got a job for you. Feed my sheep."

The pastor's first love is a love for Jesus Christ.

~

I want to call one other thing to your attention: What was Jesus really asking Peter? I believe it was not so much that Peter love him as that he love him back.

Luke tells an aspect of this story that I wish John had captured. It seems to me to belong in John's story. Luke says that after Jesus was arrested and taken to the high priest's house, Peter was warming his hands by an open fire there. Remember, the building to which Jesus was taken seems to have been built around a courtyard, and so the fire was in the open space at the center. While Peter was in that courtyard, he denied Jesus a third time, and as he did, a cock began to crow. It was nearly morning. And Jesus, who was being led from one station of the building to another, looked directly at Peter. The look cut through Peter's soul. And, as Luke writes, "he went out and wept bitterly."

As I imagine it, Peter brushes past the girl at the entrance and goes out into the darkness. In utter anguish he thinks, "That man loves me and look what I've done to him. What a coward I've been." Outside, he leans his arm against a wall, rests his forehead on his arm, and begins to weep bitter tears. Tears that come out of the depth of his being. He has denied this most special of friends.

All of that is in his head now, weeks later, as Jesus is having this dialogue with him on the beach by the lake after breakfast.

Jesus is not saying, "Peter, I want you to reach deep into yourself and somehow get into contact with some self-generated emotion and with that emotion love me." Rather, he is saying, "Peter, you have experienced my love for you. You're the object of my love. Will you return that love?"

You don't think that's so? Let me remind you that another of Jesus' followers, Paul, much later said, "God demonstrates his own love for us in this: While we were still sinners, Christ died for us" (Romans 5:8). Let me remind you also of John's later words when he says, "This is love: not that we loved God but that he loved us and sent his Son to be an atoning sacrifice for our sins" (1 John 4:10). Or consider Peter's own later words when he describes those who have been exiled for their faith as "elect according to the foreknowledge of God the Father, through sanctification of the Spirit, unto obedience and sprinkling of the blood of Christ" (1 Peter 1:2, KJV). That's how great his love is.

I think of these words from an old hymn:

I sought the Lord, and afterward I knew
He moved my soul to seek him, seeking me.
It was not I that found, O Savior true;
No, I was found of thee.

Our Lord's question is not, "Peter do you suppose that out of your brilliance and stamina you can generate a kind of love that I can accept?" No, it was, "Peter, I have loved you to the end, and now I want to know, will you return that love? Do you love me?"

Can we find ourselves in that picture?

~

I suppose I should put in a word here about the "how," because we preachers often hear the charge that we fail in our preaching to tell people how. So I take a little excursus here to say that love for Jesus Christ, like love for any human friend, is not automatically self-perpetuating. It has to be renewed, or refreshed. And if I may speak from my experience as an overseer of ministers, I see that the ministers who come to the end of a life of service fresh and radiant in faith are those who know, and have carried out, the discipline of the regular, ongoing, and, of course, Spirit-enabled renewal of their love for the Lord. The love that we have for Christ is a love that must be renewed.

Some years ago I took part in a series of board meetings that continued for three weeks, overseeing one organization after another. This was arranged in order to limit travel expenses. Sitting in back-to-back board meetings is an experience you wouldn't want to miss. Exciting as board meetings are, when they go too long, the excitement drains away. One doesn't maintain the same level of spiritual fervor. I started each day in prayer, as I always do, but there was something debilitating to the daily routine. By the end, I was weary and spent in spirit.

Then I went home from Indiana to Toronto and within a day or two I flew to Miami, waited in the terminal there several hours, and then took an overnight flight to Brazil. I got to Rio in the morning, wandered around in a bit of a mental fog, and took another flight to Sao Paulo, landing there in the noonday heat.

Friends picked me up, fellow Asbury graduates, and they told me the good news that I had no assignments until a committee meeting in the evening. I saw that I could catch a couple of hours of sleep. But when they told me that my schedule the next morning was open, I said to myself, tomorrow morning I'm not going to go downstairs and visit with my friends. Instead, I'll stay in my room and have a personal retreat.

And so I did. When the time came, I cranked the windows wide open, because in Sao Paulo summer was approaching and the air was fresh and the sky bright. I looked across the red-tiled roofs in all directions. I sat in a chair in this bedroom looking toward the windows with my stockinged feet up on the bed. The neighborhood was well populated with dogs. They had barked all night, but now had gone silent; they were getting rested up for the next night. I took my Bible and opened it on my lap and started reading Luke. It was wonderful. I had the whole morning. I went from chapter 1 to chapter 2 to chapter 3 and on. It seemed that the light in the room was on a rheostat; it got brighter and brighter with each chapter. When I reached chapter 8 – the story of Jairus – the light seemed especially brilliant.

Remember Jairus? The synagogue president who had a twelve-year-old daughter? To me that is what's important: the story of the twelve-year-old daughter. Do any of you here have a twelve-year-old daughter? I'm a father and a grandfather – a passionate father and a passionate grandfather. Now, twelve-year-old girls back then were really entering adulthood, or at least moving toward it. At that age they could begin thinking about marriage. And here's Jairus, a father who feels he's got past those nurturing early years and is seeing the first traces of womanhood in his little girl, and now she has become seriously ill. Jairus falls to his knees and begs Jesus to come and heal her, but Jesus is delayed, and Jairus receives a message from home that says, "Look, forget it; don't trouble Jesus about this. She is dead."

But Jesus goes on with Jairus anyway. He takes in to the home with him only three of his followers, plus the mother and father. He goes to the room where this girl is stretched out, dead, and calls out, "Child, get up!" The passage says that her spirit returned to her, which means the passage is not talking about someone who had swooned.

The Bible is a lens through which we see God, and in my spirit, in that Sao Paulo room, I was deeply conscious of his presence. I saw Jesus take her hand and say, "Little girl, it's time to get up now." I saw her sit up, and then stand up. I heard Jesus say, "Give her some food."

Dear friends, in that experience, my heart was revived. It was not that in the quietness of that room I generated some kind of love that had been there all the time and which I just needed to pump up. No, it was that this tired servant of the Lord saw Jesus again in the Book and saw his love and imagined his carriage and identified with his feeling of compassion for a distraught father and a twelve-year-old daughter.

And I said again, with fresh conviction, "He will have my devotion for the rest of my life."

~

Now we come back to the end of the story I was telling you about Peter.

Jesus says, "Simon, when you were young you had it your own way. You clothed yourself; you went where you wanted. When you get old others are going to clothe you and they're going to take you where you don't want to go." John adds the editorial note that Jesus was talking about how Peter was going to die.

Simon's nature is predictable. He suddenly catches a glimpse over his shoulder of John coming toward them. He thinks, Look, Jesus seems to be in a mood to prophesy, so why don't I ask him about John? But when he does, Jesus replies, "That's not your business, Simon." Then he adds the invitation that he used back when he uttered Peter's first call: "Follow me."

I see Jesus and Peter standing face to face. I see Jesus using his hand to direct Peter's eyes away from John and back to him. I hear Jesus saying, "Simon, follow me – *me*."

Of course there's a word in this encounter between Jesus and Peter for pastors today – for seminary graduates, in fact. You may leave seminary wondering: What are my peers going to do? Will they get promotions that pass me by? Are they going to lead bigger congregations? Will they have more prestige?

If Jesus were here he'd say, "That thinking will mess you up every time." He wouldn't use that language, but that is what he would mean. He would say, "Don't worry about others. Follow me."

Notice, as you read the account, that Jesus says it again. He says, "Simon, your task is to follow me." Because love, after all, is not a sensation that makes our head airy; love is, rather, a commitment. The love that Jesus was asking for was a love that would always serve him, out of devotion to him.

And pastors, new and old, that's your assignment, whether to a rural church or an inner-city church, whether to an assignment here in North America or overseas: What he is saying to you is, "I want your absolute allegiance. That's what I call love."

And so to this graduating class I ask: Have you had an encounter with Jesus that makes him the love of your life? That's the question. Is it a deep and genuine love? Can you answer Jesus' question deeply and consciously in the affirmative? Do you really love him? And out of that love will you take whatever assignment he gives you, whether it's a direct assignment or one mediated through a body that you're working for? Will you take whatever assignment he gives you and not worry about what's happening to others and simply give yourself to the task he has assigned?

The pastor's first love is a love for Jesus Christ.

CHAPTER 2

What Does It Mean to Be Ordained?

UNDERSTANDING the task of a pastor – understanding how a pastor is to fulfill it effectively for Christ, out of deep love for him – drives us to look at what it means to be ordained as a pastor. Although some form of ordination – setting apart or assigning – has existed since the beginning of church history, ordination is not always well understood or fully accepted as necessary, even among pastors themselves.

~

He was a big man, about forty, with clean-shaven face and friendly eyes. I'll call him Seth. He had come to pastoral ministry by an unconventional route. Though he was not yet ordained he had planted a church and the church continued to grow. The annual conference had wanted him to finish some coursework toward ordination, but he was conflicted about having to go through the process.

He felt that his resistance was justified: "Why should I have to jump through all the hoops?" was his way of thinking about it. After all, he knew his Bible fairly well, and he could lead a worship service. His attitude was by no means hostile, just perplexed and subtly uncooperative.

Those charged with the ordination process in the church

should not be surprised at Seth's response. There have always been some who found the ordination process tedious and unnecessarily demanding, sometimes overbalanced on the academic side. However, this sort of response has grown more common in recent decades. What counter-response should the church make?

The church has certain questions in mind from the start for men and women who present themselves for possible ordination. Have these candidates been genuinely converted to Christ, and is the resulting relationship rich and growing? Do they show a serious love for Christ? For his scriptures? Are they likable in ways that will draw others to Christ? Do they show signs of a good work ethic (because ministry can be hard work)? Do they have a growing ability to communicate the Word of God to listeners? Do they come with a good reputation among those who know them best? The questions are many.

But one more question should be in the thoughts of those who work with candidates throughout the process: Are these ordinands developing a Christian mind? That is, are their minds committed to a biblical worldview that includes not only salvation by faith and the call to holy living but also a deep respect for the God-ordained institutions of life: family, church, and state? Do the candidates have a proper understanding of authority? The neo-pagan influences of our times make questions about the Christian mind for ordinands more important than ever.

To delineate the obstacles to a Christian mind, it may be useful to review some of the philosophical underpinnings of the modern mind – ideas that often seep into the mindset of those seeking to follow Christ. When undetected, these ideas foster incompatibilities with the mind of Christ and may make living under ministerial orders difficult. Consider, in a general way, three such notions: postmodernism, anti-intellectualism, and anti-institutionalism.

Postmodernism

In our culture, unexamined ideas, like germs in the air, wait to be inhaled and cause "illness." These ideas can be found not only in things people on the street might say, but also in our media, and even among college and university faculty members. These unexamined ideas can cause even committed Christians to unconsciously harbor an ambivalent attitude toward ordination. Today a whole constellation of ideas threatens the very foundations of our society. This constellation is commonly referred to as postmodernism.

The various strands of postmodernism are difficult to identify because they are numerous and not necessarily coherent. They may include a repudiation of values of the past – call them traditions – in favor of fresh and untried values. They sometimes question the validity of rational thought, casting doubt on the concept of objective truth. Postmodern influences are highly individualistic and relativistic. That is, they hold that the choices an individual makes should be of concern to no one but that individual, and that there is no truth but one's personal truth. In some individuals, these ideas have taken over; in others, they color or compete with more traditional ideas.

To whatever degree these ideas are embraced, they are antithetical to the gospel of Jesus Christ. The gospel repudiates subjectivism in favor of eternal truth as it is revealed to us in Jesus; the gospel is rooted in a worldview that has its origin in an ancient book, the Bible; it counters a radical individualism with its truth about interpersonal relationships in family and society and the church of Jesus Christ. Pastors approaching ordination must be helped to work these issues out in fellowship and study during their years of preparation.

However, we should not think that people like Seth come to the possibility of ordination with a full cup of this postmodern brew. That would be unlikely. But it is possible that, in some inward way, they have been exposed to postmodern ideas; thus, while they seek ordination in a long-established church, they may feel ambivalent about what they are seeking, and this may show in some resistance to the process.

Anti-intellectualism

In the middle of the nineteenth century, revival experiences among conservative churches sometimes moved converts quickly from a godless life to a life of serious Christian devotion. These converts' gifts flourished and some rose rapidly to become self-made preachers and leaders. It was a from-plow-to-pulpit phenomenon that meshed well with the American idealism of "rugged individualism" and "the self-made man." Such preachers often asked, Who needs book learning if God has called me to preach? If I open my mouth, God will fill it. In some cases, a corresponding resistance to diligent study and careful training lurked just under the surface.

This cultural phenomenon did not disappear with the closing of the nineteenth century, nor of the twentieth. Even today anti-intellectualism is a more common response to education and training than we might suppose. Educators identify it in the high school and the university. It may, therefore, exist among well-meaning Christians when they are required to meet standards, and among ministerial candidates when they are asked to complete prescribed disciplines as qualifications for ordination.

Anti-institutionalism

Another and more common influence that may undergird resistance to ordination comes to us from a culture-wide revolution that surfaced in the 1960s. For our purposes let's call this influence anti-institutionalism. Though its explosive period roughly spanned the years 1960 to 1975, the revolution continues in a more deliberate way to the present. Consider, for just one instance, the various efforts to overthrow traditional ideas about marriage. These efforts have blossomed from countercultural roots of decades earlier.

The 1960s revolution was marked by a great upheaval in the youth culture, and by an overthrow of societal norms, particularly sexual norms. In extreme cases it produced mass riots against law enforcement and university authorities. In fact, at the core of this multifaceted phenomenon was the impulse to overthrow established authority and to establish, from the ground up, new moral and societal norms. In its less radical expressions, this revolution simply showed contempt for established ways of doing things. To be sure, there are good and civil ways to question existing norms, and norms should always be under review. The revolution, however, wanted nothing of this approach; it wanted a radical overthrow.

For example, during those years I attended a lakeside picnic of a Christian college. There I saw the young people spontaneously baptizing one another in the lake as a religious act while several ordained clergymen stood on the shore and watched. Even if unconsciously, these young people were making an obvious statement, mixing anti-institutional impulses with religious fervor.

This sort of thing surfaced in many ways. In extreme cases, some Christian young people during those years left their established congregation and formed their own house churches. This was another obvious statement. In the more secular realm, young people in great numbers abandoned family and societal connections and established communes with new rules and new and untried ways of relating.

During that decade and beyond, I witnessed hostility toward authority in several forms, whether in the home, the church, or the state. I was there and I heard the stories. I remember that those sharing their stories were hurting deeply from the breakup of societal connections. But the revolution prevailed.

It is unrealistic to think that young people steeped in this revolutionary ideology would seek ordination in a conservative, traditional denomination. But, in succeeding decades, some young people survived the revolution and came back to accept the ways of the established church. Yet they did so with raised eyebrows. Sometimes they brought with them unexamined anti-institutional feelings of lesser but still damaging intensities. It was as though they accepted what they found in the church but with a whisper of skepticism.

Other young people professed, with genuine sincerity, a call to pastoral ministry but had a hard time accepting the long-established procedures of the church, particularly those leading to ordination.

This, it appeared to me, was Seth's case. His sense of discipleship was genuine. You could not question his call to ministry. And his work was effective. But the ordination process with its "institutional hoops" seemed to create resistance and dampen motivation.

How Should the Church Respond?

It seems to me that any denomination that runs into such influences has three options:

1. When it detects these impulses, it can just ignore them and hope that, in the process of ordination and beyond, they will go away. Is such a response wise? Is it not careless to leave intact the notion that candidates for ministry can dig out on their own all the things they need to know and the procedures they need to understand to be effective? Is it not more likely that directed education and training can sharpen, accelerate, and deepen their development? In the recent past, ignoring this has proven damaging both to candidates for ordination and the church. Simply put, unexamined ideas can go on influencing motivations in ways that are hurtful.

2. It may reject outright any candidates who are suspected of having anti-institutional leanings. Again, such a response is shortsighted and is likely to turn away promising candidates who are teachable and may bring freshness and spiritual vigor to the church.

3. Or it may include in the early stages of the candidacy process a seminar to highlight culturally derived impulses foreign to the church and give candidates an opportunity to identify them and discuss them. The rest of this chapter is partial to this third option.

Is Ordination Necessary?

The basic question to be explored is whether ordination is necessary. For Seth or for other men or women such as he, denominations have an obligation to restate to generation after generation the long-established reasons for requiring careful steps to ordination. Consider three reasons why ordination is necessary.

Ordination Is a Form of Certification

At the purely human level, ordination is a form of certification.

The captain of the plane my wife and I flew on recently had gold bars decorating the epaulets on his shoulders. These symbolized years of supervised training, classroom courses, piloting under expert supervision, and even refresher procedures from time to time. If we had noted when we boarded the plane that he was dressed in sweats and sneakers, we would have turned away and inquired about other flights, unsure whether he was qualified for the task of flying 262 people from point A to point B, 1,400 miles in distance. The gold bars attested to the fact that he was certified.

The same holds true for the doctor I saw recently. His credentials were posted on his office wall, telling me where he had studied medicine, what specialty he was qualified to practice, and any special certifications he had gained beyond these.

Certification is a common-sense reason for ordination. As Moses learned from his Midianite father-in-law, so we can learn from the secular world. All such serious temporal enterprises, whether dealing with life, health, or valuable property, should be conducted by qualified personnel, and that requires some form of certification: evidence that the person has been examined and approved by experts who were qualified to judge.

Admittedly, even then, there are degrees of excellence within the ranks of the certified. Some certified practitioners reveal themselves to be undeserving of the trust we are asked to place in them. However, we should not use the incompetence of the few as an argument against the certification of the many. In fact, in the church, it is the very standards and expectations of certification that help to sort out legitimate from illegitimate shepherds.

Ministers Benefit from Ordination

Here is an important distinction: ordination is not intended to bestow honor; it is intended to bestow authority for service. When you think of this authority, the need for certification becomes obvious. A pastor is authorized to teach the scriptures and the doctrines of the church. This requires more than a Sunday-school level of knowledge; it calls for serious prior supervised study and eventual certification. In their line of duty pastors may enter the homes of the community to visit a young family, or to pray with a housebound elderly person. They may call on hospitalized patients before surgery. Or they may be called on to counsel parties to a crumbling marriage, or to hear the painful confessions of a deeply troubled conscience. Pastors may also be called on to represent their church at a community function.

In each case, the pastor is conducting a "representative ministry." That is, in a sense, each member of the church is a minister but does not have the time or training to carry out all such pastoral duties. So the church is provided with a pastor who can represent the body in such situations. These pastoral tasks should not be assigned to an uncertified novice.

THE NEW TESTAMENT ON ORDINATION

The detail about the required preparation of persons for ordained ministry is buried deep in the history of the New Testament church. We are not told everything we would like to know. Even so, although the explicit word for ordination does not appear in the Greek scriptures, there are a number of indications to show that care was taken to set apart certain believers for the special task of ministry or oversight. For example, from his wider throng of disciples, and after a whole night of prayer, our Lord set apart twelve of his followers as "apostles" (Luke 6:12-16). The word means "one sent with a commission." Jesus gave them authority to carry out a special ministry on his behalf.

Later, after the Spirit's outpouring at Pentecost, the developing church had to face the need for a fairer distribution of resources to needy widows. The whole body was asked to choose seven men "known to be full of the Spirit and wisdom" (Acts 6:3) and to bring them before the apostles. In Luke's record Stephen is singled out among the seven duly chosen as "a man full of faith and of the Holy Spirit" (6:5).

In turn the apostles, by prayer and the laying on of hands, set apart seven to be deacons (servants) to the church (Acts 6:6). In this brief account we can see that the whole company of believers was consulted, but the authority of the apostles was exercised for the actual ordination by means of prayer and the laying on of hands.

The fullest insight into the developing practices of the early church is given in the Pastoral Epistles. In writing to

Timothy, the apostle Paul exhorts, "Do not neglect your gift, which was given you through prophecy when the body of elders laid their hands on you" (1 Timothy 4:14).

Three things stand out in this concise instruction.

First, what Timothy was to exercise was given to him as a gift (*charisma*); in other words, a spiritual endowment that he would need for the work of ministering.

Second, the gift was apparently bestowed in his case through a prophetic message.

And third, the gift was conferred by means of the laying on of hands.

There are also other references to the act of setting apart for ministry that we refer to as ordination. Paul may be referring to the same ordaining event as above when he writes, "For this reason I remind you to fan into flame the gift of God, which is in you through the laying on of my hands" (2 Timothy 1:6). Apparently Timothy tended to be timid, and the apostle, his spiritual mentor, was reminding him that whatever was given in the initial ordination was not to be left to smolder but to be kept aflame through spiritual discipline and earnest application.

One thing that comes to the fore in the pastoral references to the setting apart of leaders in the New Testament church is the emphasis on integrity of character. Much is said about this. The overseer must fight the good fight, "holding on to faith and a good conscience" (1 Timothy 1:18b-19a). He must be "above reproach, faithful to his wife, temperate, self-controlled, respectable ..." (3:2). The same verse says that he must be "able to teach" and therefore is expected to be well taught in the scriptures and the formulation of Christian doctrine.

Given such high requirements, it is not surprising that Paul's instructions include that an ordinand "must not be a recent convert" (3:6), a statement that is matched by the apostle's later instruction, "Do not be hasty in the laying on of hands" (5:22). This is an obvious reference to what the church, through the centuries, has called ordination.

The New Testament makes clear that the act of ordination must not be seen as some sort of a terminus for the minister. Development must go on. Ministry must continue to be fresh, ardent, and effective. It is to have a growing edge, especially in the teaching and preaching of the Word. Paul writes these words to Timothy long after Timothy had been set apart for ministry by the laying on of hands and had been Paul's companion in mission: "Work hard so God can approve you. Be a good worker, one who does not need to be ashamed and who correctly explains the word of truth" (2 Timothy 2:15, NLT).

ORDINATION PRACTICES SINCE THE FIRST CENTURY

As can be seen above, ordination is not a recent invention of the church. But minimal detail is given regarding specific procedures. As the Christian church of succeeding centuries developed, it locked onto the insights set forth in the New Testament, holding to them firmly and then filling out the details.

For example, the word "ordinand" is related to the word "order." It has to do with how the church orders its life and particularly its leadership. It suggests that a person is set aside in the church for holy office.

Ordination, however, is not just an event during a Sunday-morning service at an annual conference; it is a process. This is reflected in the fact that, from the time candidates enter the process, they are ordinands. This reflects the historic concern shown that people who are set apart for full-time ministry are to be as prepared for the task as possible before they are ordained by prayer and the laying on of hands.

With the passing of the centuries different Christian bodies have developed ordination procedures they believed to be consistent with the will of the Lord of the church. Sometimes, it appears, concepts have gone well beyond New Testament standards. For example, by the end of the Middle Ages, the Roman church had developed doctrines and procedures that established the primacy of the clergy over the laity. This is not supported in the New Testament, and it made the church too hierarchical. The Reformation theologians repudiated it.

Ordination does not bestow some special grace over that of ordinary Christians. Ordination is intended to bestow a special power and authority for service. With the laying on of the hands of the ordained elders, ordination implies the bestowal of a divine gift for service. This is generally agreed on by most Christian communions.

One Denomination's Way

Seth's ambivalence about the process of ordination may have been the result not only of his unexamined anti-institutional feelings, but also of the neglect of church authorities to sit down and explain the whole process. In the following, I lay out highlights of the Free Methodist Church's approach, an approach that is in harmony with many evangelical traditions.

What authority? The church assumes that at the end of the process, the ordained elder should be supported by a threefold authority.

1. There is the church's validation of the candidate's internal call of God. Throughout the process, care is taken to ensure that the person under training understands and possesses an authentic divine call to the ordained ministry.

2. There is an external authority bestowed by the church in the ordination service itself. The ordaining officer will say, "Take thou authority ..."

3. There is the authority of a godly life. Ordination must

not be thought of as an event only, a one-hour service of public worship; it must also be seen as an ongoing process.

Throughout the training period, the ordinand is prompted to develop a devotional life that is daily and authentic and to gain a basic understanding of how to preach and teach the scriptures, as well as to master the issues of ministerial ethics, and to live a life that is blameless before God. For pastoral effectiveness there is no substitute for this third aspect of the minister's authority. Neither the divine call nor the certifying action of the church can be a substitute for a godly life.

Who Ordains?

Candidates for ordination need to know who, from a human perspective, is really doing the ordaining, because that will indicate to them the body to which they are accountable. In the Free Methodist Church, historically, the ordaining of ministers is the responsibility of the annual conference, although this body assigns certain details of the task to a special committee called the Ministerial Education and Guidance Committee; no one can be formally ordained until that committee makes a recommendation to the annual conference and the conference affirms the recommendation by vote. This vote makes the issue of accountability clear.

This approach also reflects the degree to which the episcopal system, on which the Free Methodist Church is based, has been "democratized." That is, the ordination itself is not the sole responsibility of the bishop; nor is it the sole responsibility of the special committee; nor even of all the ordained elders who lay hands on the ordinand. It is the responsibility of the whole annual conference. The conference is a representative body governed by all conference ministers plus an approximately equal number of laypersons delegated to the conference by its local churches.

Beyond providing ordinands with a clear sense of

accountability and support, there are distinct advantages to having the ordination solemnized while annual conference is in session, which is the process with rare exceptions.

For one thing, the progress of all ordination candidates is brought up to date by the report of the special committee to the annual conference. By this means ordinands are made aware of the body to which they will be accountable and by which their character and performance will be reviewed on an annual basis.

For another, the annual meeting gives ordinands the opportunity to observe the workings of the conference in its many aspects. It also gives new ministers a chance to know and become known by colleagues and major laypersons of the conference. That is, it encourages a sense of collegiality.

For yet another, new ordinands coming in to the fellowship may be made to feel they belong by being assigned minor responsibilities, such as serving as tellers for the business sessions.

All of this together enlightens, encourages, inspires, and develops community interdependence.

One final advantage is that the annual structure makes newly ordained ministers aware that ministers in the Free Methodist Church are held to a permanent standard both for their character and performance. Once a year the Board of Ministerial Education and Guidance is required to review the list of ministers and report to the annual conference. This is a sign that the denomination is concerned that all ministers live under the disciplines of the church and are called to excellence in the performance of their service. It is a feature of being "in orders."

The Bishops' Role

With rare exception bishops are the ordaining officers in the Free Methodist Church. It is of special interest why this is so and how they serve as strong links in the denomination. They are elected by a general conference, which is a grouping of one or more annual conferences and which is convened every three or four years. Bishops are in office under the authority of the general conference, but at the same time, they are assigned to be presidents or chairpersons of annual conferences, which they convene yearly. One of their most important functions during this yearly event is to officiate at the ordination services. Their presence gives dignity and weight to the event. As a result, the office of bishop is one means of linking churches in the denomination and nurturing a sense of uniformity and denominational identity.

Candidates for ordination must understand that in Free Methodist ecclesiology, bishops do not function as bosses or managers. According to long-standing Free Methodist ecclesiastical procedures, and as argued later in this book, they are not CEOs. Like all elders, they are servants of the church, but they are set apart for a special leadership assignment. Moreover, they are not elders who are then ordained to a higher office; rather, they are ordained elders who are then elected to serve as general overseers. Historically, the office of bishop has been highly respected in the denomination, and this gives those who fill it leverage and authority. Within the bounds of the constitution and Book of Discipline, they lead through preaching, teaching, writing, vision casting, counseling, and administrating. They are to be models of representative ministry.

WHO CARES FOR THE DETAILS?

Each annual conference is expected to keep records regarding the progress of ordinands and the specific credits they have gained, whether in education or service. This is a large task. Add to this the work of evaluating ministers who are transferring from other bodies, ministers transferring out, ministers retiring, and so forth, and it is clear that careful secretarial work is required.

But after all details have been considered, the excellence

of a system is determined by the excellence of the people who apply it. Therefore, the spiritual intensity of the whole process and the amount of diligence on the part of all personnel – ordinands, conference committees, recording secretaries, superintendents, bishops, and in fact the entire conference body itself – will determine the quality of ministers whom the church prepares and ordains. It is always hoped that the result of all these details will be ministers with a passion for the work of the gospel and a pastoral concern for those the church enfolds in membership.

A Calling with Benefits

Candidates for ministry who follow the course described can garner great value from the process. Here are some of the benefits.

1. Ordination confirms that a careful effort has been made to be assured of a minister's subjective, inner call from the Lord and affirm it with an objective and outward call of the church. And this recognition is important not only to the ordinand and his or her family but also to the body to which ordained ministers offer their services. For example, in any congregation there are likely to be many who have taken pains to be certified for their respective vocations. It is only right that the minister sent to lead them should be one who has seriously prepared for his or her spiritual leadership assignment.

2. Ordination, in its crowning step – the prayers of the worshiping body and the laying on of hands of all elders at a conference gathering – authorizes the candidate to carry out the demanding work of ministry on a day-to-day basis. Ordinands are not long in the work of representative ministry before it becomes evident to them that they "wrestle not against flesh and blood." Real ministry is warfare, but warfare against the powers

of darkness, not against people. It is good at such times for the minister to look on the call not only as divinely given but also as sealed by a company of God's people. Ordination is a moment to look back to and draw from.

3. Ordination gives those ordained a sense of belonging. Ordained ministers are not adherents, hired hands, salaried workers, performers, careerists, or mercenaries. They are people living out a divine calling in company with other men and women who labor under the same mandate. Ordination should give ministers a collegial sense of having been taken in to a company of people on whom both Christ and his church have laid hands of commissioning.

4. The sense of calling involved in ordination anchors ministers and gives them a sense of purpose that can't be easily reduced to a mere "career." This sense helps a minister when the temptation to seek easier work is brought on by the kind of stresses that only ardent ministers know. Ordination is really a testimony that we believe God has set us apart for a special ministry and the church has set us apart to live out that calling.

5. When ordination is taken seriously by both the ordained and the church, it tends to cultivate respect among all concerned. It is not that ordination is for the sake of honor. Rather, it is for the sake of service. Ministers are often called to suffer as an element of their calling. For some, the cost has been persecution and death. Nevertheless, when the work of ordination is done seriously and men and women are well prepared for their task, this tends to nurture respect – the respect ministers have for themselves, the respect congregations have for their ministers, and the respect ministers show their congregations.

THE BLESSINGS THAT FLOW FROM ORDINATION

I hope men and women like Seth will find this overview of ordination, and the ordination process in the Free Methodist Church, to be of value. The process is more than simply a series of frivolous exercises – a jumping through the hoops. It is a serious effort, bathed in prayer on the part of all participants, to find, direct, guide, and certify those people on whom God has placed his call to ordained ministry. And it is a serious effort to bring them to that moment when the prayers of the church and the laying on of the hands of all the elders links them to the chosen company of the ages who have accepted God's special call and have responded in obedience.

CHAPTER 3

A Week in the Life of Pastor John Doe

MEET Pastor John Doe. His work as a pastor (a shepherd and teacher of God's people, the scriptures would say) is not widely understood in a secular age. But he is willing to give a glimpse into the variety of tasks entailed by his work.

THE WEEK STARTS ON TUESDAY

It's 8 o'clock Tuesday morning and Pastor John Doe is in his study laying out pulpit plans for the following Sunday. On Sunday morning he'll preach the last sermon in his year-long series from Jesus' Sermon on the Mount. He's calling the sermon The Bedrock of Obedience (Matthew 7:24-27). In the evening he'll give one of his ongoing moral issues sermons: Stewards of God's Good Earth (Genesis 2:4-14).

His administrative assistant comes in at 9 o'clock. The phone in her office, adjacent to his study, begins to ring, but according to long-standing agreement, she shields him during the morning from calls that can wait. At 11:30 she breaks his solitude to tell him that the conference superintendent has called and wants a call back, and that the new Smeaton baby has arrived – a boy – and that Jane Hewlett of the Mother's Morning Out circle phoned to ask if he would lunch with the group this coming Thursday noon and bring a brief devotional. Oh, yes, and Mrs. Grider phoned to complain that the sound system was not loud enough this past Sunday morning and if this problem isn't fixed she'll just stay home and listen to the television preachers.

By 12:20 Pastor Doe is enjoying his lunch and by 1:15 he's on his way to the hospital, first to visit the Smeatons and offer a prayer of thanksgiving on the arrival of their new son, and then to bring God's comfort to Grandma Simms, who is dying of cancer.

The hospital is nearby, so by 3:15 he's back at the church to keep an appointment (unfortunately fifteen minutes late) with a distraught single mother. She fears that her thirteen-year-old daughter, Alene, may be getting into drugs. The symptoms are ominous. Alene has become secretive, her grades have fallen sharply, grocery money recently disappeared from a kitchen drawer, and she is experiencing mood swings. Pastor Doe has a good relationship with Alene. He assures the troubled mother that he'll get in touch with her, and that he'll put the mother in touch with a support group. He prays with her, but both know that the problem is far from solved. If her fears are true, there are hard days ahead.

In the few spare minutes before a 5 o'clock appointment with a young couple, he goes through the hymnbook and chorus sheets to choose congregational songs for next Sunday morning's service. His administrative assistant will need time to get the PDFs ready.

At 5, the couple arrives. They're both home for a long weekend from a college in a nearby city, and they want to talk about marriage. As yet only their parents know. They're shy, but as they unfold the story, they confide that they want to wait until they're married – they want to be chaste – but the struggle is intense. They are deeply in love and speak with emotion. The pastor's sympathetic ear calms them and enables them to talk rationally about solutions. He suggests they talk to their parents about an earlier wedding date.

He makes another appointment to see them; this will strengthen the couple's resolve and help them to be accountable.

At 6:10 he arrives home for dinner. After a pleasant meal he has time to play a computer game with his twelve-year-old, Thomas, and read a Bible story to his five-year-old, Cheryl.

At 7:50 he returns to the church to look in on a meeting of the newly formed building committee. He's back home by 9:15. In the quietness of the family room he chats with his wife about down-to-earth matters: a new treatment for Cheryl's asthma, the need for new tires on the car, the scrawled letter from her aging mother, the stresses at the child-care center where she works part-time, and the lawn, which needs to be mowed before what threatens to be a rainy weekend.

In all, it had been a fairly successful Tuesday, and that was surprising, considering the way it had started. Before leaving home that morning he had spent time with the scriptures, but he had been distracted by anxious thoughts. He tried to read from the Psalms and meditate but found himself meditating instead on some unresolved stresses in the church. They were interpersonal, and they involved him.

There were three men in the membership – close friends – whom he couldn't seem to please. They were influential members. It appeared to him that his vision for growth was what was at issue. So far as these men were concerned, all was well: the church was paying its bills, the building was well kept, membership was holding steady, and the people liked to be together. Talking to them didn't help. They always dismissed any changes that he suggested. The recent formation of a building committee had seemed to increase the tensions. These were men of influence in the congregation. Was big trouble ahead? He couldn't help but feel anxious.

This was not the way he liked to spend his prayer times, but he found it hard to be buoyed and balanced before the Throne when such stresses nagged at him. He knew better.

He knew he should just put the stresses in the Lord's hands and press on bravely, and before he left his room he had tried to do that, but he wasn't pleased with the way he had let the men get to him. He confessed his worries as sins and moved along to face the day.

That was not his only concern. He was bothered by what he had heard at a ministers' conference two weeks earlier. There, an engaging guest speaker reported on how, in five years, he had taken a church with eighty-two members and had grown it to nine hundred.

First of all, this speaker explained, he eased out of the membership a few who were obviously not going to go with him. He gave them their walking papers, he seemed to boast. Then he revamped the forms of Sunday worship without any strategies to take the whole congregation with him. That would take too long. A few more members left. The speaker told the conference that he had made it clear from the outset who was in charge. Sometimes, he said with ill-concealed aggression, you have to get rid of a hundred to gain a thousand. He was a skilled speaker, and there were moments of laughter, but was it nervous laughter?

He didn't know how other pastors felt, but while he felt that his Tuesday had been honoring to God, and he loved pastoring as he understood it, local church "politics" and these kinds of outside voices were causing moments of disquiet.

WEDNESDAY TO FRIDAY

Now that Tuesday had launched the week well, the rest of Pastor Doe's week brings a variety of other pastoral challenges: a visit in the home of an anxious elderly couple scheduled to be moved to a nursing facility from their home of fifty-four years; pastoral visits in the homes of two families new to the church; a visit with a young man who had just been served divorce papers; part of an evening at the nearby school gym with a growing youth group; a telephone conference with the chairperson of the membership committee; and as many solitary morning hours as he could capture to study and pray and plan.

Phone calls bring both good news and bad. He learns that one of his members has been bringing a neighbor to the women's morning Bible study, and this week her neighbor had come to a knowledge of salvation. He also hears from a distraught father who says his teenage daughter is pregnant and is hostile and defiant about it. The father says he needs prayer.

Friday Night Is Family Night

Friday night for the Doe family is special. It's family night. No phone calls. No television. Just games or a good movie or reading aloud from books that the children love. He and his wife had become aware of the need for this special night when it dawned on them that the children were getting lost in the shuffle of the busy church. The children had shown their distress by an unusual amount of crying and complaining. They needed more attention, and now they were getting it. The children loved family night; they had an instinct for it.

Pastor Doe finds that the days race toward Sunday. They always do. But in spite of challenges that come up day after day, he is frustrated that he can't shake the discomfort he feels over his strained relationship with the three men. He wants it to be different. He has tried. He tries not to let this matter cast a pall over all the good things that are going on, but it isn't easy. Sometimes it awakens him in the night. In moments of weakness he wonders why his cabinet doesn't see the problem and surround him with prayer as a gesture of support.

Of one thing he is certain: he is not going to do anything that even appears to be running these members off. That would be too simple. It doesn't fit with his understanding of pastoring. If they leave on their own, that will be different. But running members off or inviting them to leave isn't his way of doing the Lord's work. He resolves to try to win them to a bigger vision, but if that can't be done, he will be gracious with them and love them in the Lord and wait.

Saturday

It's not easy for Pastor Doe to look after every detail for Sunday by Friday, so he spends Saturday mornings in his study. He usually reserves the early hours of that day to prepare and review the content of his pastoral prayer. He has to reflect on the events of the week and check any special missionary updates in his e-mail to clarify what is important for that great moment of worship. And sometimes he needs the last part of the morning to complete his notes for his sermon.

After he attends to these matters and makes a couple of necessary phone calls, he locks his door and goes home to be with his family. Saturday afternoons are for his wife and children. They may go to a park or do some grocery shopping together or watch a football game or a video. They try to keep the remainder of the day quiet in preparation for a busy Lord's Day, which isn't always easy to do in a modern parsonage.

Sunday's Big Challenge

Pastor Doe awakens earlier than usual on Sunday morning. Immediately his thoughts are on the special responsibilities of the day. He lies in bed a few minutes and reflects on the week just past. Is this a worthwhile way to spend his life? Is pastoring just another job, or is it a divine calling? Given the interpersonal tensions and the financial stresses and the heavy workload, there must be easier ways for him to make a living. Is he really under appointment from God? Were all his comings and goings of the past week just so many unrelated elements in the life of a church generalist? Or can he say that, in spite of their great variety, they are linked by an overarching concern?

Then his mind turns to the morning worship service only a few hours away. There's a satisfaction, he remembers, even a pleasure, that only a pastor can know, in caring for a flock of God's dear people, in spite of periodic stresses and even the ones that just won't resolve. Every part of the task has its rewards, but as he faces this Lord's Day, he reminds himself that there is something special about seeing the people gather on a Sunday morning and knowing that he will have the privilege of leading them in divine worship.

As he showers and shaves, he thinks about how this hour of worship seems to pull all the activities of his week together. He has a conviction, formed while he was in seminary, that worship in its various forms and venues is central to the life of God's people: worship in the home, private worship, worship while carrying out the normal, sometimes tedious tasks of everyday life, and especially corporate worship when the people gather from their many stations to sing and pray and listen to God's Word together. It's not just the sermon he has prepared, about the two men who built their houses on different foundations – one on sand and the other on rock – and the vastly different consequences when nature threw its fury at their work. For him, every part of worship has its own appeal.

He enjoys singing praise choruses with the people because they are colorful and spritely. But they are like garnish on a meal; he can't do without the great hymns that link the people of God to many generations of believers, hymns with the rich content of the Christian faith put to music. Who could sing Bernard of Clairvaux's "Jesus, the Very Thought of Thee" without recalling warmly that believers in many lands and for several centuries have sung these words together? Such hymns link his congregation to the universal church, and that is critically important.

He has similar feelings about the reading of the scriptures as an act of worship. A portion from the ancient prophet Isaiah, God's mouthpiece eight hundred years before Christ; a Psalm of David, the shepherd king; words from the mouth of Jesus himself – what believer can help but sit up and take notice? He believes that putting the scriptures in this important place is the congregation's way of bearing witness to the authority of God's Word. For Pastor Doe, the exercise links him and his people with the Reformation of the sixteenth century, when new life came to the people through rediscovering the richness and authority of the Bible. But even beyond that, it also links his people to the practices of the New Testament church and, even before that, to the synagogue.

While dressing he remembers the special reason that this act of worship is so important to him now. He had taught an introductory course on Christian ethics to a high-school youth camp only months before. The experience had brought home to him the moral rootlessness of many of today's youth. He had heard them argue: There's no such thing as objective truth; we all have to find our own truth; right and wrong are merely matters of personal opinion; what's wrong for one person may not be wrong for another. Only two or three in the class had argued this way openly, but he could sense a certain attraction to their way of thinking among those who remained quiet. Against this mentality, Pastor Doe recalls, God's people read the scriptures publicly Sunday after Sunday as a testimony to the authority of God's unchanging truth.

As he prepares to leave the house this Sunday morning, while the rest of the family is still sleeping, thoughts like these continue to play through his mind. For him, it's a review that will freshen his leadership a few hours from now and give resonance to the morning service. He is sure again that the worship of God is the foremost activity of the people of God. Whatever other pastors might think, his conviction is that leadership in worship is the pastor's most important task, that from authentic worship flows everything else the pastor and people do together. He teaches his people how to have family devotions, he disciples new converts, he serves the Lord's Supper (a high act of worship), he answers mail and counsels the troubled, but all to this one end: worship.

Pastor Doe's long reverie ends as he pulls in to the parking lot of the church. It's time. It's time for worship.

Monday Is for Fishing Rods and Russian Novels

Pastor Doe always feels the greatest sense of fatigue on Mondays. It's not just that Sundays make so many demands on him; it's also that the long week leading up to Sunday seems to demand a great output of energy. Monday is his day to let down, to give body, mind, and soul a rest. When the season is right, he sometimes potters around in the little vegetable garden he and his wife have planted behind the parsonage, but this is dangerous because things always come up on Monday and can easily lure him to the church. In fact, it's on the day after Sunday that congregational needs seem to surface in greatest number.

It is best for him to get out of town, and his favorite spot is a quiet river a few miles to the south. He loves to sit on the bank of the river under a large willow and let his fishing line dangle in the scarcely moving current. He can think or pray or read and let the freshness of nature renew him. Whether he catches any fish or not, he finds that the experience clears his mind. He can't quite choke back the interpersonal problems that so trouble him, but he can put them in perspective. And by late afternoon he's ready to gather up his tackle, stow the Russian novel he has brought to read, and get back to town. The new week looks challenging.

CHAPTER 4

Exploring the Pastoral Task from 30,000 Feet

WHEN pastors are assigned to a church as the only or lead pastor, they should arrive with a fundamental understanding of their task. At the same time, they should always be open to reviewing and adjusting their understanding, because every church has unique features: certain doctrinal emphases, customs, board dynamics, and congregational expectations.

To explore the universal elements of the pastoral task that must be intermeshed with the above-mentioned individual features of individual congregations, I offer an outline of three main and often overlapping pastoral responsibilities. They are: (1) to preach and teach the Word of God; (2) to tend the flock; and (3) to organize and oversee the life and ongoing ministry of the body.

PREACHING AND TEACHING THE WORD OF GOD

When we read the Pastoral Epistles, we are taken with how they emphasize the pastor's major assignment to preach and teach the Word of God with constancy. Overseers are to be able to teach (1 Timothy 3:2); they are commanded to teach (4:11); and to "devote [themselves] to the public reading of Scripture, to preaching and teaching" (4:13). Paul exhorts

Timothy to "do your best to present yourself to God as one approved, a workman who does not need to be ashamed and who correctly handles the word of truth" (2 Timothy 2:15).

This primary assignment tends to fade at times but periodically, as in the Protestant Reformation, returns to prominence through the quickening of God's Spirit. Today the local church, however large or small, is a complex body with subtle features sometimes not apparent on the surface. Even so, in the light of the Pastoral Epistles and Reformation rediscoveries, it is fair to say that the operational center of each local church should be found in its pulpit. The local church grows from this center outward. That is, if a congregation and its ministries are to be fruitful, the preaching and teaching fare it receives from the pulpit week after week must nourish spiritual health and growth.

Along with leading the church in corporate worship, of which preaching is a part, this is a pastor's primary responsibility, but the responsibility does not end with the pulpit. Pastors must see that the scriptures are being given a central place in all the activities of the church: the Sunday school, small groups, the children's programs, etc. This focus on scripture is so broad and demanding that the pastor must count on staff or lay committees to share the burden of oversight.

Tending the Flock

In earlier times, the clergyman was called a curate – that is, one charged with the care of souls. There is an element of this in the preaching and teaching function, but pastoral care more typically means finding and meeting personal needs through counseling, home visitation, and appropriate support for those in various kinds of trouble such as illness and bereavement. In this aspect, the pastor has a role quite unlike that of any other profession. Lawyers and doctors do not typically go into the community uninvited and uncompensated. Pastors, however, are expected to seek out those who have needs. That is what it means to be a shepherd. They offer pastoral care whether to parishioners or people on the fringes or outside the community of faith.

Ezekiel gives a rebuke to shepherds of God's people who were not doing this aspect of their job, and in his rebuke he develops the metaphor of what committed shepherds do: they search for the lost and bring back the strays; they bind up the injured and strengthen the weak (Ezekiel 34:16). Because Israel's shepherds had failed in their task, God says, "I myself will tend my sheep," a foreshadowing of the words of Jesus, "I am the good shepherd. The good shepherd lays down his life for the sheep" (John 10:11).

Pastoral visitation is still a very important and useful function of the pastoral task. But the conditions of modern life make it much harder to do than in the past. People are more mobile. Two or more adults in the family may work outside the home and are harder to connect with. There are single parents who need pastoral care but who can hardly find a moment free from work and home duties. Furthermore, apart from hospital calling and visiting in other institutions, it may be more difficult to find a suitable place where pastors can offer pastoral care.

The wise pastor will see these problems and develop creative means to solve them: perhaps by using the pastor's study more as a meeting place when visits to a home or apartment are not suitable, or by inviting especially needy persons to his home for dessert, or by visiting as a husband-and-wife calling team. Whatever the difficulties, lead pastors must do some pastoral calling or see that it is done.

Organizing and Overseeing the Life and Ministry of the Body

Who can fail to see that Jesus not only taught his disciples in individual and group sessions (Matthew 5:1) but also organized them into teams and sent them out to minister (Matthew 10)? In both activities he was working to a plan. Today we would call it the administrative aspect of the pastoral task.

Jesus even incorporated administration into the dispensing of his miracles. When he fed the hungry five thousand with five loaves and two fish, he directed his disciples to have the people sit down on the grass in groups. These, Mark tells us, were groups of hundreds and fifties. And when the great feast ended, the leftovers were gathered to the extent of twelve full baskets (Mark 6:35-44). There is no disorder or waste in the miracle.

In the pastoral life, administration should be addressed not as an end in itself but as a means to ministry. It may come into play when planning a worship service, when guiding the Christian education program of the church, or when meeting or leading the church board. Pastors may generally be seen as weak administrators, yet churches must be led into a degree of order and structure for the sake of community life and to enable ministry beyond church walls.

For example, time not spent on careful administration in the spring will be expended needlessly in the fall when knotty problems must be untied and confusion untangled. A church that moves forward with well-defined purpose will be more likely to be a happy church.

The Three Primary Pastoral Tasks Often Overlap

Preaching and teaching, pastoral care, and administration are not independent of one another. A pastor may call on a parishioner with an administrative matter in mind, only to learn of a need for pastoral care in the immediate family. A pastor may teach a Bible study and through that discover the need to pay special attention to a serious administrative matter in the education department. Or a pastor may preach a sermon that leads a parishioner to make an appointment for counseling.

GODLINESS AND COMPETENCE

When the pastoral task is so broad, how does one pare down or simplify the basic qualifications required of a pastoral candidate? As an overseer I faced the question scores of times, and I came upon an answer two decades ago, when preparing a series of lectures to be given at a seminary. From a careful reading of Paul's letters to Timothy I saw that all pastoral qualifications may be subsumed under two heads: godliness and competence.

Godliness is a personal attitude of reverence for God that is cultivated moment-to-moment. It is powered by a deep love for Christ, as explored in the first chapter of this book. It includes a sense of accountability to him that underlies all attempts to serve God and his people. Quoting 1 Timothy 1:5 we might say that the godly person is marked by "a pure heart and a good conscience and a sincere faith." Godliness shows itself in a piety that is genuine, not affected.

It is not, however, a once-and-forever gift. The apostle Paul exhorts the young Timothy, "Train yourself to be godly" (4:7) and "pursue ... godliness" (6:11). Godliness is a dominant word in the Pastoral Epistles, representing a never-ending goal.

But to godliness must be added competence. Competence involves a broad knowledge of the pastoral task and a developed skill in carrying out its diverse responsibilities. Godliness without competence may appear sincere but is likely to lead to bungling and ineffectiveness. On the other hand, competence without godliness may appear efficient but is likely to show itself to the discerning as shallowness.

I saw, while pondering 1 Timothy, that at the core of competence is an insightful recognition of sound doctrine. In fact, Paul's first issue in his letter is doctrinal competence in countering those who teach false doctrines (1 Timothy 1:3). Paul reminds Timothy that he himself had been appointed by God to be "a true and faithful teacher of the Gentiles" (2:7). He exhorts Timothy, "Until I come, devote yourself to the public reading of Scripture, to preaching and to teaching" (4:13). As noted earlier, the proclamation and vigorous defense of truth is at the core of competent pastoral ministry.

Competence also includes skill in relating to parishioners. "Do not rebuke an older man harshly ... Treat younger men as brothers, older women as mothers, and younger women as sisters, with absolute purity" (5:1-2).

And it includes caring for administrative matters such as seeing to it that the special needs of believers in the family of God are met (5:9-16).

Competent preaching and teaching, pastoral care, and careful administration: these are the essence of the godly pastor's task in all ages.

Pastors or CEOs?

I spoke recently to a seminary class made up of mature students from several denominations. As we discussed pastoral roles, one young pastor offered the opinion that at least 60 percent of the pastors in his district openly admitted that they wanted to function in their churches as chief executive officers, CEOs. This trend is waning, but its influence (and perhaps behind it an unscriptural desire for power) is still there.

That comment reminded me of a conversation with a friend, David, who had recently gone to candidate for a church. He said the search committee had told him frankly,

"What we need is a CEO." They were repeating what they had been advised by their regional overseer.

David, who has good administrative skills and an undergraduate degree in economics, replied to them, "I can function as a CEO, but what I think you need is a pastor who can also do some of the things the CEO does – like vision casting and giving direction to the church – but within the historic pastoral model."

Later in the interview he asked them, "If one of you were in hospital for surgery, would you want a visit from a CEO or a pastor?"

When this CEO model for church leadership became popular a decade or two ago, reports began cropping up of parishioners who had received ill-treatment from pastors. "If you don't like my style of leadership," one CEO-style leader told a startled church member recently, "go somewhere else." The member of another church reported that his pastor had repeated a statement from the seminar circuit that "you may have to lose a hundred (current church members) to gain a thousand." Another long-term parishioner reports that he was literally ignored, treated as a non-person, because he dared to have an opinion not in full accord with his pastor's.

These were not troublesome people. And the cases are not exceptional. The stories of mistreatment, based on an assumed new style of acceptable leadership, are numerous.

Consider a composite example of pastoral thinking not guided by scriptural principles. He arrives at his new pastoral assignment, and before he knows the names of half the flock, before the children of the congregation have warmed up to him, he begins talking about what this church needs in order to grow. His well-underlined collection of books on the management and marketing of the modern church crowds out Bible commentaries and other reference books. His Sunday-morning sermons – supported by overheads – become lectures on church growth.

Meanwhile, as the poet John Milton put it, "The hungry sheep look up and are not fed."

When "new ideas" like the CEO model surface in the life of the church, they should be aired and examined in seminars, pastors' conferences, and even board meetings; their merits and demerits, measured against the scriptures, should be exposed. The fundamental question is this: Will today's churches prosper better under these latest ideas of what a pastor is? Or does the ancient title, pastor, or shepherd, still best define what the church needs in the twenty-first century?

CEOS HAVE A PLACE

It is evident that CEOs have an important place in our society. They are expected to have special skills in making things happen, whether in small businesses or in large organizations such as multinational electronics or automotive empires. They pull down seven-figure salaries, have eye-popping perks, drive high-end BMWs, and carry a certain mystique. They are power people. When a new CEO takes over, workers tighten up, knowing their jobs might be on the line. CEOs – accountable only to their boards and stockholders – are there to affect the bottom line.

This pushback against the idea of pastors as CEOs is not to demonize the role of the CEO. Big and complex operations involving hundreds or thousands of employees need skillful management, and large industries exist to make a profit. Being a CEO is a high-pressure job and sometimes involves signing orders to downsize affecting the future of loyal and long-standing workers. Decisions have to be crisp and somewhat detached; concern for the individual may factor in but can scarcely be foremost.

The newly expressed desire on the part of some pastors to handle their duties as CEOs, though misdirected, should not surprise us. A minister friend in a large denomination believes that pastors are having a particularly hard time these days. Their boards tend to boss them, the congregations hold them to a wide and often conflicting variety of expectations, power blocs frustrate their efforts, and society at large gives them little status. In some cases pastors do indeed function from a stance of uncertainty and even ambiguity. Yearning for greater leverage is, in a sense, understandable.

Though there are points of overlap in the skills of pastors and CEOs, by no means do they fully mesh. A church is a voluntary organization, not a unit in an industrial complex, and relationships must be built and tended with this in mind. A church should not measure its success in membership numbers alone nor in dollars and cents, and church leaders should not operate from a posture of power and prestige. Thus, scuttling the title pastor, with all it embraces, viewed biblically, is not the hope of the church's future.

There are still many pastors who embrace the ancient title shepherd and live it out with joy – though also with twenty-first-century stress. I met two recently.

A Tale of Two Pastors

My wife and I were in the home of a pastor near Ottawa, Canada. On Saturday night he and his wife gathered us with their four children, ages eight to seventeen, around their dining room table for tasty food and good conversation. It was apparent that this pastor was a shepherd to his family. The next morning I watched him lead his congregation in worship. His authority was strong but not overbearing. The connections between him and his people were warm. He obviously loved them, and they loved him back. His love appeared real, not sentimental or manipulative. He was a leader, without question, but a shepherding one.

In a conversation afterward he outlined for me the significant outreach of his congregation into the community.

He also shared with me some of the congregation's collective goals for their growing church – a congregation now of 175 or so.

One weekend later I was with a pastor near St. Louis, Missouri. Again, the table fare on Friday night was delicious. The mealtime was orderly but blessed with lively conversation in which the three children, ages twelve to sixteen, could share. Then, in the Sunday services, this pastor affirmed his people graciously and prayed for them with pastoral concern. I could see, standing with him at the door after the service, that he knew every one of them, even recent newcomers, in a personal way. This growing congregation of two hundred or so was secure in his strong but tempered leadership. The congregation was growing, he told me, with new people turning up every Sunday.

They were two different pastors, both boomers, about ten years apart in age, and they had never met. Their cultural circles were in different countries a thousand miles apart, but the underlying ways in which they operated were strikingly similar. No one would question that they were in charge, but they functioned with a gentle strength. They were godly men and had mastered the art of leading in godly worship.

These pastors were not free of stress, and they shared this with me when we were alone. Both spoke with healthy concern about their children. Raising a godly family is a special challenge today. Moreover, the demand of serving a modern congregation in a libertarian culture is not easy. In the trying moments of church life Christians do not always respond as sheep to a shepherd. The very brokenness of our society keeps committed pastors on the stretch to meet human need. Their churches serve troubled families, those struggling with addictions, lonely souls, those out of work, the bereaved, and afraid. It can be an exhausting life. Yet, I could see the metaphor under which both worked. These pastors were not CEOs; they were shepherds.

Is the Shepherding Metaphor Obsolete?

Shepherding is the dominant biblical metaphor for Christian leaders. Moses, Israel's great deliverer, is called to his life's ministry from a long stretch of caring for his father-in-law's sheep. David, Israel's greatest king, got his early training as a shepherd. Perhaps it was while he was on some quiet hillside watching over his grazing flock that he composed the beloved psalm, "The Lord is my shepherd, I shall not be in want." It is an audacious song – the shepherd God? – but the Sovereign Lord himself forever elevates the picture by declaring, through the prophet Ezekiel, "I myself will tend my sheep and have them lie down" (34:15). Israel's leaders had failed to watch over God's people selflessly, and this was God's response. Centuries later, our Lord fulfilled God's earlier promise, when he said, "I am the good shepherd. The good shepherd lays down his life for the sheep" (John 10:11).

Moreover, we can never forget that our Lord's final recorded words to Simon Peter included the order "feed my sheep" (John 21:17). This is the task of a shepherd, with all the seeking and leading and protecting that go with it. The task, so described, cannot be explained away as an understanding of pastoring that belongs to an ancient world where animal husbandry was dominant. A generation later, when Simon Peter, then a mature and aging leader, wrote to elders and churches widely spread and many of them in cities, he continued the metaphor by exhorting, "Be shepherds of God's flock that is under your care, serving as overseers – not because you must but because you are willing, as God wants you to be; not greedy for money, but eager to serve, not lording it over those entrusted to you, but being examples to the flock. And when the chief shepherd appears, you will receive the crown of glory that will never fade away" (1 Peter 5:2-4).

"Not lording it over those entrusted to you." As usual,

the Bible hits the nail on the head. Those who aspire to be shepherds of God's flock must repeatedly ask whether their motivation is to lord it over their flock or to serve them in pastoral ways.

CEOs have an important place in our modern world as they execute their complex assignments. But to bring the title in to the church as a replacement for the shepherding metaphor is to misunderstand the nature of the church and the purposes of God as revealed in his holy Word. Therefore, both laity and clergy today must rediscover the meaning of the pastoral calling. This could be a necessary first step in raising up a whole new generation of Christian leaders who will renounce worldly substitutes and embrace a calling to be shepherds, living out that calling to the glory of God.

However we approach the task, Jesus is forever the model. Was he a strong leader? Picture him as he speaks comforting words to a child in the presence of his disciples, deals with turbulent crowds, confronts disease, stands up courageously to enemies. Did he follow a strategy in his work? Indeed! When some followers begged him to settle for a while in one place, he said, "Let us go somewhere else – to the nearby villages – so I can preach there also. That is why I have come" (Mark 1:38). Was his love steady and relentless? When Judas came to betray him, Jesus addressed him as "friend." Did his work sometimes exhaust him? Picture him asleep at the back of a boat in the midst of a storm.

We can never do more than approximate Jesus' matchless example. But we can't escape the foundational attitude found in all of Jesus' dealings with his followers. He said, "I am the good shepherd. The good shepherd lays down his life for the sheep" (John 10:11). The least this can mean is that in every age a truly pastoral life includes an element of sacrifice for the well being of God's people. Every impulse modern church leaders have to be bosses must be measured against our Lord's timeless words.

THE PASTOR AS SHEPHERD

What else does the Bible say about shepherding?

The Christian scriptures have a variety of names for leaders: apostles, ministers, elders, deacons, bishops, teachers, rabbis, priests, chief priests, scribes, liturgists, deaconesses, and so forth. Foremost among them is the term "shepherd" (*poimen*), or pastor: a leader, provider, and protector of a flock of sheep.

References to sheep occur in the scriptures more than five hundred times if we include references to rams and lambs. References begin with Abel, second son of Adam, who "kept flocks" (Genesis 4:2). Scripture gives us insight into the nature of sheep. They are: affectionate (2 Samuel 12:3); unaggressive (Isaiah 53:7; Jeremiah 11:19; John 10:3-4); relatively defenseless (Micah 5:8; Matthew 10:16); and in constant need of care and supervision (Numbers 27:17; Ezekiel 34:5; Matthew 9:36, 26:31).

There is a corresponding and complementary relationship between sheep and shepherd. That is, what the sheep need, the shepherd provides.

It should be remembered that shepherding is an analogy, and analogies cannot be used to prove a claim; they only illustrate. Moreover, analogies do not have to apply in every respect. If there are as many as three similarities, an analogy can be acceptable. For example, being asleep can be analogous to being dead in the sense that in both states there is loss of consciousness, inertness, and non-communication. But it is not analogous in terms of duration. For the analogy of shepherding, although pastors are caregivers, they do not look on parishioners as helpless or stupid.

The single most arresting application of the shepherd analogy in scripture is the picture of God himself as the shepherd of his people. Consider:

- A statement by God: "For this is what the Sovereign

Lord says: I myself will search for my sheep and look after them. As a shepherd looks after his scattered flock when he is with them, so will I look after my sheep" (Ezekiel 34:11-12).

- A prayer to God: "Shepherd your people with your staff, the flock of your inheritance, which lives by itself in a forest, in fertile pasturelands" (Micah 7:14).

- Another prayer to God: "Save your people and bless your inheritance; be their shepherd and carry them forever" (Psalm 28:9).

The New Testament finds its most profound application of this analogy in Christ as the good shepherd of all his sheep. This is spelled out in John 10.

The scriptures give no support for so-called marrying and burying pastors. From Ezekiel 34:4, it is clear that pastors of God's flock are to (1) strengthen the weak, (2) heal the sick, (3) bind up the injured, (4) bring back the strays, (5) search for the lost, and (6) rule gently.

There are contemporary illustrations of the kind of closeness between sheep and shepherd reported in the scriptures (John 10). Two shepherds can call their sheep from a common fold at the same time, and the sheep will know and respond to their own shepherd's voice.

The above passages should be studied to evaluate modern images of pastors. Are they bosses managing an enterprise? Psychiatrists waiting in their offices? Activists always on the go? Or even ecclesiastical technicians spending large amounts of time on the Internet? Or are they men and women of godliness and competence, giving their attention to the spiritual leadership of their flock, to pastoral care, to administration?

CHAPTER 5

Seven Characteristics of Effective Pastors

UP to now, we've reviewed the pastor's first love; the nature, purpose, and logistics of ordination; a week in the life of a pastor; and the three primary roles of a pastor, along with some popular counterfeits. Now we turn our attention to a type of "seven habits of highly effective people," with specific reference to the life of a pastor.

As mentioned at the very beginning of this book, for a dozen years I have been going once a semester to Northeastern Seminary in Rochester, New York, to spend four hours with a class that will be a new generation of pastors, dealing with down-to-earth, practical aspects of the pastoral life. These visits are highlights of the year for my wife and me.

Several weeks before each visit I begin to reflect more deeply on my assignment. I call up memories of my own experience as a pastor and an overseer of pastors to share with a new generation. Sometimes I write a fresh paper to use as a basis for discussion.

Seminary is a time that rightly focuses on the tools of the pastor: increased knowledge of the Bible, preaching, pastoral care, the administration of a church, pastoral ethics, and so forth. In preparing for one of these visits, I decided to set down some wide-ranging insights that might not otherwise be part of a seminary's curriculum – insights that some might consider ancillary, but which, in my view, get at the heart of what it means to be an effective pastor.

In our secular culture there are still many effective pastors. As servants of the Lord, they carry themselves with dignity, go about their work with purpose and passion, and cultivate their personal relationships with integrity. They are respected by the majority of the people they serve, and often by people well beyond the borders of their own congregations. These pastors are a tribute to the Lord of the church.

Admittedly, they are not perfect specimens of humanity. Their treasure is in earthen vessels, as is the case with all of us. They have their own struggles and foibles. They often live with personal disappointments – in themselves or others. But their lives are integrated by a genuine faith in Jesus Christ, a clear devotion to their calling, and a hard-won personal integrity that is evident even to those who do not always agree with them. Here are my reflections on the characteristics of an effective pastor.

1. The Effective Pastor's Evangelistic Zeal

You can't read the apostle Paul's letters to Pastor Timothy without noticing his strong urgings to Timothy to do his work as a pastor with holy zeal. "Fight the good fight" (1 Timothy 1:18). "… devote yourself to the public reading of Scripture, to preaching and to teaching" (4:13). "Do not neglect your gift" (4:14). These are especially telling exhortations when we learn that Paul wrote them between his first and second imprisonments in Rome. Timothy was to do his pastoral work with ardor.

It is in this same spirit of urgency that Paul exhorts Timothy to "do the work of an evangelist" (2 Timothy 4:5). He does not mean that Timothy should leave the pastorate and go into full-time evangelism. Rather, he means that, in his pastoral ministries, Timothy should include and share the good news of Christ – the gospel – both within the congregation and beyond its borders, inviting a response.

Nor does he offer this as casual counsel. It is given in the context of dealing with serious doctrinal issues. For example, he writes in the same passage that the day is coming when "Christ Jesus … will judge the living and the dead" (2 Timothy 4:1) and that we work knowing the time will come when Christ and his kingdom will appear (4:1). He reminds Timothy that the day is near when men will not endure sound doctrine (2 Timothy 4:3), and for these very reasons he tells Timothy to "discharge all the duties of your ministry" (3:5). The work of an evangelist was one of those duties.

When we have a passion to spread the good news and to see those outside Christ's kingdom become insiders, we discover that there are more fields around a congregation than we might have imagined. Many congregations contain one or more people who have never been approached with the claims of the gospel in a personal way and who can often be led to experience conversion. Such new believers will need follow-up teaching regarding the gospel's implications for their lives.

As a subset of the unconverted, there may be young people who would be open to a pastor's evangelism if sought out in a non-threatening setting, such as a hamburger stand. There are people who seek pastoral counsel, which sometimes leads to the offering of the gospel.

And as a pastor becomes known, respected, and then trusted in a community, other opportunities are sure to present themselves. All of these possibilities may be included in the work of evangelism.

2. The Effective Pastor's Integrity

For pastors, integrity is built and maintained one day at a time, across a lifetime. It involves health of soul and wholeness of character. Pastors can achieve integrity only if they are fully aware of the corruption of human nature through the Fall, and, at the same time, of the marvelous possibilities of God's grace. These two companion ideas are never forgotten in prayers for integrity: "repentance toward God and faith toward our Lord Jesus Christ" (Acts 20:21, KJV). This twofold bearing exists in the lives of pastors whose love for the Savior is genuine, and who regularly monitor their thoughts and behavior in the light of that love.

I find the lines of one of Charles Wesley's hymns an excellent gauge for maintaining integrity in the face of all of life's trials and temptations:

> *False and full of sin I am,*
> *Thou art full of truth and grace.*
> *Plenteous grace with thee is found,*
> *Grace to cover all my sin.*
> *Let the healing streams abound;*
> *Make and keep me pure within.*

"False and full of sin I am" – a confession of our fallen state; that is, our human condition both by nature and personal choice. "Plenteous grace with thee is found, / Grace to cover all my sin" – an acknowledgment that God's grace is abundant and is more than adequate to wash away, and free us from, sin's power. "Let the healing streams abound; / Make and keep me pure within" – a humble prayer, asking in confidence that God's grace may be applied like a healing agent to "make" and "keep" us pure at the unseen centers of our beings. These two verbs belong on the sanctification side of our salvation.

Effective pastors take the issue of integrity seriously,

because integrity – inner holiness – is commanded in the New Testament. Jesus treated with great compassion those who acknowledged their fallenness, but he also unmasked religious professionals who were at the same time pious and devious. "They devour widows' houses," he said of the teachers of the law, "and for a show make lengthy prayers" (Mark 12:40). Their piety was a sham.

Also, when Paul wrote to the Corinthian church, he asserted his own radical integrity: "… we have renounced secret and shameful ways; we do not use deception, nor do we distort the word of God. On the contrary, by setting forth the truth plainly we commend ourselves to every man's conscience in the sight of God" (2 Corinthians 4:2).

So, what must we do to maintain integrity in our ministry? It begins in the cultivation of a genuine prayer life. As Thomas Hooker wrote, "Prayer is my chief work, and it is by means of it that I carry on the rest." Many great Christian leaders of the past have given similar testimonies. Here are four suggestions to help you work toward such authenticity:

1. Develop a daily routine of prayer. Start every day with time in "the secret place." If necessary, use a scripture-reading guide such as the one provided by the National Association of Evangelicals or the Canadian or American Bible societies.

2. Cultivate the use of a prayer list. Make it active and current.

3. Write your prayers, if this helps, or make notes to help you concentrate.

4. Build a small, inconspicuous kneeling bench for your study.

In other words, do whatever it takes. But, however you tailor the practice, make sure it is ardent and real. The late

E. Stanley Jones said, "Most of the casualties in the spiritual life are found at the place of a weakened prayer life."

3. The Effective Pastor's Relationship with Spouse and Family

Pastors can be breathtakingly busy doing kingdom work. Still, ministry should never steal away time from family. Whenever possible, pastors should eat at least one meal a day in which they focus their undivided attention on family. Observing a special family night when the cell phone is turned off and the TV is silent is a capital idea. Little children love it. Take time to laugh and chat together.

Keep lines open and honest with your beloved. Your spouse has a right to know where you have been and what you have been doing. Secrecy or even lack of communication about such things is a danger signal. Above all, if there is unresolved trouble in your marriage, take the initiative in seeking counsel. Marital strength is basic to effective ministry and to reducing the risk of moral failure.

4. The Effective Pastor's Dwelling

The pastor's living space, whether personally owned or provided by the church, reflects on the pastor's character. If the community comes to see the outside as unkempt, with grass not mowed, entrances littered, windows streaked, and paint flaking, this is sure to tarnish the pastor's reputation and thus his or her effectiveness. If the inside gets to be known as perpetually messy, with dirty dishes in the sink, beds unmade, and clothes littered about, the Christian influence of the couple is seriously damaged, especially in the eyes of the women of the church. This is so, even if, out of courtesy, the disapproval is never mentioned. Even the most excellent of sermons cannot erase this pastoral shortcoming.

Admittedly, those responsible for the care of the home do

not all have the same skill and diligence in making a home and yard attractive. And by nature and temperament, one person's level of commitment to cleanliness, beauty, and order may be different from another's. Also, there are down times in every home, when children may have made a mess with their toys, or adults have gone through an illness or the birth of a baby or otherwise have been incapacitated for a short while. But effective pastors know that there is a line below which, for the sake of the gospel, they should not let themselves slip.

It seems to me that this issue is increasingly challenging. After all, many pastoral spouses themselves work in demanding jobs. And time spent in the home is encroached on not only by work, but also by eating out, the distractions of incoming information and entertainment, and so forth. As an example of this phenomenon in non-pastoral families, it is reported that wealthy people who build "monster homes" and install the latest kitchen equipment often use their kitchen very little. Further, a realtor in the wealthy western suburbs of Chicago says, "You just wouldn't believe how half of the people in this area live. The insides of the homes should be condemned by the health department." For many, the home is no longer a safe haven, a place of beauty and comfort.

Is the problem really this serious? Kathleen and I have a place in Florida where we spend the winter months. It's no secret that cockroaches thrive in that state and the only way to be free of them is to have a company come quarterly and spray widely around the outside of the residence, and sometimes even inside.

During the agency's visit this past winter, my wife fell into conversation with the technician. "You must get inside a great variety of homes during the course of a year," she said. His response was unexpected. He described conditions that would make you gag – dirty dishes sitting around with mold on them, half-eaten food strewn near the TV and left to spoil, cupboards that desperately needed attention. He suggested that such conditions were all too common.

Given the trends, it can be an uphill battle, but, to carry on an effective ministry, setting an example, the parsonage family must see the importance of keeping the home presentable inside and out – for Christ's sake, if for no other reason.

5. The Effective Pastor's Dress

Let's agree that all across our culture "casual" has been in for a long time. Try this experiment: Walk through a Walmart on a busy day and look for a man wearing a shirt and tie. You may find him, but likely only after a search. Then look for one wearing a suit, as well. That will prove even more difficult. Then, over a ten-minute period, count the number of T-shirts you see. The count will take more than your fingers and toes. The situation may be different in more upscale stores, but less than you might imagine. Just about any busy store is a microcosm of today's dress standards. I do not mean to say that people should dress up when they go shopping; I simply wish to illustrate that comfort, convenience, personal taste – these are everything.

Comfort in attire is important. We give thanks for the flexibility of today's dress standards, but, at the same time, as pastors we pray for wisdom in how to apply this freedom properly. Furthermore, it is still true that various occasions call for specific ways of dressing. We wear one type of attire for a Sunday-school picnic, another for the beach, another for a wedding, and another for a visit to the doctor. A man dressed in swimming trunks is welcome at a swimming pool but would be ushered out of a corporation.

Once, while I was preaching in the Midwest, I was invited to a Saturday-morning reception for a new pastor in a small town about thirty miles away. The finger foods were admirably prepared and presented. The women of the church had taken their assignment seriously. The mayor came, along with another local dignitary. But the new pastor to be honored came late. He was dressed in a soiled pair of work pants and an unpressed, open-necked shirt. He might as well have come from changing the oil in his car. I was embarrassed for him. I was embarrassed for his congregation. The message of his attire was clear: neither the event in his honor nor the people who attended mattered that much to him. There are times when we should dress for others as much as we dress for ourselves.

So, how should pastors dress while on duty? That's the key: "on duty."

The famed radio news commentator Paul Harvey told our son, Robert, his doctor, an interesting story from his own experience. Harvey, at the time past eighty, broadcast with the help of his staff from a self-contained studio. The venue was in no way public. He told Robert that, with the swing to casual dress more than twenty years earlier, he had thought he could dress casually while preparing materials and even while on-air each day.

But his engineer soon told him, "Mr. Harvey, you need to wear your suit and tie again. Your broadcasts just aren't the same." Experienced though he was, he dressed ever afterward as though in public. Moses learned some things about his work from his Midianite father-in-law, and we could learn a thing or two from those who have succeeded in the secular realm.

I heard recently that "casual Friday dress," allowed for years in business and industry, is going out of favor in many workplaces. It has been observed that people who come to work in casual dress tend to work casually, too.

Here is my opinion of how an effective male pastor should dress when on duty. If he is seeing people in a study or attending a board meeting or visiting the hospital or going to a parishioner's home or otherwise appearing in public, his most informal attire should include at least slacks and a sport jacket. Neatly pressed slacks would, in my opinion, be best, but if he wears jeans, they should be dress jeans, with no tears or other decorations. If he wears an open-necked shirt, the collar should stand up within the jacket lapels, not droop crumpled beneath them.

For Sunday morning, I suggest that the pastor stick to the long-standing custom of wearing a dark suit with white shirt and conservative tie. For Sunday evenings (if evening services are held) or for other less formal services, slacks and a contrasting jacket are fine. Some may prefer loud colors and highly patterned clothing as a means of self-expression, but the truth is that such clothing will distract at least some members of a congregation.

Shoes should be of a material that can be cleaned and polished or otherwise renewed. I know of one pastor who wears sandals and no socks during Sunday services. There is no scriptural prohibition, but why offend even a few? Church is not the beach. Moreover, in all our work, the Lord himself is our guest of honor.

Pastors with an aversion to dressing in suit and tie to lead in the church's high hour of worship should ponder such questions as: How would I dress to argue a case in court? Or to be interviewed for a job by the CEO of one of the country's great corporations? Most likely not in casual clothing but in clothing that is conservative, non-distracting, and suitable for serious business.

The above two illustrations show us that the choice of clothes we wear is determined to a large extent by the situation in which we wear them. They also show that our choice indicates the importance we ascribe to the situation. Were there not reasons that the Lord showed Moses how the high priest and his sons were to dress when officiating over worship in the tabernacle? (See Exodus 28:1-5.) And is not leading in the worship of the Triune God – Father, Son, and Holy Spirit – one of life's elevated moments?

My wife's sage advice, for female pastors, is that they should dress in ways that do not call undue attention to their attire, either by its flamboyance or skimpiness or poor fit.

When it comes to both men and women's dress standards, modesty seems to be an appropriate word.

I believe the same principle applies for both male and female pastors: they must dress as workers on duty, appropriate to the particular aspect of duty before them, whether to lead a Sunday-morning service or visit in the hospital or spend the weekend with their teens at a youth retreat.

In this matter, we can take a hint from John Roberts, the Chief Justice of the Supreme Court of the United States. He said recently that he and his fellow justices wear black robes because "this is not about us." As pastors, our work is not about us but about the Lord and his people.

We dress for others. And we dress to show respect for the Lord and his people. The Lord's instruction to Moses for the Levitical attire for worship was summarized thus: "Make tunics, sashes and caps for Aaron's sons to give them dignity and honor" (Exodus 28:40).

6. The Effective Pastor's Management of Family

Imagine a church in which three very young children have a reputation for running wildly through the church while their parents – the pastoral couple – are nowhere to be seen or are looking on uncomprehendingly. Or where pre-teen daughters routinely dress provocatively, following the lead of the culture and their school friends. Certainly, some children pose a special challenge, and every child can have his or her moments. Still, children who are disobedient, loud, and disruptive, or "wild," can seriously weaken pastoral effectiveness – and in severe cases can disqualify a pastor, whether male or female.

Such scenarios can help us understand why the scriptures indicate that management of family is an issue for the effective pastor. The "leader," as the New English Bible translates the word, "must manage his own family well and see that his children obey him, and he must do so in a manner worthy of full respect. (If anyone does not know how to manage his own family, how can he take care of God's church?)" (1 Timothy 3:4-5). Similar requirements are set before the deacons: "A deacon must be ... good at managing his children and his own household" (3:12, NEB).

Pastors who read this and who have no parenting issues may skip to the next of the seven characteristics. And perhaps they will offer a prayer for those who struggle to take higher ground in parenting – for the sake of their family and the kingdom of God.

Our culture certainly does not help parents and their children in matters of discipline. It is in a parenting – and perhaps especially a fathering – crisis. Some believe the development of the problem began as far back as two or three hundred years ago. David Blankenhorn's book *Fatherless America* gives the details with frightening clarity.

Pastors may come to pastoral ministry having been poorly parented themselves. This can weaken or distort parenting and especially fathering skills. For example, one young minister got in trouble with the social services agency in his community for spanking one of his children severely, leaving marks. His intent was not evil; those who knew the family noted that this was how his father had dealt with him.

Parenting skills are, to some degree, innate. Still, with study and practice, parents can correct their deficiencies. Pastoral couples may benefit from written and video resources from such organizations as Focus on the Family. They may learn by observing and modeling the parenting style of others. For extreme needs, professional counsel or parenting classes may be required. Effective parenting, and especially fathering, is a biblical mandate; therefore, pastors who need help in this area must take advantage of every possible resource.

Another reason that the culture is corrosive to good parenting is widespread permissiveness, the seeds of which were sown by people such as Dr. Spock some generations ago. Too often this permissiveness, as it applies to the practices of parenting, goes unchallenged. Rather than being free to do whatever they want, children need to learn boundaries through the loving authority of both parents. Steady, loving, fatherly authority is especially helpful for children navigating the rough years of adolescence. Permissiveness is not consistent with the scriptures. It appears to be based on a defective understanding of human nature.

I don't propose to unravel this knotty problem of the wholesome functioning of the pastor's family in a paragraph or two, but I think it is worth mentioning that parental and especially fatherly oversight will include daily prayer with the family. It will also include teaching children to pray, forming their conscience to know right from wrong, and teaching them to know and observe boundaries and to contribute in age-appropriate ways to the operation of the home. Above all else, it should include teaching the children the way of salvation and the rules of wholesome and upright living. How all this is realized must be worked out in the crucible of the family, or with outside help, if necessary.

Firm and wise parenting can minimize the danger that children will go astray, but it cannot rule it out, because children have free will and can choose to go in directions that parents do not approve. Our three children and their spouses are serving the Lord, for which we give thanks to God daily. But we cannot take full credit: God's grace was beamed toward our family through the three churches we served. Members of these churches created a spiritual community that helped us greatly in raising our children. We wish this blessing for every pastor.

In summary, why should parents who wish to be effective pastors consider it so important to raise an orderly family with well-behaved, respectful children? Most of all, because, as may be seen in scripture, this is God's plan. Beyond this, wholesome, happy children who are learning to respect others and the moral and relational boundaries of life will be welcomed into the company of parishioners. And for another, an orderly pastor's family tends to prompt church families to raise their expectations for their own children. Example is a powerful teacher.

7. The Effective Pastor's Management of Money

Consumerism is an ideology that is prevalent in our times. The feeling that we need "more" seems to work on us like a tranquilizer. It makes us more at ease even when we succumb to its impulse to acquire what we often don't need.

Consumerism is the often-unexamined notion that happiness comes from spending; that we are measured by what we have; that debt is acceptable if it keeps us from needing to wait; that we get our fixes from the mall or in the mail. The business world fuels this urge, putting almost any merchandise, small or large, at our disposal on terms of "possess now, pay later."

Society has experienced a sea change on this issue in little more than half a century. For example, according to the U.S. Federal Reserve database, total household debt (debt minus assets) in the U.S. in the 1950s was $0 (yes, zero), but by 2008 it was $13.8 trillion. According to a 2012 *Wall Street Journal* article by Francesco Guerrera, consumer debt in the United States increased 37 percent in the previous ten years. And according to CreditCards.com, in 2012, the amount of credit card debt carried by the average American household with at least one credit card was $15,950.

It's not that the whole of society is participating in this

spending and debt binge. After all, even high-school courses on consumer economics are flagging this behavior as a poor financial approach to life. But just as we're not aware of the existence of germs until fever sets in and we ache from head to foot, so we don't realize we are afflicted with consumerism until we have maxed out two or three credit cards and are shuffling funds anxiously from one account to another to keep the collection agency from the door. Once that happens, consumerism has taken us down.

When we present ourselves for pastoral ministry, and do so because we believe we are divinely called, we must take a hard look at the degree to which our debts limit us. We may have school loans to reckon with; this is common and often necessary these days. In addition, we may be burdened by additional credit card debt. I write with a feeling of sympathy when I imagine the burden some aspiring pastors carry because of school or other debts. Even so, let me make some suggestions for you to consider.

First, if you live with the sense that God has called you to a special ministry, nurture that sense. Ask the Lord to help you resist the consumerism of our times – for his sake. My best counsel, if you are already in the vortex of debt, is to seek a Christian business person whom you can trust with the details and whose influence you will allow to guide and even press you to follow a plan.

Second, tithe your income to the Lord's work faithfully. When you set aside 10 percent as a starting point, you acknowledge that all of your income belongs to the Lord and you are his steward, or manager. It is surprising how much this Bible-supported practice enhances our skill with the remaining 90 percent. My own opinion is that when we take the trouble to give the first 10 percent wisely, our practice in doing so will transfer to a wiser and more careful use of the other 90 percent. It is as though it amplifies our understanding that God cares about how we use the 90 percent.

Third, be realistic about what the burden of debt does to your spirit. Some experts say that taking on debt is justifiable for education and housing. And in fact, for almost everyone, buying a house involves going into debt. For many, so does buying a car. But the experts tell us that if paying our credit card bills, mortgage, and other debts takes more than 50 percent of our income, we have entered the danger zone. The anxiety that this creates is inconsistent with a life of contentment and trust.

If none of this wins your favor, look back to your call to the pastorate and the example you want to set before your flock. Wise money management on a modest income in the parsonage sets a good example for struggling families.

If you are at risk in this area of life, here's another suggestion: for at least one month, operate on a cash-only basis. Put your credit cards where you can't get at them easily. Pay cash for groceries. Pay cash at the mall and at the gas pump. We have been told that those who pay by cash spend up to 30 percent less than those who use credit cards. The reason is obvious. It's painless to make an impulsive purchase by offering a piece of plastic to pay for it. It's another matter when a purchase requires you to fish a $20 bill from your wallet and in so doing you notice that there are only four more of those bills left until payday.

Another idea that can help is to identify cash drains. For one month keep a journal of your spending, right down to the penny. It will take effort, but what it reveals may be priceless: coffees on the road, fast-food stops, impulsive purchases at the grocery store, unnecessary meals out – it all adds up.

I have one final down-to-earth suggestion: Let every prospective pastor or spouse read the book *The Millionaire Next Door* by Thomas J. Stanley, not to strive for riches but to see what millionaires know about money management. It will expose the lie of consumerism.

CHAPTER 6

Ten Tips for Young or Soon-to-Be Pastors

YOU'RE a third-year seminarian about to graduate, or you've just been appointed to serve your first church. You've got three years of seminary notes neatly filed away and you've kept every textbook. But these resources are not quelling your anxious thoughts and unanswered questions about the new experience just ahead.

Here are some basic practical and logistical suggestions from a seasoned pastor and long-term overseer of pastors. I hope they will give you some markers to put down as you start out your new, challenging, but somewhat frightening venture.

1. Ground your ministry in thirty to sixty minutes of daily Bible reading and prayer for your people at the beginning of each day. Pray often at other moments throughout the day as well. Consider that pastoral labors grounded in prayer are the "gold, silver, [and] costly stones" that the apostle Paul speaks of as durable building materials used in pastoral labors (1 Corinthians 3:10-15).

2. If your study is at the church, be there at a set time each workday. I suggest 8 a.m. God honors a good work ethic.

3. Spend your mornings in sermon preparation, reading, and related study. Be diligent. If you have a church secretary or office assistant ask him or her to guard these hours. Don't allow legitimate resources such as the Internet, TV, newspapers, and news magazines to become time wasters. Beware, as well, of the potential time lost in long phone calls, even with family. "If in the morning you throw moments away, you will not catch them up in the course of the day."

4. Get an exercise program and stick to it, whether it be jogging or swimming or walking or exercising to a DVD. If you have no better idea, consider, as one possibility, incorporating some exercise into an extended noon hour. A jog, then a sandwich, apple, and beverage need take no more than an hour and a half.

5. Do not have favorites in the congregation. If your attachment to one person, or couple, or family becomes obvious – you meet regularly for meals together, or even go camping together – this will make other members feel second-class. It is a long-standing principle that the pastor must be pastor to all the people all the time, although special needs may at times need special attention. It is worth self-denial to maintain this in both reality and perception. If you need more intimate friendships, form them outside the congregation – with a neighboring minister, for example.

6. Never discuss church problems – especially difficult people – in the presence of growing children. They do not have the wisdom to handle adult problems. If they come to think that their parents are being hurt, their trust may be damaged, and eventually their respect for Christ and his church, too.

7. If congregational division develops over some issue (whether launching a building program, adding a staff member, changing the music program, or even painting the church kitchen), give good leadership through proper boards or committees. But don't take sides by talking informally with one faction or the other. To do so will cause a congregational rift and likely shorten your tenure.

8. Develop a clear understanding of your social boundaries and observe them – with the opposite sex, the aged, children, young people, church officers, staff members, and so forth. Insofar as it is possible, keep all pastoral relationships above reproach.

9. However modest your income, set an example of responsible stewardship. Show leadership in tithing your income. The church treasurer will be aware of this. If you have debts that are out of hand, seek professional counsel. Your care with money will increase the congregation's trust in your leadership.

10. Never ask to borrow money from your parishioners. To do so puts parishioners at a disadvantage. It may reduce their respect for you, and if money borrowed is not repaid as agreed, this may create a rift that puts your pastoral tenure at risk.

Pastoral ministry is built on the abilities to preach and teach the Bible, provide pastoral care, and administer. But each of these is built in turn on genuine godliness, integrity, good interpersonal skills, and beyond these, common sense.

The ten points above do not tell the whole story, but they offer some time-tested suggestions to help a minister's tenure be more effective and enduring, for the sake of the congregation and the Lord.

CHAPTER 7

Your First Thirty Days at a New Church

A young pastor's first church assignment is usually to the oversight of a modest-sized congregation. When I was finishing seminary, the professor of pastoral care cautioned us, in our search for a pastoral assignment, not to look for the biggest church available, or the one with the largest salary or most impressive building or greatest prestige in the community. Instead, he said, we should look for a church that presented us with the biggest challenge or where we sensed we were most needed.

But, once the new pastor has been given such an assignment, what first steps should he or she take? Here are my suggestions for the first thirty days.

1. Prepare and make available to your contact person (chair of the church board or of the transition committee) a fact sheet to share with the congregation before you arrive. This should tell who you are, where you come from, what other work you have done either as a layperson or a pastor, any special achievements you have accomplished, who your spouse and family are, and any special skills you bring to the situation. I'm not suggesting that it be a brag sheet, just a simple outline of basic facts.

2. Try to have your living quarters basically (note, basically) settled in a week's time so the congregation can see that you have come to stay and to work. A week may not be long enough if you have to find housing or await completion of renovations or must buy furniture or otherwise deal with unusual distractions or delays in getting settled. Every situation is different, but try to be fully on the job within a week.

3. Get a pastor's study settled as soon as possible because this will be your major workroom. Call this from the start your "study," not your "office." The church office is where secretarial and other staff do their work, records are kept, the phone is answered, and people make appointments. A study is where the minister prepares sermons and lessons, conducts personal devotions, and receives people for counsel. This is an important distinction to teach to your congregation.

4. Ask the secretary of the church board for the board minutes of the last six months. Read them to get a sense of how business is done, what issues have been addressed recently and are still active, any positions that need to be filled, and stresses in the congregation that are unresolved. If the secretary is sensitive about releasing them to you, let the chair of the board know of your interest and leave it to him or her whether the minutes are produced or not. In any event, return the minutes as soon as possible.

5. Lay plans to pay a short visit to the home of each of the church board members. This will show an interest in them; enable them to get better acquainted with you, and you with them, at the personal and social level; and generally prepare the way for you to work with them. Offer prayer in each home. You are their pastor.

6. Introduce yourself to any key business people or civic leaders in the community who may or may not be members of your church. Depending on the size of the community, this may include bank managers, major merchants, funeral directors, the mayor of the town, and hospital administrators. A cordial visit in the early weeks of your pastorate will shorten the time you need to become acquainted with and known in the community. This is harder to do in a large city but still worth the effort.

7. Set yourself a schedule for a working day and get the schedule under way as soon as your household is settled. I suggest the following:
   - 8 a.m. to 12 noon – In your study with your books and other study materials
   - 12 noon to 1 p.m. – Lunch
   - 1 p.m. to 3 p.m. – Administrative matters such as letters, phone calls to board members, checking administrative details with secretary
   - 3 p.m. to 5 p.m. – Visits to hospital, retirement homes, shut-ins, new contacts; counseling sessions in the study
   - 5 p.m. to 7 p.m. – Home with spouse and family
   - 7 p.m. to 9 p.m. – You may find it necessary to give some evenings to committees that meet in the evening or to make some visits that are possible only after people's work hours. Try not to make this a nightly schedule.

Pastors of a busy church may question the workability of the morning part of this schedule. However, pastors who are in it for the long haul learn to make their mornings count.

You will find as you become busy with church and community matters that you cannot keep this schedule exactly. But it is still a good idea to establish a pattern when you're new to the church and the congregation has not yet begun to draw on you. Doing so will say to yourself and others that these are the tasks that matter and these are their proportions. Thus is a pastoral conscience formed. Thus are key tasks (such as preparing sermons) not so likely to be overlooked or be done superficially. They will continue as priorities even if schedules have to be changed.

8. Make careful preparation for your first appearances in the pulpit because "first impressions are lasting."
   - Prepare yourself with ample prayer.
   - Prepare your sermon early (no Saturday-night specials).
   - Prepare the pastoral prayer – this particular prayer should not be impromptu.
   - Don't enter this new assignment in the spirit of a revolutionary who is going to make the church over in every respect as quickly as possible. Instead, acquaint yourself fully with the church's order of worship and follow it at the beginning of your tenure unless there is some glaring need to make changes. Even then, make them sparingly; try to remember that, if needed, opportunities to redesign worship practices will present themselves with less resistance after you have won the congregation's trust.
   - Come directly to the pulpit from the study, from your knees; socializing before service, moving about opening or closing windows, should not be necessary. Trusted laypersons should be assigned to such tasks. And there will be time to greet the people individually after the service is concluded.
   - Plan your personal attire carefully because in our culture our clothes speak volumes.

9. Establish at the outset (not necessarily for general publication but for personal direction) which day you

will take each week to renew yourself in body and soul – to fish, or picnic with the family, go out of town to a retreat setting, or otherwise change your pace, laying off the harness for a few hours.

The schedule I lay out as a pattern may seem too tight to some who wish to have a more leisurely 9-to-5 life. Effective pastors do not think in 9-to-5 terms. They come to the task as servants of the Lord and of his people; while intending to live a life of balance, for reasons of health and mental well being, as well as good family dynamics, they recognize that servanthood can't be lived entirely by the clock.

10. Understand that the trust you develop as a basis for good working relationships with the congregation will form fairly quickly if you meet four conditions:
    (1) The members experience you early as authentic, approachable, and graciously honest.
    (2) They sense early that you know what you're doing and that you work to a plan (learning what the pastoral task is about and how to work to a plan is one of the greatest values of seminary training).
    (3) They see that you have a good work ethic (laziness, or what someone has called "random path" procedures – moving from one issue to another without much order – is quickly detected).
    (4) They find you credible and competent in the pulpit, with a good blend of spiritual depth and down-to-earth wisdom and competence.

I wish for all pastors a pastoral experience that stretches them, tests them, and at the same time gives them a sense that in carrying out the pastoral task under God they are doing what they came into the world to do. This is my understanding of vocation.

CHAPTER 8

The Blessing of Church Order

AS a young pastor just out of seminary, I was chairing the monthly board meeting in the education center of the church. I could feel the warmth and respect of the people for the six of us – Kathleen and me and our four young children – and previous board meetings had gone well.

But when I opened the floor for new business during this meeting the members turned from me and entered into animated debate. A new subject had cropped up: The first wedding in the new sanctuary had been scheduled. What would the guidelines be for decorating the place?

The meeting became a bit disorderly. There was the protect-the-new-paint faction and the opposing let-the-kids-decorate-it's-their-day faction and the exchanges were getting more intense.

I called them to order and decorum returned. I told them I could offer a solution. They were polite and interested. Drawing on a course I had taken in seminary called simply Church Administration, I explained that each congregation has at least two committees of the official board: a board (or committee) responsible for "spiritualities" and another for "temporalities."

The first, the one for spiritualities (called the board of stewards), was responsible to work under the pastor for the care of persons: shut-ins, the hospitalized, new babies, etc.

They were responsible also for preparing the elements for the Lord's Supper.

The members of the board of temporalities (then called trustees) were responsible for the care of property. They were to deal with repairs, or review insurance policies, or monitor the condition of church equipment.

The people listened quietly. I explained that these two boards or committees were both accountable to the official board. I went on to suggest that they could refer the question of decorating the sanctuary for a wedding to the board responsible for temporalities and expect them to bring back a recommendation at the next meeting.

In due time the issue was resolved. More importantly, a peril had been averted: the peril of opening the way, by poor administration, for power struggles over the uses of the new building.

All this came back to me this morning when Kathleen and I were reading from the book of Numbers. As the great throng of Israelites was about to set out from Sinai for their wilderness journey, they received special administrative instructions from God. They were to take a census of all the people, especially to count all the men twenty and older, because these were to be the fighting men. The number reported was 603,550 (Numbers 1).

Then the Israelites were given instructions on how the camp was to be laid out when they were not on the move. The Tent of Meeting was to be at the center because God was the center of the community's life. The Levites, as servants of the tabernacle, were to locate on its three sides. Then the twelve tribes were to locate one row behind them from the tent, placing three tribes on each of the four sides (Numbers 2).

Should the organization and structure of today's church be any less clear? Whether it is a local church, an annual conference, or a general conference, the body that has rules and prescribed procedures and adheres to them is more likely to be administered in a godly fashion. Its leaders will always be given rightful authority but with clearly defined limits. The life of the body is then ordered to guarantee that each member will have a voice at some level of the organization. Across the years I have seen how simple organizational parameters, when applied and maintained, generate trust and harmony.

The Bible has so much to teach us about church life, and when we follow these teachings, God's people are more likely to be wholesome in their deliberations and open to the blessing of God in their endeavors.

PART II

THE PASTOR AS PREACHER

CHAPTER 9

What Congregations Want Most in a Pastor

IN an age that finds it easy to lament the ineffectiveness of the church, it's good to ask, What are churches doing right? Are there common features to churches that are thriving and consistently incorporating new converts into the life of the congregation?

Thom S. Rainer wanted to know, and he chose a little-used way to find out, which he details in his book *Surprising Insights from the Unchurched*. He did not seek out the unchurched to ask what they would look for if they were searching for a church. Rather, he asked those he calls the "formerly unchurched."

A formerly unchurched person, by Rainer's definition, is "one who has not been in church, except sporadically, for at least ten years (most for a lifetime) but has recently become active in the church. They are to be Christians, not merely church attenders."

In his very first chapter he explodes nine myths about the unchurched. For example, contrary to the opinion of some, the unchurched are not turned off by denominational labels. His study shows that this is not a big concern to them. He also shows that pulpit fare does not have to be thin gruel – essentially a form of entertainment – to hold their attention;

in fact, the opposite is so. He also found that pastors do not have to be superstars to succeed.

At the time of his writing of the book, Rainer was founder and dean of the Billy Graham School of Missions, Evangelism, and Church Growth at Southern Baptist Theological Seminary in Louisville, Kentucky. He had been pastor or interim pastor of ten churches, had written broadly in his field, and was sought after to speak at conferences about church growth concerns dear to his heart.

His book reports on a study that he and his research team conducted. It is organized and written with such care and skill that it makes for very interesting reading. The author and his team interviewed 353 of the "formerly unchurched," asking them many open-ended questions. This involved thousands of hours of interviews. The team also talked to 350 "transfer Christians," Christians of longer duration who also had interesting insights into what drew them to the church where they were now members. Add to all these, extensive, in-depth interviews conducted with 101 effective evangelical pastors and six years of study involving more than 2,000 effective evangelistic churches.

Only evangelical congregations were included, but those chosen were from seven different denominations (including Wesleyan, Nazarene, Assemblies of God, and United Methodist), plus 37 independent congregations of varying traditions. These churches were from all regions of the country and included African-American, Hispanic, and other segments of the population.

An effective evangelistic church, according to the study's definition, is a church that has no fewer than 26 conversions a year and a conversion ratio of less than 20:1. That is, to qualify, a church of 300 members should have at least thirty conversions a year.

The study's insights are sometimes arresting, sometimes affirming of already held viewpoints, and in several respects deeply convicting.

For example, one chart shows responses to the question, "What factors led you to choose this church?"

The most common response, from 90 percent of respondents, was the pastor and his preaching. The second most common, from 88 percent of respondents, was doctrine. Put these together and it becomes immediately evident that the formerly unchurched touched by the study were hungry for the content of the Christian faith to be presented well by pastors they were attracted to. Only 11 percent of respondents said a church's worship style/music determined their choice; this was second to last on the list.

Interest in preaching and clear doctrine – this was not a one-shot response but one that comes up repeatedly in the book, making it all the worthier of deep reflection. And the insights gleaned from the 101 pastors interviewed were essentially the same as those gleaned from the 353 formerly unchurched. Rainer writes that the formerly unchurched were "not only interested in knowing about doctrine, they were attracted to conservative, evangelical churches that were uncompromising in their beliefs."

Getting the formerly unchurched to come to church for a few Sundays is one thing; assimilating them into the church as active participants in ministries is another. At this point, the study turned up another significant fact. Rainer writes, "We found an overwhelmingly convincing relationship between effective assimilation and involvement in small groups. Most of our data was on Sunday school …"

The importance of a well-directed Sunday school comes up several times in the book. The combined findings of a Barna study and one by Rainer's researchers was that "new Christians who immediately became active in Sunday school were five times more likely to remain in the church five years later than those who were active in worship services alone."

Small groups provide a basis for friendship, Christian fellowship, and further scriptural teaching.

Rainer's study ranges wide. The physical facilities of churches that were reaching the formerly unchurched are characterized generally as clean, attractive, with excellent, up-to-date nursery equipment in service; good signage; well-maintained parking lots; and friendliness everywhere. Worship services were joyful events.

The positive influence of the pastor in a thriving and growing church came to the fore so regularly in interviews with the formerly unchurched that part two of the book devotes five chapters to the review of findings gleaned from 101 pastors of effective churches. What do they say are their greatest strengths? And their greatest weaknesses? Rainer reports that to a person they were quite willing to speak freely of both.

In a list of twelve strengths, 72 percent said their greatest strength was vision casting. As for their comments on their greatest weakness, 72 percent said it was pastoral ministry: counseling, hospital visitation, weddings, and funerals. This, plus the other eleven acknowledged weaknesses, indicate that this type of leader tends to be more managerial than pastoral.

However, the larger picture gleaned from the formerly unchurched plus the self-evaluations of the 101 pastors show pastors of thriving churches to be leaders who engender trust, demonstrate integrity, have a strong work ethic, have a good sense of humor, and tend to be impatient when things don't progress. They are forthright about both their perceived weaknesses and strengths. To their followers, they are "real." Above all, they are committed passionately to their belief system and to reaching the lost for Christ.

To a large number, the ministry of preaching is primary. Rainer writes, "The leaders whose churches are reaching the unchurched are passionate about preaching." They list preaching as "the most exciting and challenging task." They give ample time to preparation. In fact, this note concerning the centrality of preaching and doctrinal teaching is so prominent throughout the book that a whole chapter is devoted to preaching. These leaders have a conservative, biblical theology about the lost and a passion to reach them, a passion that is contagious to their churches.

CHAPTER 10

How One Preacher Prepares a Sermon

THE study summarized in the previous chapter highlights the importance of preaching to recently converted churchgoers. Is it important enough to move us pastors to develop a trusted method of sermon preparation?

In his book *Fire in Thy Mouth*, Donald Miller notes wryly that if the Protestant church ever dies with a knife in its back, that knife will be the Protestant sermon. The comment reflects a sense that preaching in the Protestant pulpit is often far below standard. Perhaps things have improved since 1976, when he wrote those words, but good preaching is so central to Protestantism that what he says should capture our attention. There are good preachers sprinkled across the continent, to be sure, but we should not rest until every pulpit is alive with God's truth, clearly and passionately delivered.

This chapter suggests a method of sermon preparation that can contribute to that goal. Arguably, no one method will fit all personalities. Pastors will develop their own procedures by trial and error. What is important is that they develop a method that will produce a certain consistency of results and will ensure that, with each sermon, the scriptures receive a fair and accurate treatment. I do not wish to suggest that a sermon is a purely human achievement. I will speak later of the spiritual dimension of the task. For now, I simply want to put on paper the sequence of steps that I have found necessary.

STEP 1: EXPLORE THE TEXT

I customarily begin by making notes in a spiral notebook. I first write, verse by verse, the passage on which I'm going to preach. Even if I am to speak from one verse, I establish the context first. For example, if I am preparing a sermon on as short a text as, "... you will always be rich enough to be generous" (2 Corinthians 9:11, NEB), I begin by reproducing the verses for the whole chapter, or at least from verse 6 to 15. In some cases I paraphrase a verse if its meaning is clear to me. In other cases I may write the full verse word for word, or I may try to restate its essence.

This discipline has significant value for me.

For one thing, it brings me face-to-face with the passage I hope to draw from, saving me from the peril of superficiality. It also keeps me from drawing conclusions about what a text says until I have acquainted myself with its context. In literature, every text is shaped by its context.

For another thing, this discipline makes me pay tribute to the importance of a whole passage.

For yet another, the exercise sometimes makes me aware of important insights right at the start. For example, in this first exercise I may note a word that is repeated or a contrast that is made that gives me a hint, right at the outset, where the text may be taking me. In reading 1 Peter 2:13-3:7 recently, I underlined the word "submit" each of the four times that it occurs. Such a notation may prove to be the starting point of the sermon.

STEP 2: REVIEW PRESENT KNOWLEDGE

I may then jot down anything I know about the text before seeking the counsel of the commentaries. In the above case, my notes would be on the word "submit." Moreover, the initial exercise may already show me a pattern, or may disclose the significance of a certain sentence or phrase. Or it may make me aware of another portion of scripture that I should keep in mind. For example, a reading of the conversion of Zacchaeus, the chief tax collector (Luke 19:1-10), may lead me to think about Leviticus 6:1-7, which instructs Israel in how they are to make restitution for wrongs committed. These initial jottings may show their worth later in my preparation.

Step 3: Assemble Tools

I make sure my tools are at hand and prepare to use them, though I may not use all of them every time I study a text. I refer to such tools as a lexicon for the definition of words that are uncommon; a good concordance to help in the deeper study of important words; and a Bible dictionary for questions about background. Some go further and include a grammar to help in the study of syntax – showing how words go together to create meaning – and word-study books. Haddon W. Robinson, in his excellent homiletics text *Biblical Preaching: The Development and Delivery of Expository Messages*, suggests some of the best resources under each of these categories (pp. 60-64).

Of course, as a second tier of resources I make sure I have within easy reach a good and adequate dictionary of the English language, a useful text on Old Testament theology, and another on New Testament theology. It is sometimes surprising the clarity that may be brought to a text by considering the meaning of a word in English or looking up a subject in the index of a book on biblical theology.

Step 4: Consult Commentaries

I consult commentaries for deeper insights, making notes as I go. One wise pastor stated that reading without a pencil in hand or laptop accessible is a waste of time. Even though there are commentary aids on the Internet, it can still be argued that very serious preachers should build a physical library that gives access to good commentaries for every book of the Bible. I suggest, for starters, owning three commentaries for each biblical book: one that is expository; one that is homiletical, or at least that has a devotional quality; and one that gives the fruit of contemporary scholarship. Over time, I achieved this goal for a number of the books of the Bible. However, I wish I had seen the value of this practice earlier in my ministry.

Some experts counsel against buying sets of commentaries without evidence that the volumes that constitute them are of consistent quality. Sometimes a preacher can find used commentaries in a used bookstore and even more easily online, or by helping a retired pastor to thin out portions of his library. The Internet provides some good staple digitized commentaries. If you're unsure of what is the best commentary for your money or best use of time on the Internet, seek the advice of a good and trusted biblical scholar.

One word of caution: if you try to include in your sermon all that you discover in your study time, you can be sure that at least half your congregation will go to sleep. The research and study I refer to is meant to enrich the sermon. The late Dr. Turkington of Asbury Theological Seminary taught that the material a preacher gathers is like the scaffolding used to build a house. Once the house is built, the scaffolding is taken down.

I find it helpful, when possible, to consult commentaries of both Wesleyan and Reformed persuasion on the same text. On major texts, there is often little disagreement between these traditions. For the former, Adam Clarke's *Commentary on the Bible* is still a worthy choice. And for the latter, you might consider Jamieson, Fausset, and Brown's *Critical and Explanatory Commentary on the Whole Bible*. Both are available on the Internet. I have found a little set by William Barclay, the Daily Bible Study Series, a wonderful resource that often combines the exegetical with the devotional and homiletical. Barclay's Greek word studies are rich and illuminating.

In nineteen years of visiting pastors' studies, I noted a correlation between the richness of the resources gathered and the quality of pulpit fare delivered. Lean shelves usually went along with lean fare.

An aside: In the preparation of sermons, the difference between spaced vs. massed preparation is worth considering. Learning theory has long told us that twelve hours parceled out at two hours a day for six days will produce a much more fruitful result than twelve hours spent in a block on one day. The amount of time is the same in each case, but twelve hours spent in one block doesn't take into account the mind's ability to work on an issue "in the background," while otherwise occupied. Pastors who have spent some time in the morning studying a text may find that its meaning becomes clear, or a sermon outline suggests itself, while they are on the way to the hospital in the afternoon. Insights sometimes come after a night's sleep.

A further value of spreading the study time across several days is the time this gives a preacher to correct conclusions or clarify difficult points. Even further, spreading sermon preparation across most of the week increases the likelihood that illustrations will present themselves from here and there.

About illustrations: You may catch insights for illustrations from reading newspapers or hearing newscasts or from recalling personal experiences or memories. It is wonderful how the mind cross-references matters when given the time to do so.

STEP 5: CONSIDER INITIAL IDEAS

As I collect my notes, thoughts may come to me that are not from commentaries or other reading. I save them in writing, because good ideas are elusive if not captured. I may have an idea how to introduce the sermon I'm working on to pique listeners' interest. When these thoughts come up, I jot them down right in the midst of my notes. If the thought is for an introduction, I will write in the margin beside my notation, "intro?" But I do not commit right away to use this because doing so may dry up the flow of ideas that my mind may have for me. (Sometimes I find that by week's end my notes may have two or three suggestions for an introduction followed by a question mark. The same may be so for a conclusion.)

STEP 6: ESTABLISH UNITY

As the week moves along, I begin to look for the key idea, or the major issue, or the central question. The reason for this is that a sermon – if it is to be remembered by the hearers – must have unity. That is, it must say one thing. One test of unity is to ask, can I summarize the sermon in one sentence? The outline may be divided into sub-points, but the one idea or one question or one thought must never be far from my mind or that of my hearers.

I recall a sermon preached by a Methodist lay preacher named Rex Moon. He announced that "people are not doing very well without Jesus." That was his thesis. From then on, his insights, illustrations, and repetitions stayed with the point he had made at the outset. It may be an extreme example, but it serves to make the point that creating sermons that are memorable requires finding a central issue and presenting it for all it is worth. The wisdom of this is evident when I tell you that I heard that sermon sixty years ago.

STEP 7: ESTABLISH SHAPE

I have always tried to remember, whenever I preach – whatever type of sermon it may be, and whatever the mean age of my listeners – that a sermon always has a beginning, middle, and end. I have heard many attempts to order a sermon otherwise, and have tried some of them myself, but have found that no new style of communication, however strongly it is commended, can safely violate this rule.

I construct the beginning of my sermons to speak to an assumed "ho-hum" on the part of at least some of my listeners. They are likely asking why they should listen to this sermon. Their interest must be aroused. I do this with a statement, or a question, or the findings of a study, or a story, or a quotation, or a combination of these. Any one of them will do so long as it is interesting, capable of arousing curiosity, and directly related to the theme of the sermon.

I always set forth, between the beginning and the body of the sermon, a clear intimation of where the sermon is going to go, what I will attempt, how I'm going to get to my goal. Fred B. Craddock, former professor at the Candler School of Theology, Emory University, puts this concretely: "People will get on the bus if they know that it's going somewhere and they know where it's going." I find it is best to keep this part short, to make it a simple map or signpost. Doing this helps people to listen. It's always good to assist the listener as much as possible. The Southern preacher's explanation of how he proceeded is worth considering: "First, I tell 'em what I'm going to tell 'em; then I tell 'em; then I tell 'em what I told 'em."

The middle is the body of the sermon. If the sermon is based on 1 John 1:7, for example, the middle of the sermon may be built on the three verbs involved: we walk, we have fellowship, and the blood cleanses. If it is built on the opening words of Psalm 13, "How long, O Lord?" it may address the question, Why doesn't God answer my prayers sooner? The sermon may draw some of its answers to the question from the psalm and some from outside the psalm. The psalmist's question is worth wrestling with in the presence of a body of God's people.

Most times I follow the generalization that the end of the sermon should answer the question, "So what?" That is, why should this matter to me and what do you want me to do?

A seminary professor asked his class to write and then deposit their sermons in his office. He was slow in returning them with his comments. One day a seminarian noticed the professor's office door was open and the professor was in. Eager to get a response to his sermon, he stuck his head in the door and asked, cheerfully, "Will it do?" The professor replied, "Do what?"

That is always an appropriate question to ask of a sermon: What do we expect it to do? How do we want the listeners to respond? What do we want them to attempt, to change, to believe, to do? It takes creativity to avoid predictability in writing a conclusion.

Moving past this generalization about conclusions, there are more ways than one to conclude a sermon. The conclusion can be a story or a recapitulation, or a gospel appeal, or even a question. W.E. Sangster, the famous English Methodist preacher, makes the point that the conclusion should not be merely an add-on. It should somehow flow out of the body of the sermon. That is, it should be integral to the matter at hand.

It is reported that some preachers prepare their conclusions first, but I think this is not the best procedure. Often, for me the effective conclusion has come hardest, if at all. This may be because I have not developed my imagination as I should or because I have not been as clear about the importance of the conclusion. I'm still working on it.

STEP 8: CONSTRUCT THE SERMON

Once I have gathered ideas, notations, insights, and questions, have established unity, and have roughed in the shape of the sermon, it is time for me to begin constructing the message. I attempt to do this from the body of the sermon outward. That is, I want to be sure I know what the message is before deciding how to introduce or conclude it. Once I have set down the sermon's essence, I rake through the notes and find the most suitable introduction. By the time I come to this stage I often have ten or more pages of notes in my notebook.

To me this step is one of the most difficult to take in preparation because it calls for me to commit: that is, to put my sermon notes into a fuller statement on paper. Sometimes (not very often, unfortunately) the sermon presents itself from my study notes. The outline may form spontaneously.

For example, one afternoon during my pastoral days I decided to walk to the hospital to visit patients from our congregation. It was about one mile from the church. The week was wearing on and I had made my notes, but no outline was presenting itself. Then, as I walked past Prof. Miller's house on Elm Street, the outline suddenly came to me fully formed. I stopped, took an envelope from my pocket, and, standing there on the sidewalk, I wrote it down.

Even when the development doesn't present itself so easily, there is usually something nestled in your notes that will give you the lead you need to continue.

An aside: What place does prayer have in the preparation of a sermon? If the sermon is prepared without prayer, this will show in its delivery. It will come off as an academic exercise, a human achievement, or even a time-filler. On the other hand, if a sermon is prepared mainly as a devotional exercise, it will come across as nice to know but not very compelling.

The ideal is to get a balance between prayer and the hard work of sermon preparation. To achieve the balance, it is good to begin each study session with a prayer. Pray for wisdom and insight. Pray for divine direction as you begin your search. When I come to an impasse in breaking open the meaning of a passage, I often stop and pray – sometimes with remarkable results. Since, as we affirm, the passage is the Word of God, then he is the one, better than anyone else, to open its truth to the humble seeker.

It is especially important to pray when you begin to form the sermon from the work you have done. Your hope is to come before a congregation with a fresh word of divine insight formed into a "message" that can bless the hearers and glorify God.

STEP 9: PREPARE FINAL PULPIT NOTES

Next, I put my notes together in the form I plan to take them to the pulpit.

Some preachers put together a full manuscript. In such cases, notes must be clear enough to not preclude eye contact with the congregation. Eye contact is crucial to real preaching. On one occasion I went to hear a preacher who was having a hard time satisfying the expectations of his congregation. I estimated that he had eye contact with his listeners only about 5 percent of the time. The sermon was tedious. Some preachers learn how to use a manuscript very skillfully, but in my opinion this is not the best procedure for the delivery of a sermon from the heart of the preacher to the hearts of the congregation.

At the other extreme, some preachers master the art of speaking extemporaneously. That is, they know from careful preparation what they're going to say, but they leave the exact words to the inspiration of the moment. This ensures eye contact and usually adds vitality and emotional tone to the event. It is a good idea for the extemporaneous preacher to have a full manuscript back in the study. If nothing else, this preserves the fruit of his preparation to save for another day. I have found that I may remember the essence of a sermon I have prepared, but see, when I look back at the notes, that some valuable insights or details had vanished from my memory.

Most preachers I know anything about find themselves somewhere between these two approaches. I place myself in this third category. I usually have two or three pages of notes in front of me, but they are there largely as a safety measure. I may turn to them to prompt a second point or to remind me of an illustration or to otherwise support my aging memory.

If notes are skillfully used, hearers have little awareness of them.

STEP 10: ABSORB THE SERMON

When I make final preparations of a sermon far enough ahead of the event, the message becomes more a part of me. I have time to review my notes, memorize my points, and tell the stories to myself or rehearse them in an empty sanctuary (or in the woods, which is where the young Billy Graham practiced) until they are ready for an energized delivery.

A confession: I envy the preacher who can end his devotion to study time sometime on Friday with a finished sermon in hand. I've never been able to do that unless I was reworking a sermon I had delivered before. My tendency is to keep digging until the time is perilously near. For that reason, I should not be offering advice on this point. But be assured, the experts will tell you of the worth of giving yourself time to absorb, gestate, identify with, and feel the truth you are going to deliver. The preaching of the sermon may last from twenty to thirty minutes, but when it is given clearly, forcefully, and in the power of God's Holy Spirit, the effects can last a lifetime.

CHAPTER 11

Six Questions Preachers Can Ask Themselves About Their Sermons

THERE is a story about a young soprano in the Midwest whose voice showed great promise – even operatic possibilities. She was an unusually fine singer with a keen ear who could memorize music quickly. Her teacher sent her to audition with a famous voice coach in New York. The coach, however, refused to take her as a student. The reason he gave? "She lacks the power of self-criticism."

Self-criticism is essential in all artistic endeavors; and, in one sense, preaching is an artistic endeavor. If we preachers lack the power of self-criticism, we may not be overtly rejected by our people as this young singer was by a coach, but we may preach for a lifetime, all the while falling far short of our potential. To avoid this, it is good to have a method for critiquing our own sermons.

The key is knowing the right questions to ask and then to answer and act on them. Here are six questions preachers can ask of every sermon they preach.

1. Is This Sermon Biblical?

Just exactly what is biblical preaching? Haddon Robinson, prince of contemporary preachers, has the question in mind when he says, "Expository preaching is the communication of a biblical concept, derived from and transmitted through a historical, grammatical, and literary study of a passage in its context, which the Holy Spirit first applies to the personality and experience of the preacher, then through him to his hearers."

The definition seems complex, but here are its elements in question form: Is the thesis of my sermon in harmony with the mainline of biblical truth? Does the sermon show that I have studied the passage in terms of its historical setting? Have I examined its grammatical elements? Is there evidence that I am aware of the literary category the passage belongs to, for example, prophecy or parable? Has the passage made its impact on me first? Finally, will the hearers get the message?

One might quibble that Robinson's definition says nothing about Christ, the one to whom all preaching should point. Aside from that, is his definition too academic? Many a biblical sermon has been preached without meeting its exacting criteria – at least consciously. Nevertheless, on my repeated reading of it, the definition registers as being on the mark. Without this arduous background work, sermons are usually mediocre at best.

The question "Is the sermon biblical?" asks whether I have taken seriously the passage on which the sermon is built. Have I carefully determined its central issue? Is the sermon in some way related to a major biblical truth, for example, the Creation, the Fall of humanity, Redemption? When we take such questions seriously in the early stages of our study, our sermon is more likely to be biblically accurate.

But the issue of biblical preaching is not fully addressed until one further question is asked – the premier question: Is the sermon Christ-centered? John Calvin said that preaching consists substantially of the clarification, exposition, interpretation, and reappropriation of the writers of the written Word in witness to the revealed Word. For example, Paul wrote to Timothy, "From childhood you have known the sacred writings that are able to instruct you for salvation through faith in Christ Jesus" (2 Timothy 3:15, NRSV).

Biblical preaching thus involves the convergence of the written Word, the scriptures; the living Word, Christ Jesus; and the proclaimed Word in the language of our own day. When these come together, a sermon can be called biblical.

2. Does This Sermon Have Unity?

Was it not A.J. Gossip who said the last and hardest task for him in preparing a sermon was to reduce it to one sentence? That's how we can test a sermon for unity.

When Norman Vincent Peale was a young pastor, he committed himself to send his father a telegram no longer than ten words each Saturday night stating the essence of his sermon for the next morning. A telegram for a sermon on the prodigal son might read: God has a big surprise for sinners who come home. Or, forgiveness is always a big surprise.

Unity is a principle all artistic endeavors must follow. For example, a composer strikes a theme in a symphonic movement and then works with that theme in the strings and then in the woodwinds. Or he may invert the theme, introduce sub-themes, and tuck in interludes to rest his audience. But once the theme is struck, he unifies the movement around it from beginning to end. The same can be said about a choice oil painting or even an award-winning quilt. So it should be with a sermon.

If a sermon is preached in points, the points may be parallel, or they may be sequential, so that one point leads naturally to the next; but the one issue of the sermon must always be in view. By contrast, if the points don't show unity in the way they are stated, they are likely to come through as individual mini-sermons – or even wandering thoughts. How can you tell whether a sermon is unified or not? When it has unity, people will remember it. When it doesn't, they won't.

3. Does This Sermon Speak Concretely?

A word is abstract when, of itself, it does not elicit a visual image. Words like "helpfulness" and "truthfulness" and "weariness" are abstract. To be sure, we can't think precisely without abstract ideas such as these. But the preacher's task is always to make the abstract concrete to the hearer. Concreteness in speaking makes our communication vivid.

The best source for concrete preaching is the Bible. The story of Creation is concrete. It draws pictures even though it deals with truth beyond the full grasp of the human mind. The Bible doesn't teach us about marriage by giving us a definition; it gives us the story of Adam and Eve, which concretely confronts us with deep and essential truths about marital union.

The word "greed" may create only fuzz in the hearers' minds until they meet Achan and see his conduct during the conquest of Jericho.

The New Testament does no less with its stories: stories about conversion (Philip and the Ethiopian eunuch) and kindness (Dorcas making garments for the poor); stories about providence (Paul's divine deliverance from shipwreck on his way to Rome) and treacheries (Judas betraying Jesus). The cross of Jesus Christ will forever stand as the supreme concrete picture of the utter coarseness of humanity and sin, the fathomless reach of divine love, and the cost of redemptive suffering.

Consider the Proverbs. They give pithy insights into life for the training of the young, but they might remain opaque if not for the vivid similes they often draw. How about this one: "Like one who seizes a dog by the ears is a passer-by who meddles in a quarrel not his own" (26:17). Similes like this contribute to vividness in preaching. So do metaphors. For example, these words of Jesus to his disciples: "You are the light of the world" (Matthew 5:14). Concrete allusions are easier to come by for some than for others, but we can all strive to reach for them in order to make truth vivid. Preaching that always has a sense for the concrete will make its mark, because the mind of the hearer is not so much a dictionary of definitions as an art gallery where pictures can be easily hung. Preaching exploits this fact – concretely.

4. DOES THIS SERMON SPEAK RELEVANTLY?

The word "relevance" is easily misunderstood or misused. A college student attending the first week of classes for a course on western civilization finally closed his text and barked out in frustration, "This course is not relevant to me." It turned out that he couldn't see how the course would help him in his after-school job cleaning dorms. Being relevant in this case required the teacher to bring her subject matter to bear directly on the larger but overlooked aspects of his life. For that student to live in the here-and-now without any idea how he got here would be to live a narrow existence.

The preacher's task is also to give perspective to the here-and-now – eternal perspective – but we preachers sometimes confuse relevance with novelty. We cast about for a new and sometimes startling way to get our messages across. Indeed, innovation can be good, and we want preaching that is fresh and imaginative. But preaching that is only cute or clever or sensational is not necessarily relevant insofar as the Bible's message is concerned.

The sermon is relevant when it connects some basic biblical truth with the real needs of the people who hear. A missionary to an Indian tribe many years ago was discouraged because he could not seem to reach through to his people. The tribe had lost several children to an epidemic, and the parents were grieving stoically but deeply. Finally, the missionary began a message with the words, "I can tell you where your children are." Immediately he had their interest, and he was able to give them the gospel of eternal life in a way that was relevant to their sorrow.

We can test the sermon for its relevance by asking: Does the sermon speak to some universal human need – the need for hope, forgiveness, mercy, love, repentance, purity, holiness, or Christian assurance? Does it link the Bible's message with life as it is lived in the community? Is it faithful to truths that can be known only by divine revelation, such as the promised return of Christ, the certainty of final judgment, the revealed destiny of saints and sinners? Humans who are lost may not be aware of the need for these truths, but when they are preached with clarity and power they establish their own relevance.

P.T. Forsyth said that the preacher's first duty is not to secure his audience but to secure his gospel. Understanding the importance of relevance will save us from any effort in our preaching to be cute or clever or artsy. As Thomas Oden writes in *Pastoral Theology: Essentials of Ministry*, "Preaching that has lost touch with the vitalities of scripture is easily captivated by egocentric faddism, pretentiousness, and sentimentalism" (p. 135).

5. Can This Sermon Be Preached with Unction?

Unction is defined by Oden as "an intense awareness of the holy in the midst of our concrete life revealed through human speech" (p. 139). This question, then, unlike the previous four, centers attention on the preacher. But that is appropriate if, as Phillips Brooks, a nineteenth-century American clergyman, put it, preaching is truth mediated through human personality. Warren W. Wiersbe cites him as follows, in his book *Phillips Brooks: A Preacher of Truth and Life*: "The truest truth communicated in any other way than through the personality of brother man to men is not preached truth."

The spiritual state of the preacher matters, and this raises the issue of unction, or anointing, in preaching. Again, Oden describes anointing as "this subtle, compassionate, firm, set-apart quality of blessed speech – when firmness is accompanied by tenderness, when all is engendered in common worship, when moral commitment is bound with love."

We ought not to surrender to charismatic television preachers the exclusive use of the language of anointing. It's a biblical word used in both testaments to suggest a special divine endowment, and it should apply to all preachers. The word is applied to kings (2 Samuel 2:4), prophets (1 Kings 19:16), and priests (Exodus 28:41). Essentially, at Pentecost, the apostles, prophets, and evangelists spoke with compelling power. It was evident that the Spirit anointed them for the task.

Given this breadth of references to anointing, both as a general bestowal on the church and as a particular bestowal for special ministries, we ought to expect that every time we preach, we do so under an anointing, and to pray regularly to that end.

But this calls for further clarification. For one thing, the Spirit's anointing is usually consistent with our personalities. It is more likely to be experienced as a heightening and intensification of who God created us to be than as a radical change of our make-ups. Extroverts will likely continue to be extroverts, introverts to be introverts; proclaimers will proclaim with extraordinary power; teachers will teach with fresh clarity and persuasiveness. Barnabas will still be Barnabas; Paul will be Paul; but each will work with a particular anointing as a servant of the Most High.

6. Does This Sermon Have Bite?

You'll not find the term "bite" in a homiletics text. It's a term coined by my wife, Kathleen. She is a quiet person, but there are times when she is moved to share an idea with conviction. One of those times came when she was serving breakfast to three or four ministers who were attending a Christian education seminar in a church nearby.

During the meal in our dining room that morning, the conversation turned to sermons.

"The trouble with most sermons," she told the visiting ministers, "is that they lack bite."

The men were taken with the term and asked for an explanation.

She told them that earlier in her life she had attended a liberally oriented church. There were many good features to the services, she said, and the preachers often said uplifting things, but the sermons didn't come out anywhere. They were little more than nice talks, giving the hearers something to think about. There was no application. This sort of preaching, she said, could actually inoculate people against the gospel.

Kathleen had been trained as a teacher. She knew, for example, that a lesson must have a beginning designed to capture interest, a middle that gives the essence of the lesson, and an ending that calls the children to do something to show they had taken the lesson in. For example, after a teacher has taught a third grade class on the perils of pollution, he or she may list four things the children can do around the home to reduce the problems of pollution, urging their commitment to this new regimen. What was missing in many sermons, my wife contended, was this calling for some sort of response to show comprehension and agreement or the willingness to change.

A few days later, Kathleen got a call from one of the ministers, who lived 165 miles away. He said that, after that breakfast conversation, he had gone home and reworked his Sunday-morning sermon, and four people had responded to the invitation publicly. Later, another minister met her and told her that his preaching had not been the same since that breakfast table discussion.

Not every sermon needs to call for a public response. That could get predictable and perhaps tedious. But every sermon should call its hearers to do something about the truth. Recently, via television, we've been educated to the way that lawyers plead with great seriousness for a verdict. We preachers should do no less, making certain that our sermons call for response.

Here, then, are the six questions that we should ask of every sermon we preach. Is the sermon biblical? Does it have unity? Does it speak concretely? Does it speak relevantly? Can it be preached with unction? And does it have bite? Submitting our sermons to these questions will increase our powers of self-criticism and thus increase the impact of our preaching.

If we learn to answer these questions courageously, two things are sure to happen. First, when we know that we have preached poorly, the commendations of even a score of worshipers will not comfort us. And second, if we know in our hearts that we have preached well, we'll not be downcast even if not a soul offers a word of appreciation.

CHAPTER 12

Writing Your Way to Clearer Preaching

"I'M a preacher," you say, "not a writer." It's true that preaching and writing are different genres of communication, but both use the same material: words. Therefore, I believe that preachers who sharpen their skills in writing will enhance their effectiveness in preaching.

So, here's a simple thesis: Every preacher should constantly study how to use words both cogently and economically, and, across a lifetime, writing is the best discipline for this.

We preachers are not called to use slide rules as architects do or transits as surveyors do or wrenches as mechanics do. That's not to say we can't don an apron at a barbecue, or repair a lawnmower when necessary. However, faulty lawnmowers are not the reason we're in town. Our tools are words, and our skill with words is fundamental to our effectiveness.

Words are our stock-in-trade. Our work involves not only sermons but talks, Sunday-school lessons, hospital calls, home visits, counseling sessions, chairmanships, civic gatherings, and even conversations on the street. Effectiveness in all these activities in large measure depends on the skillful use of words.

Moreover, we preachers are judged a great deal by our words. Unlike many in the workplace, we do not keep office hours in a professional building at city center and then disappear for evenings and weekends. Instead, we live and work among the people. They see us in all of life's circumstances. Yes, we are judged by how we keep our lawns, the tidiness of our cars, the neatness of our homes, and the way we treat our spouse. But in terms of our competence as pastors, the way we use words is a major measuring stick.

WE ARE SERVANTS OF THE WORD

Perhaps the most important reason we should write to sharpen our skill with words is that we are called "servants of the Word." The main word for "word" in the Old Testament, *dabar*, occurs fourteen hundred times. As a verb, "to speak," it occurs another eleven hundred times. The expression "the word of Yahweh" occurs hundreds of times. The same is true of references to God and his word to his people, and expressions that identify a particular message as a word from God.

In fact, here's a summary of how one writer sees it: By God's Word the universe flowed into existence – "And God said, 'Let there be light,' and there was light" (Genesis 1:3). By God's ten words (commandments) the moral order was established (Deuteronomy 4:13). By his words of covenantal promise, Israel's existence was ordered (Exodus 20:22 and 23:19; Psalm 147:19-20). Through the prophets, God's word of judgment and salvation was uttered, and through his words he gave shape to the future before it happened (Isaiah 46:10).

The New Testament caps all this by calling Jesus "the Word." Mark traces Jesus back to the baptism of John as foretold in the prophets, and Matthew and Luke trace him back to the miraculous birth from a virgin. But John says he is the Word that was "in the beginning." Whenever the beginning was, the Word was already there.

This very Word – Jesus Christ – came to our world to make God's deepest thoughts and most serious intentions known to us. That's what words do – they make what is internal to a person and otherwise shrouded in secrecy external in order to be understood by another. Here's the wonder: Jesus is God's Word in human form, and we preachers, redeemed sinners though we are, are called to be servants of that Word.

Francis Bacon, scholar and scientist of the late sixteenth and early seventeenth centuries, gave the world a timeless aphorism about a connection between speaking and writing. I edit his words slightly to make them more contemporary: "Reading makes a full person, dialogue a ready person, and writing an exact person." Exact! For those who preach, writing adds the element of precision, thus clarity.

The ancient scriptures counsel us on this economical use of words: "The more the words, the less the meaning, and how does that profit anyone?" (Ecclesiastes 6:11). The writer identifies himself at the beginning of the book as The Preacher and later exhorts to economy with words in the activity of worship: "Do not be quick with your mouth, do not be hasty in your heart to utter anything before God. God is in heaven and you are on earth, so let your words be few" (5:2). This caution can be extended beyond preaching to include pulpit announcements, the "patter" of welcome offered to visitors, the wordy introductions singers give before they sing, and so on.

But what power when the right words are used simply! Blaise Pascal wrote, "Jesus Christ said great things so simply, that it seems as though He had not thought them great; and yet so clearly that we easily see what He thought of them. This clearness, joined to this simplicity, is wonderful."

WE HAVE AN INBORN CAPACITY FOR WORDS

We preachers, of all people, should be aware that humans have the capacity for language shared by no other creature. It is distinctive to our humanness. Researchers are now telling us that infants are born with an inherent sensitivity to language as spoken by the human voice.

My wife and I have a grandson, now in his early thirties, who spoke remarkably well long before he was two. Even discounting the bias of a grandfather, he would have been judged ahead of his age in that regard. I recall his first sentence.

One Sunday afternoon his father was resting and Ian was playing nearby with a paint stick. Knowing how rambunctious a little boy can be when armed with a stick, his father warned him, "Don't you hit anyone." Then dad slipped into a state of drowsiness verging on sleep. But he had dropped an idea into little Ian's mind.

Soon enough, Ian whacked his inert father, who came up with a start, which frightened the little boy. Ian went crying into the hall where his mother met him.

"What did you do?" she asked.

Then came his first full sentence: "I hit Daddy."

There you have the perfect simple sentence: a subject, a verb, and an object. The subject showed who was making something happen; the verb told what was happening; the object said to whom it was happening.

"And what did Daddy do?" his mother asked.

"Yell," Ian replied through his tears.

"And what did Ian do?"

"Cry," he answered.

Before two years of age – a simple sentence plus the verbal sequence for a paragraph – hit, yell, cry. No one had ever said to the child, "Let me explain verbs and how to use them." Of course he had heard many conversations, but something innate was expressing itself here, something fundamental to his humanness. Yet, there is evidence in our culture that this unique gift is all too easily trivialized. Words have become very cheap, and we preachers face the peril of cheapening them, too.

English deserves better, and especially so when used to give forth the Word of God. I recall reading, "English is the richest, most colorful, most poetic and at the same time the most practical language in the world. It has absorbed words from many languages – Latin, Greek, Hebrew, Arabic, German, French, Spanish, and Italian as well as Anglo-Saxon. Language alone is a human treasure but the English language is a gem." One way to show that we cherish this gift is to write and speak it well. Arnold Bennett, the writer of novels and short stories, said, "… the exercise of writing is an indispensable part of any genuine effort towards mental efficiency."

The Kind of Writing That Hones Preaching Skills

You may still insist, "It's all true, but I'm a preacher, not a writer." Indeed, there are pastors who are very good preachers but not good writers. Consider two reasons. First, some pastors seem to require the stimulus of a live congregation. Looking at a blank piece of paper brings neither inspiration nor motivation. They lack imagination at this point so writing seems a fruitless activity.

Second, speaking is different from writing in at least one fundamental way: Listeners follow a speaker at different paces. To keep the slowest listeners on track, the speaker may use asides, repetitions, pauses, changes of inflection, and other devices. A writer, by contrast, knows that readers can set their own pace. The writer's task, therefore, is to pare down the content by taking out the lard – useless and unnecessary words. But here is the precise reason that writing is important for the speaker: Preachers who don't value writing as a discipline are almost certain to become wordy!

At the same time, preachers who succeed in their calling are inescapably writers. Consider the various kinds of writing we are called on to do. Every one of these tasks can be seen as a drudgery that bores us or a challenge that hones our communications skills.

- **Sermons.** Some of us pastors write one complete sermon manuscript a week. This practice preserves the nuances of thought that otherwise would be lost from memory. It's also a good way to keep our thoughts economical, exact, tight. If nothing else, the physical work of writing may keep us from writing into a manuscript the throwaway lines or even the "fluff" that we may so easily indulge in while speaking extempore. If we feel we cannot write a whole manuscript, we should discipline ourselves to write some part of the sermon each week – an introduction, a conclusion, or one of the points. The sermon can still be preached extemporaneously.

- **Prayers.** Paul N. Ellis, a minister friend, now deceased, often wrote prayers in his private devotions as a means of concentrating his thoughts. When I was a pastor I prepared the pastoral prayer on Saturday morning, writing some of it out and then filing it. The next day I then prayed for the people extemporaneously, but this practice of writing or outlining the prayers kept them fresh and free of verbosity and preachiness.

- **Letters.** We pastors show our level of professionalism by the way we write our letters. Every letter should be an exercise in good writing. We will not be with the recipient to interpret or explain, so all must be clear on the page – well composed, nicely placed, clearly stated, and all with an economy of words. A good letter takes thought, and sometimes a second or third draft.

- **Journaling.** This exercise has been recommended as a good way to cultivate the inner life. It's also a good way to capture fleeting thoughts before they escape. I have done this sort of thing only off and on – in fact, all too sparsely – for many years. Even so, when we moved to a new short-term assignment recently my wife and I bought two blank notebooks to capture thoughts, insights, and information worth keeping.

- **Bulletins.** Many churches have staff to produce newsletters and bulletins, but the pastor is still responsible for "quality control." And when we participate, by means of a devotional column or a special announcement, we should express ourselves clearly and concisely. One promoter of good writing says, "Of all the crafts and arts, writing has the widest audience and the longest life." We pastors may be tempted to dash something off for this lowly bulletin, forgetting that the bulletin may be in someone's file ten years from now. How much better to consider this as one more opportunity to hone our writing skills – and thus ultimately our preaching.

- **Memos.** If the pastor has staff, from time to time they must receive a memo. Blessed are the staff members who can understand clearly on first reading what they're being told. Writing memos gives pastors practice in thinking and writing economically but with clarity.

- **Church periodicals.** Many a sermon could be recast for publication in a religious paper. To do so gives breadth to our ministry. Recasting takes work because articles are different from sermons. But offering a piece to a church periodical from time to time keeps the creative juices flowing and, more particularly, makes us wrestle with words that stare back at us from the page without flinching. That kind of wrestling builds mental acumen. If you try this, however, don't be thin-skinned about rejections. The late Dr. Carl F. H. Henry once told me that the successful writer will receive enough rejection slips to paper a room.

- **Newspapers**. Most of us ministers when asked to write for the secular press produce a devotional. This can be good, but we need the discipline from time to time of writing a report on something current that actually happened, that is, news. We are then pressed hard to get the facts straight, to make a piece vivid and interesting. This will sharpen our skill in the use of gripping illustrations in preaching. Hometown newspapers in particular are hungry for copy. Once an editor discovers that you write well, he or she will use your offerings. But what you offer must meet three criteria: It must be (1) informative, (2) interesting, and (3) accurate.

How to Get Started

If all this sheds new light for you and prompts you to take the writing part of your ministry more seriously, here are some ideas for getting started.

Even if you do not consider yourself a writer, discipline yourself to write at least one paragraph a day. Make it a deliberate exercise and strive for excellence in clarity and economy. Or write a letter to a child, or a note to your spouse. Make what you write clear and interesting as well as sweet. Go for short, pithy sentences, strong verbs, images.

The secret of writing is not writing but rewriting. That gem was passed on to me also by Dr. Henry more than forty years ago. Great writers rewrite. Ernest Hemingway rewrote the last page of *Farewell to Arms* thirty-nine times. Margaret Landon, author of *Anna and the King of Siam* (which became the musical *The King and I*), rewrote the book twenty-five times and was starting through the twenty-sixth time when her husband pressed her to get the manuscript into a box and get it off to the publisher. For us more run-of-the-mill writers, no first- or second-draft manuscript should ever be released to the public gaze.

When you are reading – newspapers, magazines, journals – don't be hesitant to edit in your mind. The author will never know. If a sentence is not clear, make it clear. If a sentence is too long, break it into two sentences. That goes for this chapter, too. Doing so will sharpen your critical skills and make you better able to critique your own writing.

If you are writing an article for possible publication, or one section of a sermon, or preparing an announcement for a newsletter, follow these suggestions from the Famous Writers School: (1) Be direct, simple, brief, vigorous, and lucid. (2) Prefer the familiar, common word to the far-fetched. (3) Use a concrete word in preference to an abstract one. (4) Prefer the short sentence and short word to the long one. There are plenty of exceptions to these guidelines. But if your writing sticks closely to them, you won't be far from the bull's-eye most of the time.

Try these suggestions seriously over time, and I promise you one thing: ten years from now, you will be a better preacher than you are today. Your sermons will be clearer, more concise, more on target. Your hearers will remember longer what you preach. Now and then people will remind you that a certain sermon you preached long ago was a turning point in their life. And, as a bonus, via publication your ministry may go much farther afield than it does today.

CHAPTER 13

Advice I Have Gathered About Preaching

I believe that the local church grows from the pulpit outward. Sermons delivered Sunday after Sunday shape the mind, soul, and vision of the church, for better or for worse.

I do not mean that preaching alone will cause the body to flourish. The pastor is a generalist and is called to do much more than preach. There are visits to make and committees to attend and problems to solve and administrative minutiae to look after. Nor do I want to suggest that nothing less than brilliant, masterful preaching will cause the local church to thrive. Some pulpit craftsmen of average ability have disciplined themselves to a high level of faithfulness in the pulpit, and the result has been congregational health and growth.

Even the shape or location of the pulpit is not a determining factor in the church's health. Novel efforts to fashion pulpits in some new way – of Plexiglass or of diminished size or even in the shape of a music stand – and other innovations have failed to bring about the renewal and growth that pastors long for. It is the centrality of preaching, not the centrality of the pulpit, that God will bless.

That said, here is a list of preaching ideals that I hold to – advice I wish I had been given when I began my life of pastoral ministry.

1. **Read from the Bible daily.** Do this not just in search of sermon texts but to nourish and develop your own spiritual life. Read early in the morning, before you address the normal tasks of the day. The orchestra tunes its instruments before the concert, not after. Read the Bible according to a plan that takes you into all its parts over the course of a year. The National Association of Evangelicals or the American and Canadian Bible Societies have excellent Bible reading guides. Make notes in a journal if possible. This will intensify and save what you see. He who said we should never read anything without a pencil in hand (or, today, a laptop nearby) gave good advice.

2. **If you are married, read the Bible with your spouse and family every day.** Think of it this way: your family is your primary congregation, and you are their priest or priestess. As well, this practice will give you grounds to encourage the families in the pews to form the same family practice.

3. **Strive for balance in your preaching. Preach from both testaments with particular attention to the New.** Even so, preach so your congregation is aware of the riches of both testaments. Preach from the stories in Genesis, the holiness code of Leviticus, the historical lessons of 1 and 2 Samuel and 1 and 2 Kings. Preach on radical conversion from the book of Ruth. Let the riches of the Psalms spill over from the pulpit to the people. Discover the moral rigor of the eighth-century prophets: Isaiah, Hosea, Micah, and Amos. From the New Testament, preach on Jesus' miracles and parables in the gospels, and enrich your congregation with the astounding missional events of the Acts of the Apostles. Wrestle with the great doctrinal teachings in the writings of Paul and Peter. In it all, keep the death, burial,

and resurrection of Jesus at the center. These truths constitute the core of the gospel.

4. **Plan your preaching.** Take time in the summer, for example, to lay out a schedule of preaching for the year, or at least a part of the year. If you do this prayerfully, you need not worry that the Holy Spirit will be quenched. He knows the future and can guide for the long future as well as for the week ahead. If special circumstances arise – a tragedy in the community or a national issue that must be addressed – you need not be bound to your plan. However, if the plan is set aside repeatedly on a whim, it is no plan at all.

5. **Commit yourself at the outset of each workweek to the passages or texts you will use the following Sunday and then devote quality time each day to studying them.** This is vastly better than choosing a text on Monday and then changing your mind several times during the following days so that by Saturday you're still not settled on the passage you plan to use the next day. Preaching that results from this practice is likely to be thin gruel for the congregation. How can I be so certain of this? I fell into this error for a short while in the early days of my pastoral ministry. A panic sermon prepared on Saturday night is not nearly as enriching to the people as a sermon you have lived with all week. I broke from my unworthy routine by committing myself to preach three to six successive sermons on a particular subject. (For more on preaching series of sermons, see point #7, below.)

6. **As discussed in more detail in chapter 10, in your sermon preparation, commit yourself to established procedures and then follow them.** Keep your findings in a notebook, not merely in your head or on scraps

of paper. Start with your passage and get its context clearly in mind. Consult two or three good commentaries and make notes. It's best to use an exegetical as well as homiletical commentary. If ideas for illustrations come to mind, write them down. If you don't capture them, they may flee. Note especially thoughts, stories, or ideas that could serve as introductions or conclusions. Meditate on this passage as you go about your week's work. Put your sermon together toward the end of the week and give yourself time to review it before the actual time of delivery.

7. **Preach serially.** Keep your series short to start with – from three to six sermons. This may be a series on three Psalms, the Lord's Prayer, the Beatitudes, or 1 John (one sermon from each chapter). Or you may preach a topical series: on the Apostles' Creed, or the Seven Deadly Sins, or Conquering the Enemies Within (anxiety, greed, fear, envy, guilt, etc.). There are two basic rules about serial preaching: First, the individual sermons must have a clear and uniting theme if they are to hold interest. And, second, each sermon must be able to stand on its own. That is, you should be able to pull any sermon of the series from your files and preach it separately later. Never begin a sermon in a series by saying, "Now you'll remember that last week we took up such and such." For one thing, there will be some present who were not there last week. And for another, this is the laziest way possible to begin a sermon, one that is completely without imagination. Is serial preaching worth the trouble? When I was a college pastor, young people turned out in greater numbers when a series was in progress. The human mind likes to see how something unfolds, or the various ramifications of an issue.

8. **Later, when you have mastered the art of the short series, preach longer ones.** For my first full year as a college pastor, I preached from Jesus' Sermon on the Mount (Matthew 5-7). During my last three years, of a total of thirteen, I preached serially through most of the Gospel of Mark, paragraph by paragraph – not quite making it to the end of the book. I broke from the series for such occasions as Christmas and Easter. So far as I could tell, there was no lagging of interest across those three years. People knew in advance what the passage for the coming Sunday would be, and they came with interest.

9. **Read systematic theology all your life.** This will help you to keep fresh on the broad scope of Christian truth. Your own church tradition will dictate in some measure which texts you consult. In recent years, I have turned again and again to the three-volume set by Thomas Oden (recently published in one volume under the title *Classic Theology*). It appeals to me because of his declared objective to discover nothing new or novel in theology. His search, rather, is for the theological truth held through the ages, the consensus of twenty centuries. He refers repeatedly to "classic Christian theology" and "the ecumenical consensus," by the latter meaning those theological insights that have been commonly held to be true about God throughout the Christian era. When a sermon deals with a major doctrinal issue, it is good to go to such a theological text and refresh the mind on that issue in larger context. The purpose is not to preach a theological lecture to the people but to be sure of the sermon's grounding.

10. **Preach Christologically.** Remember that all Christian preaching is Christological. A sermon that does not give Jesus Christ a proper place is a sub-Christian sermon.

This does not mean that every sermon is a rant about "the gospel" or "getting saved" or "receiving Christ." To be sure, these are all bottom-line issues and must never be far from sight. But the Bible is a big book and covers many subjects that God's people need to hear. Moreover, sermons must have moral content. That is, they must have purchase on the conscience of the hearers, but all with the intention of offering Christ as God's final word to all of life's restless searchings. Notice how these two issues come together in the apostle Paul's address to Felix, the Roman governor (Acts 24:24-25). Luke tells us that "[Felix] sent for Paul and listened to him as he spoke about faith in Christ Jesus." That was Paul's central theme. But in the verse immediately following, Luke says, "As Paul discoursed on righteousness, self-control and the judgment to come, Felix was afraid …" Not every one of our sermons will have that sort of pungency, but, at the same time, only when God's law awakens does Christ's gospel really appeal. It may be that modern sermons too often do not connect with the conscience of hearers.

11. **In all your preparations, seek the anointing of the Holy Spirit.** It is he who gives that special quality of life to the sermon. Let the sermon grow out of prayer as well as study. Pray particularly when, no matter how hard you work on it, the truth of a text does not open up readily. Pray for the anointing during preparation and pray over your pulpit notes. The Spirit who inspired the truth will also enliven it, if entreated.

It is two decades now since I left the bishop's office and took emeritus status. In that time I have gone on preaching and teaching and writing with regularity. This has taken me to a great number of churches in Canada and the United States. I have often heard the clash of the music and worship wars. I have seen churches circulate questionnaires and set up committees and hold meetings all in search of the right worship style and the best way to reach their neighbors.

But the questions at the back of my mind are always the same: What authority do the scriptures hold over this body? How does this manifest itself practically? What programs are in place for teaching the scriptures systematically to the children and young people? Is this a passion with congregational leaders, so much so that they invest the Lord's resources and their time in the task?

Despite the fact that I spent a good part of my working life as a church overseer, my passion continues to be for the well being of the local church. I have not gone back and invested my life in that ministry for the simple reason that serious pastoring requires tremendous energy not available to me to expend at my age. But if I were ever enticed to do so, I would do it because of my conviction that the church grows from the pulpit outward. What goes out regularly across the pulpit should affect everything else that goes on in the church.

PART III

THE PASTOR AS WORSHIP LEADER

CHAPTER 14

Leading Worship

WHEN pastors arise from their sleep on Sunday mornings, they may well reflect on the week past before they take up the special responsibilities of the day before them. And as I have described above, in chapter 3, "A Week in the Life of Pastor John Doe," they may well wonder if there is a focal point that makes sense of their numerous responsibilities.

I believe there is. Just as I have said that the effectiveness of pastors flows from their first love, a love for Jesus Christ, so their varied pastoral activities radiate from the common concern of engaging God's people in the worship of God. You might counter: What about evangelism? Or what about leading the congregation in community ministries? These activities are authentic horizontal concerns of any lively congregation. But the vertical concern that gives them depth and stability is how the believers worship God at home and in church.

So, at the outset, let us agree that the multiplied tasks of the pastor – whether solemnizing a marriage, baptizing new converts, visiting grief-stricken parents, ministering to an elderly widow with a broken hip, teaching Bible lessons to a rambunctious class of twelve-year-olds, or carrying out personal devotions before the workday begins – must be linked intimately to the issue of the worship of God. That is my thesis.

Biblical Words for Worship

Let us begin by looking at key biblical words for worship. In the Old Testament there are two major ones. The first is a general word that means to labor or serve and usually is translated "the service of God." As well, for the specific act of worship there is a word that means to bow, to prostrate oneself.

The New Testament has two corresponding words. The general word, *latreia*, originally meant servitude, the state of a hired laborer or slave, and thence the service of God – divine worship. The second word, *proskuneo*, means to prostrate oneself, to adore, to worship.

I make two observations concerning the first word above as its equivalent appears in each testament.

First, the idea of worship as a service to God goes back to antiquity, long before the Bible took form. In those ancient times, it is speculated, the deity was conceived of as having human wants and appetites, and true worship was regarded as dutiful ministration to these wants through sacrifice and obedience to the deity's commands.

Second, I know that this idea has long since left our consciousness but remains with us in our use of language. Do we not feel that worship is still, in a sense, humble service to God? Why do we retain such nomenclature as: a worship service, a prayer service, a song service, a Communion service, a baptismal service, a funeral service, a service of celebration? In all cases, the primary idea is that we are doing something for God. He, not the leader in charge or some member of the congregation, is the central figure in the event.

I have sometimes recommended – half facetiously – that a church board meeting should be called a business service or service of business. A change in name might change the nature of what sometimes goes on. For example, just as the soloist Sunday morning does not offer up a song first of all to the congregation but instead to God, so the treasurer at the business meeting might offer his or her report not first of all to the board but to God. It is an elevating thought.

These biblical words – to serve and to adore – are highly relevant to pastors in their understanding of their work. If the words are allowed to penetrate their beings, they not only will shape their understanding, but also will affect their very feelings about their task. When they go to the hospital to visit a parishioner before surgery, are they going merely to cheer the person up or to be God's representative, pointing the patient to the sovereign care of God in all situations? When they enter the pulpit Sunday morning, do they go to raise the congregation's spirits, to speak soothing words, or to help their people improve their perspectives on life by leading them into the Presence?

To illustrate what I mean, let me tell you of a wedding I attended recently. The building was beautiful. The bride and groom were deeply committed Christians and lovely in their wedding attire. The officiating minister used a prescribed ritual.

But as the ritual unfolded, he repeatedly interjected his personal comments:

"Now I am going to ask the bride to …"

"At this time the groom will …"

He catechized, even patronized the congregation. It was bad enough that he didn't trust the powerful words of the ritual, and that he didn't trust the intelligence and imagination of the congregation. What was worse, to put it in a nutshell, he placed himself – not God, not the bride and groom, but himself – at the center of things.

Afterwards, on the lawn outside, a young man sidled up to me in disgust. Though not trained in theology, he was interested in the subject and savvy about church life. "Where was the mystery?" he asked as he passed me. "Where was the transcendence? Who invited him?" It should be a rule written into the fiber of our beings that when we lead any aspect of worship, God is first, the congregation is second, and we, the leaders, a distant third, as servants of the event.

A High Hour of Worship

It is impossible in one chapter to consider in detail every aspect of worship: public and private, formal and informal, individual and corporate, spontaneous and planned. Therefore, I will single out the congregation's one weekly high hour of worship.

Let us let our minds drift back to the early 90s of the last century when the trend toward "seeker friendly" services was developing. The desire to make what went on in church services more appealing or accessible to those on the fringes of church life or even completely unconnected to it, was noble. Services included such changes as electronic keyboards in place of pianos, organs abandoned in favor of guitars or an instrumental ensemble, song leaders replaced by worship teams, scripture portions shortened to accommodate short attention spans, and sermons focused on contemporary issues, sometimes without much Bible exposition.

As well, simple Bible or devotional choruses replaced hymns, and overhead screens replaced hymnbooks. Short and engaging monologues or skits were integrated into the services, and pulpits were removed or given much lower profile.

The success of some such services is well known in terms of attracting baby boomers or young people with no previous church experience or lapsed Christians or people who have a hard time with anything traditional. We can cite churches where Sunday-morning attendance boomed under this format.

All I wish to say concerning these or even more recent innovations is that innovations by pastors and church boards must always be based on a thoroughly understood theology of worship. Pastors whose theology in this area is thin or unbalanced may sponsor such innovations for utilitarian or pragmatic reasons. Pastors whose theology of worship is comprehensive may encourage their board to support such a service for evangelistic reasons, in addition to, but not in place of, congregational worship.

When evangelism is the issue, a thorough theology of worship will dictate that a seeker friendly service must not eliminate from church life the long-standing practice of at least one high hour of worship in the week. From the beginning of the trend, I was aware of pastors who worked out of a deep theology leading their congregations to make the Sunday-morning service seeker friendly but then to make a Sunday-evening service the church's high hour of worship. The theory was to draw converts from the morning service into the evening service of worship and fellowship. This trend may have been thwarted, however, by the cessation of Sunday-night services.

Worship is the central activity of the people of God. Read the descriptions of worship going on in the unseen world as pictured in Revelation 4 and 5; for example, here is 5:11-12: "Then I looked and heard the voice of many angels, numbering thousands upon thousands, and ten thousand times ten thousand. They encircled the throne and the living creatures and the elders. In a loud voice they were saying: 'Worthy is the Lamb who was slain, to receive power and wealth and wisdom and strength and honor and glory and praise.'"

Congregations that do not understand the centrality of worship in their corporate life will be spiritually anemic no matter how full their church's activities. And pastors who do not lead their people in at least one high hour of corporate worship each week will deprive them of life-sustaining nurture.

The Pastor's Bearing

Consider the bearing of pastors in leading public worship.

Let us say at the outset that their bearing has two aspects: the external and the internal. That is to say, how they appear and the spirit they express. Please do not think that I'm retreating from the profound to the trivial if I ask you to move in your thinking to the externals of appearance. Appearance matters!

Elena Jankowic, in her book *Behave Yourself: The Working Guide to Business Etiquette*, writes about the Rule of Twelve in connection with the first impression people make in the business world. Jankowic says that we first notice and remember three things about people we meet: (1) the first twelve inches from shoulders up, (2) the first twelve steps taken toward us, and (3) the first twelve words spoken. It should not seem irrelevant for pastors to consider the Rule of Twelve when they enter the sanctuary to lead God's people in worship.

For example, the first twelve inches from the shoulders up: Is hair neatly trimmed? Are shoulders free of dandruff? Are shoes appropriate and well cared for? The difference between an amateur and a professional is often little more than careful attention to detail. If you resist the adjective "professional" for the pastor's role, at least let it stand for the pastor who has a keen sense of what is appropriate in each pastoral situation and who puts that ahead of whatever personal tastes he or she might have.

The first twelve steps: Does the pastor walk with confidence? Appear to know why he or she is there? Has the pulpit been cared for in advance so no time is needed to shuffle or rearrange papers? Can the pastor move directly to the assigned seat whether on or off the platform and sit and bow in prayer?

The first twelve words: Do the pastor's first comments summon the people into the Presence? Are his or her first words deliberate and well chosen? Are they pleasant but not frivolous or irrelevant? Do they address the issue at hand: the worship of God? Are they characterized by economy of words? It's refreshing to be under the leadership of a pastor who knows how to offer a call to worship either formally or informally.

More than a score of years ago, I came across John T. Molloy's book *Dress for Success* and read it with a good deal of pleasure. Later, based on the success of his first book, he wrote a second one addressed to women in the work world, which he later revised. These books were not intended to outline the etiquette of a person's dress but instead its effect. His initial book shows by a series of experiments how our dress unconsciously affects those we come in contact with. His book was set in the context of the business world, but that does not make it irrelevant to our pastoral calling.

Later, I prepared a bulletin on the subject of pulpit-wear, which I sent to our ministers across Canada. I was specific in my recommendations. I recommended, for male pastors, a dark blue or dark gray suit, an Arrow Mark shirt (a new, neat collar developed at the time), and black over-the-calf stockings. The reason I gave for these stockings was that, when a male minister sits down in the presence of the congregation, his socks ought not to droop around his ankles, revealing between their tops and his trouser cuffs a blob of flesh.

(I am scarcely qualified to write the equivalent guidelines for female pastors, although I have discussed the matter with some women whose judgment I trust. Consensus suggests the same principles should be followed by both men and women: dress modestly, so as not to attract undue attention to attire itself, wearing clothes that fit well, neither too loosely or tightly, and that are appropriate to the level of formality or informality of the occasion.)

I have not yet heard the last of that bulletin sent to male pastors. It apparently went far and wide. For example, it was reported to me that several years later, when the late Charles D. Kirkpatrick, the director of world missions in my denomination, was taking a tour group on an African missions trip, the group flew from Chicago to Montréal on the way. As the plane crossed Ontario, I'm told, he said to the group, "Pull up your socks, fellows; we're flying over Bastian's territory."

I'm aware that my counsel will not seem relevant to female pastors and may seem restrictive to some male pastors. I know well the arguments for casual attire as a way of identifying with people of this casual generation. I agree that those who come as laypersons to worship in the congregation should be free to come dressed as they choose. What I write now has to do with those who in some way offer leadership in worship.

I acknowledge, too, that there is always room for exceptions with ministers – when speaking at a youth meeting, around the campfire, at a church retreat, and so on – but against all this, I contend that the bearing of pastors is affected by how they dress as they come before their people for that high hour of worship. If you are caught between the generations on the subject, ask yourself as you dress for worship: What clothes would I wear to lead in worship if the guest of honor in the service were the Queen of England? For Christians, the guest of honor is the King of Heaven.

You may be waiting for me to say that our bearing is affected by the deeper issues of our being: our relationship with the Lord Jesus Christ and how we nurture that relationship on a day-to-day basis. Yes, our bearing does involve profoundly more than our attire! However, it can be argued that the hour when pastors lead their congregation in worship is their most transparent hour. By their attire they reveal their respect for what they are doing. They reveal their taste and judgment by the scriptures and music they choose. They show their understanding of public worship by the way they fashion the order of service. They show their craft by the way they move from one element of worship to another. Their rapport with their people is shown in the subtle nuances of prayer and announcements. Underneath all these, their relationship with their God is discernible by a reverence they themselves are scarcely aware of.

Beyond this, consider the issue of spiritual bearing. Richard Baxter, in his great work, *The Reformed Pastor*, wrote penetratingly of the pastor's need for spiritual integrity in his work, "God never saved any man for being a preacher, nor because he was an able preacher; but because he was a justified, sanctified man, and consequently faithful in his Master's work. Take heed, therefore, to yourselves first, that you be that which you persuade your hearers to be, and believe that which you persuade them to believe, and have heartily entertained that Savior whom you offer to them." This calls for a consistent and ordered inner life, ever renewed by personal times of worship daily.

Bishop Stephen Neil says the best place for pastors to have their daily prayers is at the altar of their church. Whether there or elsewhere, pastors must set aside a place for daily Bible reading and prayer for the nurture of their own being as well as their intercessions for their people. If at all possible, it should be a place apart, not the place they use for the preparation of sermons or the reading of magazines, or the answering of mail. It may be a personal altar built and located in a corner of the study. When I was a pastor, I had such an altar built for me by a handy church janitor. It was two-and-a-half feet wide. If not an altar for personal devotions it may be a chair by a shelf of devotional books or a quiet corner in a basement. But pastors should make it a sacred place where they go to commune. What they do in that sacred space will affect their bearing in public worship.

I like to say to pastors that when they enter the sanctuary to lead the people in worship they should come "out of the Presence, into the Presence." We expect when they come before the waiting congregation that they come in to the Presence. But they will do that best if they come out of the Presence. If they teach a Sunday-school class before service, they should give themselves a fifteen-minute interval to compose their souls in private. If it is their custom to shake hands with people in the foyer or check on thermostats and public address systems – tasks for responsible laypersons – they should disappear fifteen minutes before the worship service begins.

Preparing and leading a service is a much more complex task than most people realize. I focus here on two features that I believe are in need of special attention – the reading of the scriptures and the pastoral prayer – and then offer some thoughts on aesthetics in worship.

The Reading of the Scriptures

I am referring here not to what is read as the basis for a sermon but to what is read as a separate act of worship. This separate reading of the scriptures is probably implied in Paul's instruction to Timothy, "Give attention to reading." Is this an aspect of worship that needs to be highlighted among those of us in the evangelical church tradition?

I mean by evangelical those worshiping bodies so classified, such as Wesleyans, Independents, Evangelical Presbyterians. I also mean any other bodies whose worship services are characterized as (1) having a strong emphasis on the Bible, (2) purposefully avoiding ecclesiasticism, (3) insisting on simplicity over against a reliance on set forms, (4) and in it all insisting on the need for an unhindered freedom of response. (For a more in-depth consideration of worship traditions, see chapter 17, "Three Ways We Worship God.")

Over against this is liturgical worship, that is, worship that is prescribed: the Christian year is outlined not only in seasons but by holy days and feasts to be observed; written prayers are used; a lectionary is followed; services are highly ordered; and leaders wear vestments rich in symbolism. Liturgical worship has a strong emphasis on the aesthetic.

The strengths of liturgical worship are that it emphasizes the corporate nature of worship, it ensures a broad and orderly exposure to the whole sweep of Christian truth as reflected in the scriptures, and it deliberately emphasizes the transcendent. Its peril is that its heavy dependence on form can easily lead to formalism. Its participants may come to depend on the rituals themselves rather than on the living God, and, most seriously, they may confuse an aesthetic experience for an authentically Christian experience nurtured by the indwelling Spirit of God.

By contrast, when the free-church style of worship is followed by a congregation in the full bloom of spiritual vigor, its very simplicity and spiritual immediacy are moving. But when spiritual vigor declines, it may appear thin and monotonous, lacking both in style and content. The problem is complicated if the free-church pastor lacks a comprehensive theology of corporate worship. Christian worship without basic designated borders can quickly degenerate into a sort of folk religion.

We each thank God for our own tradition, but before we feel smug about it, we should consider whether we live up to our own commitments relative to the Bible.

I have a friend who collects church bulletins. He told me some time back that he is amazed at the number of them that do not have a special place in the order of worship for the reading of the scriptures. The only scripture reading may be a few verses the pastor reads as the basis for his sermon.

Another friend sought a church to attend while on vacation. He found one whose outdoor sign advertised it boldly as a Bible church. But, he says, in the Sunday-morning service, no place was given for the reading of the scriptures, and the pastor did not even read a scripture text before his sermon.

In our secular times, can so-called evangelical worship

become so man-centered that it deadens the sound of the Word of God by the babble of the words of man?

Blessed are the pastors who teach their people that the Bible is to be read carefully and systematically in corporate worship. The people are to "hear" the Word of God. Through readings from both Old Testament and New Testament the people are to be reminded regularly that the whole of the Bible is the Word of God, not just one section of it.

Here are some suggestions for an orderly, year-round practice of Bible reading in each week's high service of worship.

1. Make it a separate moment in the service and teach the people to listen for the voice of God in the reading of his Word.

2. Plan weekly readings in such a fashion as to expose the people to all the divisions of the scriptures: the Law, the Writings, the Prophets, the Gospels, the historical narratives, and the Epistles.

3. Take advantage of Bible reading in public worship to highlight certain key passages annually, such as Psalms 23 and 91; Genesis 1, 2, and 3; Exodus 20; Isaiah 6 and 53; Matthew 5, 6, and 7; John 1 and 15; 1 Corinthians 13 and 15; Revelation 4 and 5; and many others.

4. If you have laypersons share in the reading of the scriptures, teach them exactly what you want. Urge them to prepare their own hearts by reading the passages over several times, and have the readers with you near the pulpit or microphone.

5. When you read the scriptures publicly yourself, heed the advice given once to read them as if you are listening to them, not as if you wrote them. This practice may not be followed in every service – such as an outdoor youth camp or camp meeting. But even in them the scriptures should never be far from sight.

The Pastoral Prayer

The second feature that needs special attention is the pastoral prayer. To introduce this, I share with you an incident from my own pastoral life.

Toward the end of my thirteen years as a college pastor in Greenville, Illinois, somewhere around 1972, a special committee of the church prepared a wide-ranging questionnaire and administered it to the congregation. They wanted to get input into how the people were experiencing the church's worship services. As I recall, it was three pages long. Several of the questions had to do with public worship and my leadership in that exercise. For example, about the sermons the questionnaire asked: Are they too short? Too long? Just right?

Because of the spirit of the times several questions solicited from the congregation whether they wanted more of the laity (besides choir members and instrumentalists) to participate in public worship.

One question had to do with the pastoral prayer in the Sunday-morning worship service. Did the congregation prefer that laypersons offer this prayer in rotation or that the pastor and laypersons alternate by Sundays or should the pastor himself always offer the Sunday-morning prayer? Though in some other aspects of worship there was a consensus for more lay participation, the questionnaire returned a solid response that the pastor should pray the pastoral prayer. This was especially gratifying to me because it showed me that the people had a historic sense of the meaning and function of the pastoral prayer.

My practice was to prepare the pastoral prayer on Saturday mornings. Sitting alone in my study I could review all the aspects of the previous week: the blessings that had come to God's people, the adversities they had faced, what was going on in the larger Christian community regionally and what was taking place on the world scene.

The grid against which I organized the pastoral prayer

consisted of the five classical elements of prayer: adoration, confession, petition, intercession, and thanksgiving.

1. Adoration is praising God for who he is. "My soul magnifies the Lord, and my spirit rejoices in God my Savior" (Luke 1:46-47, ESV).

2. Confession is acknowledging the sins and shortcomings of all God's people, both generally and specifically.

3. Petition is that portion of the prayer that calls for grace to be delivered from the power of sin and to live victoriously by the power of God: "Where sin abounded, grace abounded much more" (Romans 5:20, NKJV). This element of prayer pinpoints specific needs.

4. In intercession pastors stand as vocal intermediaries representing the congregation as they call on God for the needs of others.

5. And thanksgiving is the enumeration of the blessings that God has poured on us.

Not all the above elements need to be included in every pastoral prayer, but this is a good grid for the preparation of the prayer.

When the congregation learns that the pastor has been careful in preparing a pastoral prayer, and prays it with sincere engagement, they enter this aspect of worship with feeling. They do not expect to hear confidences that were shared with the pastor during the previous week, but they listen for categories into which they can fit their own blessings and needs. Pastors do their congregation a great disservice if they spend many hours preparing a sermon but count on the inspiration of the moment for the pastoral prayer.

To put this matter into a theological context, when pastors preach, they carry out the prophetic function of their office. When they pray for their people, they carry out the priestly function of their office. They should do both carefully.

Attention to Aesthetic Detail

I move now to some brief comments on aesthetics and worship. Evangelical worship is vulnerable to carelessness here. What does it mean to worship God in the beauty of holiness? How is the worship of God enhanced by beauty?

Sometimes people who have been trained in the liturgical tradition come to free-church services and go away shaking their heads. They often feel that there is a lack of content and that there is so little to excite the senses. Even worse, sometimes the service itself is chummy and colloquial, devoid of much that speaks to them of the mystery or majesty of God.

This need not be the case. Moreover, free forms of worship may have their own genius. Their motto might be, "God is a Spirit: and they that worship him must worship him in spirit and in truth" (John 4:24, KJV). Substitute for the word "truth" the word "reality." But this by itself does not mean that elements of beauty are unimportant or that "anything goes." I mention in passing some matters in public worship that need regular attention.

There is the issue of music, one of God's greatest gifts to his people. Instrumentalists must be taught how to use their instruments to the glory of God. They need to know how to play a prelude that quiets the minds of today's highly stressed people before corporate worship begins. How blessed is the pastor who is aided by instrumentalists who understand the function of music in not only rousing the spirits of the worshipers but also in calming them as worship begins.

Moreover, pastors on the growing edge develop a certain artistry in the way they incorporate quality Bible choruses in the service without eliminating hymns that represent the historical continuity of the church.

I commend to organists and other instrumentalists the simple device of playing an interlude after the pastoral prayer. This gives people time to reflect briefly and compose themselves while also giving the pastor time to be seated before moving to the next part of worship.

These few comments about attention to aesthetic detail can alert us to the great demands on pastors to ensure that beauty is a part of corporate worship. One could go on to talk about the color scheme of the sanctuary, the acoustics of the building, the state of the sound system, the condition of the hymnbooks, the cleanliness of the facility, and the regular tuning of the instruments. Again, a pastor's attention to such detail is a sign of a high view of worship.

I mention only one more matter that bears on the aesthetics of worship. I refer to the economy of words exercised by all who participate in the service. Someone I know was once the pastor of a large church in the United States. Early in his ministry in that church he had his secretary, on a Monday morning, type every word spoken during a Sunday-morning worship service.

The transcript included not only what the lead pastor had said but also what other staff had said as they took part. Then he and his staff went over the transcript as an exercise. Each considered privately the issue of economy of words.

They were amazed, in some cases appalled, at the great volume of verbiage – wasted and unnecessary words – that they had incorporated into the service. There were unprepared announcements and wordy introductions to elements of the service.

The pastor's concern was twofold: first, that wordiness made the event somewhat messy, and second, that the time wasted could have been put to so much better use in the worship of God.

So, returning to the question at the beginning of this chapter, what links the various and sundry activities of pastors? I believe the answer comes to many pastors as they move through the worship service and are themselves uplifted by it. I believe it floods their mind as they give themselves heartily to this leadership.

And I believe that after the benediction is said, after they have greeted their people warmly in the foyer, after the last worshipers have left for their cars, after they walk to their study, flicking off a couple of light switches as they go, after they drop into a chair across from their desk to relax a few minutes before going home – that after all that, it suddenly becomes clear to them: What binds together all the activities of a congregation and the ardent labors of its pastor is this – the pastor's love for Christ and the people's hearty worship of the Triune God.

CHAPTER 15

The Elements of Worship

THE pastor stepped to the pulpit dressed in a black Prince Albert coat, formal striped gray pants, and well-shined dress shoes as the congregation sat waiting. In his right hand he held three or four slips of paper. From each he read a brief announcement without additional comment, laying each one aside as he did. Then he said to the congregation, "Now let us worship God."

The organist sounded a chord, and the congregation stood and in one voice broke forth into song: "Glory be to the Father, and to the Son, and to the Holy Ghost; As it was in the beginning, is now and ever shall be, world without end. Amen."

It was 1948, and I was twenty-three years old. I had traveled from Toronto, Canada, to the Roberts Memorial Free Methodist Church in Washington, D.C., to preach a week of services. This was my third day at the church, and I was experiencing culture shock.

For example, the first night I was there, I sat during the early part of the service in a pew at the front of the sanctuary. When the congregation was invited to kneel for prayer, I found kneeling between the pews difficult. Then I heard "click, click, click," and, glancing around, saw that the pews in this beautiful colonial church were equipped with kneeling benches.

I was taken aback. The church of my childhood and

early teens on the prairies of Saskatchewan had no place for kneeling benches or even musical instruments, printed orders of worship, and prayers over the offering. Those were signs of formalism to the leaders; to that church kneeling benches would have been unthinkable. I sat in Roberts Memorial and kept my thoughts to myself.

Then came Sunday morning and the congregation's singing of the Gloria Patri. I was suddenly filled with awe, stirred inwardly, momentarily breathless. Beyond mere emotion, my spirit was awakened in a new way to the majesty, the splendor, the glory of the Triune God.

It was not that church life in my childhood had been unemotional. Sometimes emotion had been strong and openly expressed, often when the saints demonstrated their joy. But it took this more objective and unselfconscious act of worship to raise my sights above myself to the pure radiance of the God who is "high and lifted up" (Isaiah 6:1).

Today's Worship Differences

This is not a plea for Prince Albert coats as pulpit attire. And the Gloria Patri is not the only way to open a service of worship. But that event of more than sixty years ago comes to mind as I think of the way public worship is often carried out now.

Today a libertarian spirit pervades our culture. To many, freedom of expression is everything. "Norms" have been seriously downgraded in churches just as they have been in society. Hence, we have much confusion and conflict even within individual congregations over how worship should be conducted.

Some congregations have adapted their worship to accommodate the styles of the entertainment culture, but large numbers of believers find the sudden and drastic changes wrenching and, as they see it, somehow lacking the authenticity of normative worship. Others are troubled by the introduction of elements they consider in poor taste, lacking in aesthetics, and in some cases even crude.

In my travels and conversations across North America I have heard many tense discussions about worship. I have met believers who have pulled up long-established roots to leave their churches in search of congregations better suited to their worship ideals, while others have stayed behind but grieve in silence over what they feel is a profound loss.

In the midst of the sometimes-jumbled collection of the old and the new, the historical and the innovative, all sides should ask in deep reflection whether there are norms from which we can take our reckonings, basics that have endured from age to age. These questions are worth answering: What is the essence of Christian worship? And what is its substance?

The Essence of Christian Worship

I will use these two philosophical terms, essence and substance, to make some important distinctions.

In addressing the essence of Christian worship, the first question is always: Whom are we worshiping? Animists believe that every tree, rock, and animal has a spirit, and this belief regulates how and where they worship. Polytheists, such as Hindus, must necessarily figure out how to give many gods their due, while pantheists such as New Agers must design ways to worship themselves.

So, too, for us: questions about worship must begin with a clear apprehension of the God we worship.

The Old and New Testaments tell us in great detail: He is the God who spoke the universe into being, and so ours is a God of omnipotent power and creative order. He is the God who summoned Abraham to a pilgrimage of faith and appeared to him at least nine times, so he is a personal God who addresses his people individually. Our God gave Moses his divine law in the ethereal reaches of Sinai, so he is a God who not only protects but also makes moral demands on his people in accordance with his own character. Our God, through Amos, rebuked his chosen people (and us today) with stern promises of judgment for the wanton disregard of his moral law; through Hosea he assured them (and us) of his unrelenting love. This God repeatedly tells his people, "I am holy."

Above all, in the incarnate presence of Jesus Christ, his one and only son, God made full revelation of himself to his world. "For in Christ all the fullness of the Deity lives in bodily form" (Colossians 2:9). When we examine Jesus' life of service, his love for sinners, his reproach of hypocrisy of all kinds, his readiness to offer forgiveness at great personal cost, we know we are seeing what God is like. Jesus said, "Anyone who has seen me has seen the Father" (John 14:9).

This is where any discussion of Christian worship must begin. This is the God we worship when we bow down or prostrate ourselves (one meaning of "worship") and the God to whom we offer services, like a servant to a master (another meaning).

Across two millennia, Christian minds both brilliant and devout have attempted to summarize in creeds and articles of faith who God is. For example, in 1571 English Reformers set forth the following statement under the heading "Of Faith in the Holy Trinity": "There is but one living and true God, everlasting, without body, parts, or passions; of infinite power, wisdom, and goodness, the Maker and Preserver of all things both visible and invisible. And in unity of this Godhead there be three persons of one substance, power, and eternity; the Father, the Son, and the Holy Ghost." This lofty and enduring statement came only after several decades of wrestling and reflection. It is worth pondering today.

But what happens when an elevated vision of God no longer dominates every part of corporate worship? Worship may then become a combination of the lifted up and the banal – or even the utterly casual ("bring your coffee with you"). Congregations may still enjoy being together, but a serious malnutrition of the spirit sets in. The horizontal lines of human fellowship may remain intact, but they will lack the bonding power of the great atoning sacrifice of Jesus Christ for them. And the vertical lines of adoration and awe will weaken. Worship leaders become verbose because the whole event is not regulated by a deep sense of reverence. Style dominates substance, and worship and entertainment become intermixed. Ultimately God's people leave the event lacking the cleansing and renewing effect of true worship.

The essence of worship is reflected in the cry of the Heavenly Beings in Isaiah's temple revelation: "Holy, holy, holy, is the Lord Almighty; the whole earth is full of his glory" (Isaiah 6:3). It is reflected in the declaration of Peter when Jesus asked, "Who do you say I am?" Peter replied in a flash of holy insight, "You are the Christ, the Son of the living God" (Matthew 16:16, ESV).

THE SUBSTANCE OF CHRISTIAN WORSHIP

Essence must be attended by substance. It is true that Christian worship is largely internal, an exercise of the spirit, because "God is a Spirit and they that worship him must worship him in spirit and in truth" (John 4:24, KJV). But we are not pure spirits. We are creatures who partake deeply of the material realities of life. Paul acknowledges this fact when he exhorts, "… offer your bodies as living sacrifices, holy and pleasing to God. This is your spiritual act of worship" (Romans 12:1). So, what can help us physical beings to worship God in spirit? Consider four substantial means.

THE USE OF RITUAL

All congregations rely on ritual of one sort or another, and sometimes those most opposed to ritual become the most ritualistic. For example, a charismatic leader was in charge of a community-wide service in an evangelical church in our town. He began by scolding the host congregation's members for how "ritualistic" they had become over the years. He then sought to help them by calling for some hearty "Amens." Next, he faced one side of the congregation and exhorted them to say "Amen" together at the drop of his hands. Turning to the other side he made the same urgent request.

He kept this up until he was satisfied (but the long-suffering people had had too much). His intent was to deliver the people from what he considered their cold rituals. In fact, he was only substituting another ritual more to his liking.

Christians who have grown cold in their faith will find any ritual merely routine, but there is no such thing as a congregation without a ritual. Saying the Lord's Prayer together, singing the Doxology after the offering, standing for the pastoral prayer, starting each service with twenty minutes of praise choruses, singing a hymn of response after the sermon – the things a congregation does week after week are its rituals. These should be chosen wisely, because rituals must have substance and beauty to bring refreshment despite their frequent use. One elderly church member who had served the Lord since childhood said to me, "The ritual for the Lord's Supper becomes more meaningful to me with the passing of the years."

THE PLACE OF SYMBOL

The substance of worship is also reflected in the use of Christian symbols. A symbol is an object that helps the worshiper apprehend the spiritual reality behind all Christian worship. The use of symbol is not a substitute for truth but marks the point where physical and spiritual reality meet.

I once took a membership class of ten- and eleven-year-olds in to the church sanctuary. I had them sit down on the floor in front of the Communion table. Carved across the face of that beautiful walnut table were the words, "This do in remembrance of me."

For starters, I asked if they ever felt that God was present when they came with their parents to worship.

One of them, Barbara, said, "Oh yes, and sometimes it's sort of scary – well not really scary, but you know what I mean."

I did know.

Symbols can help in divine worship: the Communion table with a Bible and candles on it; the pulpit (in earlier times often called "the sacred desk"), a symbol of the authority of God's preached Word; the Communion rail, more recently referred to as the altar; a cross mounted on the wall behind the pulpit; artistic banners reminding the congregation of "faith" or "hope" or "love." It is impossible to live without symbols, so they should be chosen carefully and exploited wisely to enhance the worship of God.

SACRAMENTS AS ACTS OF WORSHIP

Sacraments, or ordinances, are a third substantial means of worshiping God. The word "sacrament," from the Latin *sacramentum*, means a "pledging." Sacraments are physical enactments that enhance our sensitivity to spiritual realities and call forth our renewed obedience. Whereas symbols consist of objects, sacraments mostly involve actions.

The two sacraments observed almost universally in Protestantism – baptism and Holy Communion – convey by action two key realities at the heart of the Christian faith.

Commanded by Christ, baptism is a rite of initiation or entrance into the church (Matthew 28:19-20). Water is used to represent the washing away of sin and the beginning of a new life in Christ. Paul refers to the "washing of rebirth and renewal by the Holy Spirit" (Titus 3:5).

Opinions differ on how baptism should be used. Through baptism some believing parents dedicate their children to God until such a time as the children can make their own faith commitment. And in adult baptism new believers pledge publicly to follow Christ. Baptismal services greatly bless congregations because the essence of the faith – the worship of the Triune God – is made substantial, visible, even palpable.

If baptism is a rite of entry into the church, Holy Communion is a right of continuation in fellowship through faith in Christ's sacrificial death. When believers regularly receive a piece of bread and the juice of the crushed grape, they celebrate again and again the death of the Lord Jesus Christ and enact their dependence on the merits of that death for their redemption. Jesus commanded this rite when he said, "Do this in remembrance of me" (Luke 22:19). His most mystifying and inviting words, reflecting the reality behind the action, may always be, "unless you eat the flesh of the Son of Man and drink his blood, you have no life in you" (John 6:53). Holy Communion enacts ongoing total dependence on Christ for our life here and hereafter.

Sacrifice in Worship

Sacrifice is the fourth substantial element in Christian worship. In fact, worship is summed up in sacrifice. In any era or place, when people have awakened to the divine, the resulting sense of holy awe fills them with an impulse to give something to the unseen Presence. When the Ammonites sacrificed their children to Molech in the fire, this was a corruption of the impulse (Leviticus 18:21). All religions appear to have something equivalent to an altar.

How does the element of sacrifice permeate Christian worship? There is the sacrifice of praise by means of hymns and spiritual songs. The offering up of prayers of thanksgiving both corporately and privately belongs in this category. Also, the giving of tithes and offerings has in it an element of sacrifice. So it is for every part of worship. Even when the soloist or choir sings, their song must first be regarded as an act of sacrifice offered up to God.

It can be argued that the proper response to musical offerings, therefore, is not a round of applause for a job well done; it is a fervent mental or audible "Amen" as agreement with the truthfulness of the song. If we say that applause is the new way of saying Amen, then applause should follow every part of worship, not just musical offerings. For example, a good pastoral prayer should be followed by a good hand.

It seems to me that applause following only musical renditions of one sort or another represents an invasion of worship by the entertainment world. This practice deserves deep and prayerful reflection. Worship is about God. In worship, the gaze is primarily upward, and only secondarily inward and others-ward. And "Amen" – meaning "truly" or "verily" – is a distinctive Christian word that belongs to the congregation (1 Corinthians 14:16). It affirms the truth in God's presence.

Above all, the sermon given at the high point of worship is preeminently offered to God as an act of sacrifice. The Reformation in the sixteenth century came about through the rediscovery of the sacred scriptures as a living message and the consequent renewal of preaching. The Methodist movement of the eighteenth century was a preaching movement out of which grew a community of transformed men and women, along with an outflow of social ministries. To the serious congregation of the present, the preaching of God's Word must be the crown jewel in the setting of Spirit-inspired congregational worship.

As Martin Luther summarized it, "When I declare the Word of God I offer sacrifice; when thou hearest the Word of God with all thy heart, thou dost offer sacrifice. When we pray, and when we give in charity to our neighbor, we offer sacrifice. So, too, when I receive this Sacrament, I offer sacrifice – that is to say, I accomplish the will of service to God, I confess Him, and I give Him thanks. This is not a sacrifice for sin, but a sacrifice of thanksgiving and praise."

What May Change and What May Not

How a congregation adapts true worship practices to its own setting may legitimately vary depending on a variety of factors: What is the culture of the people? Are they predominantly blue-collar or white-collar? Is the community rural or urban? Is it a congregation of fifty or five hundred? What is its average age? What sort of architecture frames the sanctuary? And what is the temperamental leaning of the pastor in these things?

But none of these variables should obscure the fact that in all cases, worship that is truly Christian has one essence: from beginning to end it is reverence and joy in the presence of the God who is thrice holy – Father, Son, and Holy Ghost. And it has a common substance manifested in its rituals, symbols, sacraments, and sacrifices.

In fact, here is a good test any congregation may apply: If a young man should come to worship next Sunday, as I did more than six decades ago, how would he be affected by the experience? Would the worship be dull, predictable, lacking in spirit? Or rousing but short on reverence and holiness? Would it be so sincere, so unpretentious, so Spirit-directed, so Christ-exalting, that he would be lifted into the Presence, sensing the majesty and glory of God? And might the experience be so telling that he would remember it more than half a century later? It's a good test for modern worship.

CHAPTER 16

We Cannot Avoid Worshiping

IN our human existence, we do not have the choice either to worship or not to worship. Because we are created beings – "creatures" – we are hardwired to acknowledge in some way the source of our existence. That is, we either act out our trust in God, our Creator, or we bow down to someone or something of much lesser worth.

The word "worship" is from the Anglo-Saxon root *weorthscipe*, which means "to show the shape of our worths." The meaning of the word indicates that we will find some special way to acknowledge that which we count worthy of our reverence and trust.

But this impulse to worship with which all of us are endowed can be easily misdirected. The peril of such misdirection is a fundamental issue in the Bible. Look at the world teeming with idols so dramatically portrayed throughout the Old Testament and into the New. And observe today's worship of cheap substitutes in place of the worship of the All-Glorious God.

Consider the gaudily decorated casinos spotted across the land, their thousands of patrons hunched over faceless machines as they call on Lady Luck to favor them. They are a prime illustration of the worship impulse gone awry. The widespread craze for drugs is another.

Less dramatically, one person worships nature; another

a companion's beauty; yet another, material possessions. We worship that which commands our allegiance or comes to dominate our wills.

Christians avoid the lure of these idolatries by practicing with diligence the worship of the true God revealed in Jesus Christ.

George S. Gunn, in his little book on the Psalms, *Singers of Israel*, identifies five goals that we strive to achieve when we bow in divine worship. I offer them in adapted form.

1. In worship we aim to declare openly our adoration and thanksgiving. We may do this with words, as in saying the Lord's Prayer, or in gestures, by closing our eyes or kneeling or raising our hands or pausing in silence. Whatever the method, it is worship that is visible or audible.

2. In worship we acknowledge and confess our sins. I note that it should not be necessary for Christians to live forever in a state of abject wretchedness or to be always confessing a condition of sinful failure. The gospel can do better than that for us, and the Christian life is to be a life of joy. But whenever we come before God in worship, there should be occasion to examine our lives for anything that displeases Him. Jesus said when we pray we are to say: "… forgive us our sins, as we have forgiven those who sin against us" (Matthew 6:12, NLT).

3. In worship, we aim to nourish our personal faith amidst all the problems, fears, doubts, and reverses in life. There is always some private aspect of our life that distresses us. "… man is born to trouble as surely as sparks fly upward" (Job 5:7). The worship of the living God is a wonderful antidote to despair in these areas because in true worship we remind ourselves potently of an all-sufficient God who comes alongside us in our troubles (Psalm 46:1).

4. In worship we aim to give open witness to others and especially to oncoming generations. A Christian who was diligent in attending public worship, rain or shine, was asked by a not-so-diligent fellow believer why she attended so faithfully. She replied, "I always want my neighbors to know which side I'm on." It was one way, out of many, to give "open witness."

5. In worship we aim to crown and complete our worship by "service, gifts and sacrifice." When King David wanted to build an altar and worship God, Araunah offered to give him the land and sacrificial animals free of charge. King David insisted on paying him. He said, "I will not sacrifice to the Lord my God burnt offerings that cost me nothing" (2 Samuel 24:24). The grace of God is free, but the worship of Him is costly. It calls forth our willingness to serve and to give of ourselves generously in the face of human need.

For help with real worship there is no better starting place than the Psalms. James Gilmour of Mongolia, a fearless missionary, writes, "When I find I cannot make headway in devotion, I open at the Psalms and push out in my canoe, and let myself be carried along in the stream of devotion which flows through the whole book. The current always sets towards God, and in most places is strong and deep."

CHAPTER 17

Three Ways We Worship God

CHURCHES everywhere seem to be struggling with questions: Can an organ and drums inhabit the same sanctuary? Does a cross mounted behind the pulpit take precedence over a PowerPoint screen or vice versa? If a robed choir is replaced with a praise team, is there to be any requirement as to how the latter dress? When musical instruments are used, who should determine their volume? Should hymnbooks be discarded in favor of transparencies? The questions are like smoke rising from the battlefields of the worship wars.

Are these questions deserving of serious thought? My host took me to attend his church, a large conservative evangelical church in the Midwest that has experienced remarkable growth in the past decade. As we were leaving the service, he confided to me, "There are many refugees in this church." Later, he explained that some had fled churches where debates over musical tastes had divided the congregation painfully; others from churches in which leaders had insisted on changing worship practices radically without cultivating support from the people; yet others in protest that the influence of the entertainment world was distorting for them the nature of worship.

The questions are indeed pressing. I've heard them asked again and again, and I often go away wishing they would lead to debate that goes deeper than a concern with the trappings of worship. To illuminate the debate, we can ask, "How did earlier generations of Christians worship God?" One generation will never duplicate the worship practices of another in every respect, but if God does not change and human nature remains the same, then there must be some constants to worship in any age.

Historically, Christian worship tends to fall into one or more of three categories: liturgical, word-centered, or charismatic. Each type has its place, and, enacted appropriately, each deserves respect. Those who insist that one way alone is right cut themselves off from the breadth bequeathed to us by the historic church.

Liturgical Worship

For some the word "liturgical" immediately evokes images of elaborate vestments, candles, incense, and written prayers. Those who react in this way may say under their breath, "From all these, dear Lord, deliver us."

But we need not brush this term aside so lightly. First, it derives from *leitourgia*, a gold-plated word that has an honorable place in the scriptures. For example, in the Greek-based Septuagint, it is used to describe the services of priests and Levites in the temple (e.g., Numbers 8:22, 25, 18:4; 2 Chronicles 8:14). In the New Testament, it also describes temple services (Luke 1:23; Hebrews 9:21), but as well, Christian worship (Acts 13:2), and even acts of love and devotion (2 Corinthians 9:12; Philippians 2:13). Liturgy, simply put, is the service given by the people of God.

Note the word "service." Even among non-liturgical bodies, the word holds sway. We have worship services, prayer services, song services, baptismal services, and Communion services. The word has a ring of liturgy about it.

The apostolic church modeled its worship on Jewish

patterns of temple and synagogue and fashioned their worship liturgically – in orderly ways of praise, prayer, scripture reading, exposition, and the Lord's Supper (1 Timothy 3:16, 4:13; Romans 6:3). Immediately following apostolic times, around 100 AD, the *Didache*, a first Book of Discipline for the young church, was put forth. It was basically a manual of church practices: liturgy. We also find this word in the writings of the church fathers after the first century, expressing the whole service of God, especially the pastoral office.

Liturgy does not mean merely ornate ceremonialism with its candles and incense, bells and genuflections, such as one might find in the Eastern Orthodox rites. Instead, think of liturgy as planned worship, such as through the use of worship folders that outline the progress of the service and the congregation's participation. Liturgy may include other ordered elements: saying the Lord's Prayer in unison, singing together the Doxology, hearing the rituals for weddings, or attending to the words of consecration for the Lord's Supper. Liturgy is intended, among other things, to facilitate the people's worship.

Ordered worship is especially necessary at some moments of the church's life. For example, a professional man tells me that he invited a secular friend to attend church with him. It was Communion Sunday. The pastor's prejudice against anything even resembling liturgy was so strong that he largely ignored the prescribed spoken ritual and distributed the bread and wine with no definitive statements or ordered explanations concerning the meaning of the sacrament. The Christian man was dumbfounded and embarrassed. What went on, he said, would be utterly incoherent to his non-Christian friend. And, perhaps, would be little understood by young Christians present as well.

Admittedly, the liturgy can become a substitute for genuine worship of the heart. Worshipers may be moved by the beauty and grandeur of an aesthetically pleasant service and confuse the sensation with true spirituality. To go away from church merely feeling "better" is not the same as feeling lifted up, cleansed, and renewed by the Spirit of God.

Nevertheless, the liturgy has its value. Consider: It puts a holy restraint on worship leaders, cuts down on verbosity and other distractions, keeps triteness and folksiness at bay, and provides actions or words that convey truth to God's people in inspired, established ways. Wise use of liturgy makes way for God himself to break in on the spiritual awareness of his worshiping people – bringing a sense of awe and wonder.

Word-centered Worship

At our house we occasionally listen to television preacher Charles Stanley, Baptist pastor from Atlanta, Georgia. Two things stand out to us in his telecasts. First, the hour is mostly given to Bible-based preaching that is searching, positive, interesting, enthusiastic, and practical. Here, there are no "sermonettes for Christianettes." His eccentric but inoffensive trademark, the recurrent command, "Listen," seems to spill out from his obvious passion to communicate. One doesn't have to agree with his every theological nuance to appreciate his ardent passion to feed his people the strong meat of biblical truth.

Second, as the cameras pan the congregation from time to time, resting briefly on the face of this or that worshiper, we are impressed by the attentiveness and reverence for truth so broadly in evidence. The congregation, like their pastor, is word centered in its understanding of worship. The question of authority is not at issue or confused in this body; pastor and people stand together under the authority of the scriptures.

This is a light that shines out from the Reformation of the sixteenth century. Among the most significant features of that God-blessed movement were its rediscovery of the authority and power of the Bible and the transformation that this brought to worship. Imagine Martin Luther, cloistered, quill in hand, working diligently to translate the Bible into German, sentence by sentence, so the common people could hear it in their own language. Or recall William Tyndale, hiding in Europe to translate the scriptures into English for his countrymen, and eventually paying for his diligence through death by strangling in Holland, after which his body was burned at the stake.

History gives us pictures of what should not be allowed to fade from the Christian mind: Luther and other Reformation greats preaching from the Bible with vigor and clarity; Bibles chained at several locations in St. Paul's Cathedral, London, while people crowded around to hear its timeless passages read; the early Presbyterians of Scotland waiting for the Sexton to carry the big Bible to the pulpit, signaling that worship could now begin; John Wesley mounting his portable pulpit in the out of doors, dressed in his Geneva gown, and preaching from a selected text to a sometimes roistering but soon subdued crowd. To the present, wherever the traces of the Reformation continue, the Christian scriptures hold a central place in worship.

Like liturgical worship, word-centered worship is not without its perils. Once, while in Colorado, I searched out a church within walking distance of my motel. The setting of the church could not have been finer, both inside and out: well-coiffed shrubs, immaculate lawns, a modern and splendid sanctuary, a pastor in robes, a special reading desk for the Bible. But there was no sense of joyful community, and I left the meeting as undernourished as when I arrived. Word-centered leaders may come to assume that to explain some portion of the Bible is enough. It can become merely the practice of cold orthodoxy, a duty carried out faithfully but without the warmth of God's enlivening Spirit.

Nevertheless, in Christian worship the emphasis on the

authority of the scriptures is needed. When a service of worship opens with a few verses from the Bible, an authority is established under which the whole event is to be carried out. Later, when portions are read from both testaments as a separate act of worship, this declares the worshiping body's confidence in the scriptures as both revealed in history and illuminated by the Spirit in that moment. When everything about the service builds toward the preaching of the Word, the way is prepared for the Spirit to give understanding to God's worshiping people. Word-centered worship can be transforming.

On the other hand, where reading the Word of God is diminished in worship, the words of man can be counted on to multiply, and, however cheery they may be, this leaves a void unfilled. Spirited worship should not be confused with spiritual worship. Worship that does not give the Word of God a central place tends to lean toward folk religion. This deficit does to the body of Christ in a spiritual way what the absence of important nutrients does to the human body in a material way.

Charismatic Worship

Reference to charismatic worship may bring up images of the Pentecostal movement that appeared at the beginning of the twentieth century in California and by the end of the century had become a Christian force to be reckoned with around the world. Charismatic worship places strong emphasis on the Holy Spirit and the special gifts he bestows on God's redeemed people. Whether in a Roman Catholic, Pentecostal, or evangelical setting, it is usually highly energized, open to spontaneity, and presented as receptive to the direct leadership of the Spirit.

Charismata means grace gifts. The word is found in such references as Romans 12:6 and 1 Corinthians 12:4, 9, 28,

30-31. Charismata have been defined in the Interpreter's Dictionary of the Bible as "favors, endowments, graces, offices, all bestowed by God's grace without claims of merit whatsoever on man's part." In its classical expression, charismatic worship honors the gift of tongues as the certain sign that a believer has been baptized in the Spirit. But not all charismatic worship includes this emphasis. It tends to be lively, and often intentionally emotional. In its most radical expression, it emphasizes the more sensational gifts of the Spirit: power gifts such as healing and miracles.

The evangelical church everywhere has been touched in some measure by the trend toward charismatic worship. To some, it makes the quieter, more ordered worship of earlier generations seem pale and unengaging. An age that is bombarded hourly by the sensate and sensational, and that daily gets its news in living color, is bound to be susceptible to stressing the sensational in religious practices.

Indeed, charismatic worship has support from the New Testament. The picture of the New Testament church from its earliest days is that of a community under the direction of the Spirit. The Acts of the Apostles introduces us to the outpouring of the Spirit that created the Christian church. The earliest Christians worshiped in informal and spontaneous settings. Romans 12 and 1 Corinthians 12-14 give us a picture of an emphasis on the "giftedness" of the early church.

But these are not the only pictures of worship modes in the New Testament. Paul and Silas went up to the temple to pray. The prayers they prayed in community there would be liturgically prescribed. Jesus attended synagogue worship from childhood onward where the major emphasis was on the reading and explaining of the scriptures, and the offering of prayers. In his missionary journeys, the apostle Paul went first to the ordered life in the synagogues to present his message.

Charismatic worship needs the balance of both liturgical and word-centered worship. Lacking these, certain perils exist. For example, worship may come to depend too much on charismatic personalities for its direction. Or "worship leaders" may degenerate into being merely "masters of ceremony," a vastly different assignment from leading in worship. The event then comes to be regulated more by the skills and verve of the leader than by the Spirit of God. Charismatic worship may become too caught up in sensation and end up downplaying the scriptures as preached and taught. It is charged that charismatic excess sometimes develops devotees who are highly religious but not always well formed in Christian knowledge and character.

An observer of an extremely charismatic church near the Toronto airport, a church that has become internationally known, noted that the sermon the night he attended was extremely weak and lacking in biblical content. There seemed to him to be an eagerness to get past it to "mat time," which held the major attention of the crowds for the evening. During that time, people lay prone on the floor, or twitched or laughed uncontrollably, or howled like animals. Across several weeks of public scrutiny by the media, responses were shown to be extreme. Some who attended were fascinated and could not stay away; others were repelled and would not return.

FINDING THE BALANCE

There are perils when one mode of worship is emphasized to the near exclusion of the other two. Liturgical worship can become aesthetically pleasing but devoid of the transforming life of the gospel. It may perhaps depend too much on its props. Word-centered worship can lead to a cold orthodoxy, expounding the truth with care but lacking the warmth that the Spirit of God gives. Charismatic worship can be emotion-packed while lacking the character-forming influence of the scriptures carefully expounded and energized.

One thing is sure about worship: churches that practice well-ordered and unifying rituals, that give central attention to the preaching of the Word of God, and that honor the flow of the Spirit in it all are most likely to avoid dead ends, survive unstable tendencies now in evidence here and there, and approximate a station of Christ's true church on earth.

CHAPTER 18

Some Pointers on Aesthetics in Worship

CHRISTIANS come together in several different formats. There are Bible studies, growth groups, committee meetings, Communion services, Sunday-school classes, and hymn sings. Each kind of meeting has its own order and mood.

I contend that a thriving church of any size should have at least one service a week – likely to be Sunday morning – that is understood by pastor and people alike as a high hour of worship. That goal should be reflected in the order and mood of the service. There is a spread of opinions on what the service should look like. My only contention is that the high hour of worship may be either formal or informal (depending on the personality of the pastor and the culture of the people), but it should never be casual.

As mentioned in chapter 14, the difference between an amateur and professional is often little more than attention to detail. Pastors give themselves away by how they conduct a high hour of worship. The following questions raise issues that should be formally addressed. How they are answered can make all the difference:

- **If announcements come first, how do you get from them to the beginning of worship itself in an**

orderly manner? With a musical interlude? With a period of silent prayer?

- **In a super-casual age, how much does pulpit attire matter?** The fewer comments the people are likely to make to themselves over what they see "up there" the better. Innovative attire, attire that changes in style from week to week – these do not help the cause.

- **Does excessive "wordiness" in public worship really glorify God?** Meditating on Ecclesiastes 5:2 and 6:11 or discussing these passages with other worship leaders may be helpful.

- **Is there a good way to use musical interludes in public worship, such as between the pastoral prayer and announcements?** The musical interlude should be brief, a hymn melody people can recognize, and played softly to invite meditation.

- **What is the rule for announcing a hymn properly?** Give the hymn number first, then the title, and lastly the posture you expect, e.g., "Let us stand."

- **Can hand signals sometimes substitute for words in giving directions to a congregation (such as to rise or be seated)?** Yes, but they should be gentle, clearly defined, and without words. The congregation will learn quickly to watch for them and respond appropriately.

- **Is the pastoral prayer merely an impromptu fill-in or a high point in a worship service?** If it is not thought out in advance many of the worshipers will treat it as an intermission from worship. They'll stop listening or check in and out.

- **Should the interlude for shaking hands and greeting fellow worshipers be regulated so as not to break** the flow of the service? It should not be so long that people can wander all over the sanctuary socializing. You can use the introduction on the keyboard of the next hymn or chorus to signal that the service is now continuing.

- **How is a benediction to be used to keep the service from trailing off at the end?** See my comments on benedictions in the next chapter.

- **Why should the use of good English (or whatever language is spoken) matter in the conduct of worship?** Worshipers who are not alert to good English will not notice when it is poorly used. But those who are alert will notice when it is spoken well. So, good English will be well received by everyone, and poor English will distract a few.

- **Do aesthetics in worship and evangelical passion have to be either/or? Can there be both?** God is the author of both. They need not cancel each other out.

- **Who is responsible to see that the tempo of hymns is neither rushed nor dragged? Or the volume of the praise band is regulated to congregational comfort?** This is likely to be a matter the pastor must deal with behind the scenes, gently but clearly.

These questions are worthy of discussion in a search for balance in worship. Where do the clear and careful exposition of the Word of God, the ordered and beautiful flow of the various parts of the week's high worship hour, and the free life-energizing movement of the Spirit of God meet to join hands with one another?

In my opinion, evangelical worship on this continent tends to be too man-centered. This accounts for the lack of reverence in approaching the God and Father of our Lord

Jesus Christ. It accounts for the run-on of words, the casualness, the hurry to get on to something else the moment the last word of the benediction is pronounced. One pastor takes his coffee cup in to the pulpit with him. And, in another situation, laypersons take their coffee in to the pew. These are extreme cases, I admit. I have heard of a professor in a strongly evangelical seminary who slips away every so often to attend worship in a Roman Catholic church. He claims that there is too little sense of mystery in the church he normally attends. He is like a man whose diet regularly lacks protein. Some Wheaton College students were recently in the news for attending a highly liturgical Eastern Orthodox church because what they experienced in chapel services was too often full of exhortation. That is, too horizontal.

"Let us ... worship God acceptably with reverence and awe, for our God is a consuming fire" (Hebrews 12:28-29).

Can I Get an "Amen"?

The church in many places is taking its cue from the entertainment world when it comes to how a congregation responds to truth during worship. If we like something, we applaud. The preacher makes a good point, and we applaud. The musicians sing an exciting piece. We applaud. The biblical "Amen!" seems to have lost its place.

No congregation should be faulted for wanting to make some sort of response in a service of worship. Worship in many places needs more of that. But applause is known in virtually every other context as affirmation for performance. Thus, the question: Is applause during worship the best way to affirm what is happening?

Not that there isn't any place for applause in church. For example, when a member is celebrating her hundredth birthday or another member has been chosen as valedictorian of her class, applause may be the right response. It acknowledges the achievements of God's people and the rejoicing of the community.

But applause seems to have nudged out the biblical response that is sprinkled liberally across the scriptures – the word "Amen!" The difference is this: applause is a way of saying "we like that," or "you did a good job." It's used as a measure of performance, and one isn't required to put the weight of one's character behind applause.

"Amen," on the other hand, is a way of saying, "That's the truth." That word expresses commitment.

The Hebrew meaning of the word is "surely," from a root that means "to be firm, steady, trustworthy." The Greek word has the same sound as the Hebrew and this is why in more literal translations the word is often rendered, "verily" or "truly."

The book of Psalms, the hymnbook of the ancient church, is divided into five books, perhaps to parallel the Pentateuch, the first five books of the Bible. Each division, except book four, ends with "Amen and Amen"; book four ends, "Let all the people say, 'Amen!'" (Psalm 106:48). The Amen is the congregation's special word for responding to and affirming God's truth.

When Nehemiah charged wrongdoers to return to the poor a portion of the money they had exacted from them, "the whole assembly said, 'Amen,' and praised the Lord" (Nehemiah 5:13). Again, the word carries the weight of truth, fidelity, the pledge of obedience.

David presented to Asaph a psalm for worship, ending with the words, "Praise be to the Lord, the God of Israel, from everlasting to everlasting. Then all the people said 'Amen' and 'Praise the Lord'" (1 Chronicles 16:36). This usage became common in synagogue worship and passed into the practice of the early church.

Paul writes that in Christ God's promises are authoritative. "For no matter how many promises God has made, they are 'yes' in Christ. And so through him the 'Amen' is spoken by us to the glory of God" (2 Corinthians 1:20). "Spoken by us"! When a congregation says "Amen," they are saying yes to God's truth and thus glorifying God.

It is a good word, a robust word, a congregation-friendly word, to be spoken with conviction when the scriptures are read or at the close of a pastoral prayer, or when a benediction is pronounced over a dispersing congregation. The word can echo warmth and confidence. It is a God-directed word and shouldn't be surrendered with little thought to a less-biblical way of responding to God's truth revealed in Christ.

When a prayer ends with the Amen of the congregation, we are saying, "That is my prayer, too," or "I own that as the truth." That seems more potent than applause that says, "I like that," or "Nice going."

CHAPTER 19

The Elements of a Worship Service

IN chapter 15 I dealt with the elements of worship. Now I consider the elements as they are reflected in a worship service.

SCRIPTURE READING

From my perspective, the best advice to be given to those called on to read scripture in public worship is to read the Bible as though you are listening to it, not as though you wrote it. Such advice might continue: Read clearly, with confidence and conviction. Read so the people will want to listen.

Most importantly, read the scriptures as a separate act of worship. Too often they are read only as the text for the minister's sermon. The latter is commendable in and of itself, but historically, in Christian worship scriptures from both testaments have also been read as a stand-alone element in worship.

An elderly Scot was exasperated by the young parson who repeatedly left out or shortened Bible reading to allow more time for the things he had to say. The elder finally said to him, "Gie us more o' God's Word and less o' your ain."

The reading of the scriptures was a fundamental activity in the ancient Jewish synagogue. The scrolls were kept in a sacred chest and removed reverently to be read to the gathered worshipers. Early Christian assemblies continued this practice. The apostle Paul, who was well trained as a rabbi when Christ called him, wrote to the young pastor, Timothy, "Until I come, devote yourself to the public reading of Scripture, to preaching and to teaching" (1 Timothy 4:13). Notice that the reading of the scriptures is spoken of here as an exercise separate from preaching and teaching.

It is ironic that public worship in congregations some might call liberal regularly include in their order of worship a Bible reading from both Old and New Testaments and the Psalms, while many congregations we call evangelical lack a place in their order of worship for scripture reading as a separate act of worship.

I was teaching a seminary class of fifteen or so who came from a wide range of church traditions. I asked how many of them attended or led a congregation that includes Bible reading as a separate act of worship. Fewer than half raised their hands.

In the early decades of our denomination – and indeed of many evangelical denominations – it was different. I open the Free Methodist Church's 1910 hymnbook and find an order of worship printed on the first page. This simple order includes, "Scripture lessons from both the Old and New Testaments." The forefathers of this denomination apparently wanted to ensure that scripture would be central in worship, and that the practice would be uniform among all congregations.

To recover this practice, here are some procedures for pastors to consider.

1. Well in advance of Sunday, choose a portion from each testament, usually between ten and twenty-five verses in length, giving special attention to the Psalms and the Gospels.
2. Choose lay readers carefully. Reading the scriptures in worship is not a favor to be bestowed broadly; it is an

assignment for those with the gift to do it well. Choose believers who are good readers, who articulate clearly and project their voices so they may be heard by all.

3. Give readers the passages before the Lord's Day and encourage them to acquaint themselves well with them. Stumbling over words during public reading should never be necessary.

4. If young people are chosen, sit down with them and talk to them about the importance of what you have asked them to do. I have noted a number of times that young people tend to read too fast, not being aware that many worshipers need a slower pace. Model the pace for them, or have them read for you and coach them. Also, advise readers to dress modestly for the assignment and with respect for a holy God and a worshiping congregation.

5. Require readers to sit near the microphone at least until they have carried out their assignment. They share leadership for that service and the congregation should not need to wait while they come from some distant place in the sanctuary.

Many years ago, I had a conversation with Carl Bangs, an outstanding Arminian scholar and seminary professor. We discussed the drift of some liberal churches from historical beliefs. He noted, however, that "so long as the scriptures continue to be read, there is hope." It is a pastoral duty to ensure that they continue to be read and are read well and with as few distractions as possible.

The Pastoral Prayer

My hunch is that for some evangelical services of worship the pastoral prayer is the least prepared part of the service. If so, what might the reasons be? For one thing, pastors may look on the pastoral prayer as a less significant part of the service, a sort of fill-in between important elements such as the sermon and the music. For another, pastors may have developed a casualness with sacred words that enables them to compose on the spot. It's called impromptu prayer. Or it may simply be that some pastors think this is the appropriate way to lead in prayer because, after all, when a child has a need he makes it known to his father spontaneously.

But, if my hunch is correct, I fear that the deficiency may originate with those of us who teach in that we haven't conveyed to pastors-in-training the significance of this public pastoral task.

If my confession is accurate, I hope to correct the deficiency to a small degree by offering some insights on this critical aspect of leadership in public worship. I do not intend to encourage pomposity in public prayer, or literary artistry, or a self-conscious striving for effect. I write to encourage pastors-in-training to pray public prayers that are more authentic, ordered, and fresh, that are heard not only by the Lord but also by the Lord's people.

First, what is the pastoral prayer intended to do? Very simply, it is a priestly aspect of the pastoral office, and it is intended to allow pastors to exercise this priestly function in the shepherding of God's people. Pastors move in and out among their people throughout the week and by week's end are current on many of the hopes, joys, and disappointments of many in their congregations. Pastors, of course, will be discreet in the sharing of what they learn. They will understand (1) what information to include in the public pastoral prayers, (2) what to present to the Lord in terms of universals, and (3) what to carry in their hearts as ongoing private confidences.

For example, if a pastor learns that a daughter of a parishioner has come down with mononucleosis at college and may lose her semester, this, with permission, may be included in the pastoral prayer explicitly. But if the pastor learns that a new attender is on the verge of a divorce, this may not be mentioned in prayer, but may be included as a universal petition: "Bless those who are going through dark and painful times." The experiences of the week will color the pastoral prayer in offerings of praise, words of joy, and petitions offered with urgency.

Second, the pastoral prayer also is a representative prayer on behalf of the people. That is, the prayer gathers up the interests and concerns of the congregation and voices them in a way every individual worshiper present cannot do individually. It is a corporate prayer. For this reason, the pastoral prayer should always be offered in the first person plural pronoun, "we," not the first person singular pronoun, "I." Pastors who do not understand this propriety may have parishioners in the congregation who feel as if they are listening in on the pastor's private devotions. So, pastors who are serious about leadership in public worship should be diligent in training themselves in using the plural pronoun when leading the congregation in prayer.

And, third, the pastoral prayer, includes concerns that the congregation should be praying about but may not think to do so. In a sense it leads and teaches the congregation to offer intercessions that go well beyond the bounds of the congregation itself: prayers for civic leaders, prayers for community concerns, prayers for soldiers who are in harm's way, and prayers for ministries in distant lands.

The pastoral prayer, looked at in these three lights, becomes a vital, even irreplaceable, part of the public worship service. The pastoral prayer is a prayer for the people and with the people. Henry Ward Beecher wrote, "Never in the study, in the most absorbed moments, never in any company, where friends are sweetest and dearest, never in any circumstance in life, is there anything that is to me so touching as when I stand, in ordinary good health, before my great congregation to pray for them."

What can pastors do to keep their prayers fresh and engaging – engaging both for themselves and for the praying congregation? It's an important question, because if the pastoral prayer becomes routine and predictable, the people will treat the prayer time as some sort of an intermission from real worship. If this element in public worship is narrowly patterned, centering routinely only on those who are in the hospital and those in the nursing home – as important as these concerns are to the congregation – it will suffer from lack of scope and creativity, and the worshiping congregation will not participate. No pastor wants that to happen.

As I touched on earlier, in chapter 14, I find it helpful to organize my private as well as my pastoral prayers around the five great elements in prayer – not necessarily using all five in each prayer. They serve only as an order to ensure that prayer has both depth and breadth. Consider them in brief.

Adoration

It is good to begin a pastoral prayer with some contemplation of God's glory: "Eternal God, our Heavenly Father, we worship you because your mercies are new every morning, and your faithfulness never fails." In other words, in adoration we pay our God homage while asking for nothing.

Adoration is "the homage of the creature to the Creator." In adoration we reflect on God's mercies, God's holiness, God's glory. If such reflections do not come spontaneously, we can get help from the Psalms in framing our homage. One Psalmist prays, "I will exalt you, my God the King; I will praise your name for ever and ever" (Psalm 145:1). To begin a public prayer with moments of adoration helps us and our people to focus on who our God is. It saves us from rushing in to the Presence.

For us who live in the gospel age, it is reflections on Christ

Jesus that call forth our adorations most compellingly. He is the Good Shepherd who saves us from all predators, the light who dispels our darkness, the express image of the invisible God so that when our enlightened spiritual eyes see him they see the Father. He is our at-one-ment with God. He is our solace in times of trouble and our joy in times of elation. As James Hastings records, "He that perceives Christ every day is continually engaged in adoration."

Our God is no megalomaniac who must be praised from morning to night and be constantly reminded of his greatness. Our adoration is as much for us as it is for our God. His glory is of the very essence of his being. Someone has said, his glory is the external manifestation of his holiness. It is we who need to remind ourselves of his greatness and glory in order to get our prayers on the right track. When we begin our prayers with words of adoration, we set our compass, whether in our private devotions or our public prayers. In fact, our best preparation for giving public leadership in prayer is to glorify God in our private prayers.

Confession

The Christian life, when lived at the optimum, is a life of joy. Therefore, whether in private or public, the mood of prayer should be confident, full of faith. Our God is both holy and loving. We are his children, redeemed from a sinful past at an infinite price. His grace is mightily at work in us.

Yet, within that context of confidence, our prayers should have in them a place for confession. What do we confess? We stand ready to confess our human weaknesses, our moments of failure, our sins, our regrets. And if this is an element in our own private prayers, then when we lead a congregation in a pastoral prayer we will be more certain to be identified in spirit with the confessions that other worshipers bring to the place of public worship.

However, although the element of confession in our

prayers keeps us from coming to think lightly (or not at all) of sin, it should not lead us to morbid self-examination: "If we confess our sins, he is faithful and just and will forgive us our sins and purify us from all unrighteousness" (1 John 1:9). We embrace that assurance in faith and go on.

PETITION

It is appropriate that confession be followed by petition because in confession we want to do more than acknowledge weaknesses, regrets, and sins: we want to be delivered from offending further in these ways. Thus, in petition we pinpoint those special requests for ourselves, our families, and the family of God. The pastoral prayer puts together confession and petition, though not always in obvious or wooden ways.

Petitions can be for the fundamental needs of life. The prayer our Lord taught his disciples to pray begins with an address elevated in its tone, in a sense spoken in adoration: "Our Father which art in Heaven." But before his model prayer is finished it includes a petition for daily bread. What more fundamental need do we have than one for simple food to sustain our physical beings? When we pray prayers of petition, we ask for the basic needs of life, whether physical or spiritual.

Petitionary prayer is personal and specific. As Jesus taught his disciples, "Ask and it will be given to you" (Matthew 7:7a). Then, to make his point crystal clear he added the illustration of the father who responds sympathetically and generously to his children's requests, closing with the rhetorical question, "If you, then, though you are evil, know how to give good gifts to your children, how much more will your Father in heaven give good gifts to those who ask him!" (Matthew 7:11).

In the sequence we are considering, it is reasonable for petition to follow confession because we are to desire sincerely that those matters that stir us to confess need to be followed by a sincere will to improve or change. Confessions that are repeated monotonously without any hope or sign of change are sure to lack sincerity.

INTERCESSION

In the mode of intercession we stand in the presence of the Eternal God and from that privileged position offer earnest requests for the needs of others. We are intermediaries. To use an Old Testament reference, we stand in the gap – the breach in the wall (Ezekiel 22:30) – as a protector against the enemy.

Intercession widens the scope of our requests in the pastoral prayer. In the pastoral instructions about prayer in the New Testament, we are told to pray for "kings and all those in authority" (1 Timothy 2:2). We can consider that instruction as a command for the church at prayer. And in a democratic country we can certainly extend this privilege and duty beyond those in top positions of authority. It's good from time to time to pray for officers of the law in our community, for medical staff in local hospitals, for mission workers who distribute food to the hungry, for school officials, and so on. The list can get very long.

The pastoral prayer can engage the attention and involvement of the people as they anticipate its unfolding from Sunday to Sunday. In an evangelical church, especially, it is always appropriate to pray an earnest prayer for the work of salvation in the lives of those the church touches. The number-one concern is for the efficacy of the gospel.

THANKSGIVING

How appropriate it is to offer words of thanksgiving before closing the prayer. Again, there is need for reflection on this so that thanksgiving does not become predictable. Whatever else the list includes, it is always important to offer thanksgiving for the great gift of salvation through the sacrificial death of our Lord Jesus Christ. It is in order to mention the providences of God. It is never appropriate to become so enamored of the good weather and the loveliness of nature and the well being of our families that we forget the center of all Christian thanksgiving: Christ, our crucified, risen, ascended, and coming Lord.

Two matters need to be noted here. First, the five elements of prayer briefly covered here do not need to be followed in the order I've given them. There may be other sequences that a pastor feels more comfortable with. And not all need to be included in the same act of prayer. Some pastors may have more than one place for prayer in a service. But it is good to get the elements clearly in mind and in both private and public prayer to include them as an act of worship.

Second, there will always be a correlation between pastors' prayers in public and their practices of prayer in private. If the personal prayer life is rich and growing, a discipline earnestly maintained, this will be evident in the pastoral prayer. And if the discipline of private prayer is allowed to grow cold or even minimally existent, it will be difficult to conceal this in public prayer. There is a certain transparency to the pastoral life; sooner or later the disciplines of the private life will seep through for good or ill into ministrations in public.

Preparing for the Pastoral Prayer

During my pastoral days my practice was to go to the pastor's study early Saturday morning when the church was quiet. There I would reflect on the week as I prepared the pastoral prayer. I outlined it on a 4"x 6" index card. I spent some time considering how to begin the prayer so I would not slip into a predictable routine. I filed these cards by the week. Although I tried to include each element as I've outlined here, I did not necessarily dwell on each with the same intensity or duration. Praying an edifying pastoral prayer, though anointed, is also a learned art as much as preaching is a learned art. Those who would be "full service" pastors will take this to heart. And the filing of prayers is one way to keep one's public prayers fresh in such a way as to engage the congregation.

Jesus said, "My house shall be called a house of prayer for all nations." Having said that he chided the leaders for having made the temple a house of thieves. Our houses of worship may not have the grandeur of Herod's temple, and the people who gather there may not deserve the serious charges that Jesus leveled, but the more conscious we leaders become of the place and importance of prayer in public worship, the more likely we are to preserve a sense of God's holiness when God's people gather to worship under our leadership.

Finally, a tip about the delivery of the pastoral prayer. If you are an energetic preacher who enhances your sermons with gestures, and if with those same gestures you also enhance your pastoral prayer, here's something to consider. Some members of a congregation don't close their eyes during the pastoral prayer and others close them but open them occasionally. In such cases your gestures may catch their attention and detract from the prayer you are offering. They may see your motions as an eccentricity, as though you are preaching to God.

Here's a suggestion: Before your prayer begins, place your left hand on the pulpit, palm down. Then over it place the right hand, palm down. Then keep both hands there throughout your prayer. With head bowed and eyes closed, lead the congregation in prayer, letting that extra physical energy flow into your words of petition and thanksgiving.

RECEIVING THE OFFERING

At a big family dinner, savory dishes began their rounds. When the platter, heavy with turkey, came to eight-year-old Luke, he took enough for himself and then pulled onto his plate a large turkey leg.

His mother noticed and asked, "Luke, what are you going to do with all that?"

Pointing to the leg, he said, "That's for Buster."

As his mother returned the leg to the platter, she said, "You can't take a turkey leg for your dog. Wait until after the meal, and we'll give you lots of scraps for him."

When the meal was over, Luke was heard to say to Buster, "Here's something for you. I thought I was going to bring you an offering but all I've got is a collection."

For those who lead in the Sunday-morning worship of God, it's good to ask, from time to time, are the gifts we place in the offering plates treated like offerings or collections? In other words, how do we experience the time in the service when we receive the worshipers' gifts? Is it an intermission from worship in order to collect up "leftovers," to look after mundane matters like paying the pastor and repairing the church van? That would be a collection. Or is that time a high moment of worship in its own right when we give as a conscious act of worship?

Do the worshipers think of themselves as giving not to the plate, or even the church budget, but to God himself, our Heavenly Father? Are they giving it as a portion of what he has entrusted to them as his stewards? And is their participation in this part of the service as much a moment of worship as when they bow their heads to say the Lord's Prayer or settle to hear God's Word preached? If so, their gift can be called an offering.

I love to remember the sight of ushers receiving the Sunday-morning offering at the last church I served. It took twelve ushers to receive the congregation's gifts: three ushers on each side aisle and six in the middle. When it was received, the ushers gathered at the back of the center aisle, assembled the plates into four stacks, and then four ushers walked in formation to place the plates on the Communion table. As they did, the congregation stood and sang the Doxology. It was a wonderful, holy moment.

How the pastor frames the giving of tithes and offerings has a lot to do with how seriously the congregation, young and old, worship in the giving of their gifts. And it may determine whether a congregation gives collections or offerings.

For the pastor, it should be a theological issue of great importance. Is the worship of the Triune God what we do in a service only when we sing or pray? Or is everything we do in a service an act of worship, including announcements and offering?

What pastors teach a congregation from week to week out of their own reservoir of truth becomes what their congregation learns to hold as true also. It is to be hoped that pastors resolve to say often on behalf of their people, "No collection mentality around here; no more timeouts in worship to look after paying the bills."

Every congregation needs to think of presenting tithes and offerings to the care of the church as a sanctifying moment. To sanctify means to set apart to God. It is an act of thanksgiving and trust: thanksgiving that God out of his provident care has made the gifts possible, and trust that the officers of the church will dispense the gifts prayerfully and with diligence.

What a clever distinction eight-year-old Luke made between collections and offerings. And how aptly the distinction can be applied to the stewardship moment in every worship service. If what we put in the offering plate is the leftover scraps from the week – what we can spare after all other needs have been met – it is a collection. If it is the first fruits, right off the top, set aside to be given with joy – it is an offering.

GUIDELINES FOR USHERS

Pastors need to be aware that next to themselves, the ushers are the most important leaders in a worship service, in these respects: They have the first and closest contact with visitors or newcomers who may be slightly ill-at-ease in a new situation. They also are the ones who can keep distractions to a minimum in seating worshipers, meeting special needs that may arise, and so on.

Pastors also need to be aware that they themselves can greatly improve the procedural details of a worship service as well as its aesthetics by training their ushers personally. No ushers should be put on duty without training for this ministry. I am high on ushers!

The following guidelines are to help pastors in this training.

1. Ushers should be on duty at least twenty minutes before the service begins. This means that from the time they arrive until the congregation is dispersed, their full attention should be given to their task.

2. Ushers should be aware that they are ushering at a worship service and should model the spirit of such an occasion. Teach them to work quietly and calmly. Let them know that, when the work of seating the congregation is completed, they should sit down themselves and enter into the service. They should avoid distractions such as chewing gum, talking loudly, and entering into long conversations.

3. Attire is important. For female ushers, attire that is not flashy but modest makes a statement. This is a service of Christian worship. For men, a three-piece suit may be too much to ask in these causal times. But a suit for the morning service with a conservative tie is appropriate, and a matched jacket and pants if there is an evening

service will give the sense that what they are doing is important.

4. Newcomers often seek anonymity in their earliest visits, so ushers will need to gauge the degree of their friendliness by the deportment of the visitors. The degree will vary from person to person. Ushers should avoid prolonged conversations while on duty. If the church also has greeters, let them care for any special details not related to ushering.

5. Every service needs one usher designated as head usher. This is the leader over all ushers on duty. This usher is also responsible to see that the sound system is turned on and staffed, the lights are properly adjusted, the heat is at the right level, and ventilation is cared for. (There is more to good ushering than meets the eye.)

6. How they seat worshipers is important. The first person or family to be seated usually determines the distribution of the congregation. For example, if a family enters and is seated halfway back in the sanctuary, worshipers who follow will be inclined to want to sit behind them. This phenomenon can be observed almost anytime. It is good to have stalwarts come early and take forward seats. If a small number come to service relative to the size of the sanctuary (for example, sixty in a place that seats two hundred), attempt to seat them toward the front, in the center, and in reasonable proximity to one another. This makes them a group rather than a number of isolated individuals.

7. Train ushers to treat those entering the sanctuary in this sequence: a friendly greeting, a handshake if appropriate, and an offer to take them to a seat. As they are about to enter the pew, ushers should present them with the bulletin and any other handout. (As ushers

lead them from the foyer to the pew, they should keep an eye out over their shoulder. It is embarrassing to arrive at the proposed pew only to discover that those following have popped in to a back row on their own.)

8. Ushers should never seat people while the scriptures are being read or announcements are being given, but rather after a hymn or during a musical interlude for that purpose (perhaps during an interlude after a pastoral prayer). Consider whether it is a wise policy to close the doors to the sanctuary when the service begins and open them to seat those arriving late. This may or may not be a good way to encourage on-time attendance.

9. Advise ushers to be alert and prepared to receive the offerings so that there will be no awkward delay when the offering is announced. Before service begins, they should be sure that the offering plates are in their expected location. They should come forward to receive the plates, and as they move from pew to pew, should stand parallel to the pew looking toward the front. This should keep them from gawking down the pew as worshipers put their offerings in the plate. The ushers can then regroup at the back and bring the offering plates forward together, holding them until the Doxology or prayer is finished and the minister takes them.

10. Have your ushers, either while taking the offering or later, count the number present in their section of the congregation and give their count to the head usher in writing. Accurate accounts are important for the records.

11. Let your ushers know that they are still on duty after the service is dismissed and the congregation has left. They are to check their section of the sanctuary for order,

arranging the hymnbooks and pew Bibles uniformly in the racks, removing any envelopes damaged or otherwise defaced, and picking up discarded papers from pews and floor.

12. Never forget to thank ushers, sometimes publicly, for their willing service to the Lord, the congregation, and the pastor.

THE POWER OF THE BENEDICTION

How should ordained pastors close a service of worship? Just dismiss the people with a hand signal? Have them join in the singing of a hymn? Pray over them a closing prayer? Give them a rousing exhortation to go out and be good witnesses for the Lord?

All four means have been used, but there is one better. It is to pronounce over them a benediction. In other words, bless them in the name of the Lord, and send them away with the guarantee that the Lord will go with them.

That's what a benediction is: "a word to evoke God's blessing," pronounced over the Lord's people in the Lord's name, usually at the close of a service of worship. Numbers 6:22-27 introduces us to the great priestly benediction. God ordered Moses to instruct Aaron and his sons to use this blessing to dismiss a gathering of his people. The priest was to raise his hands and say: "The Lord bless you and keep you; the Lord make his face shine upon you and be gracious to you; the Lord turn his face toward you and give you peace."

In this blessing there is a reflection of the mystery of the Trinity. Note the threefold reference to "the Lord." That is, as you go, you will be blessed by the Triune God – Father, Son, and Holy Spirit – he will be with you.

God's instructions to Moses make it clear that this benediction is no mere collection of empty words. The Lord adds, of the priests and himself, that when it is pronounced, "So they will put my name on the Israelites, and I will bless them" (Numbers 6:27).

Some pastors may feel that this is all too Old Testament and priestly. Not so. When rightly understood, the pastor's ministry is both prophetic and priestly. Think of such priestly ministries as the pastoral prayer, the wedding ritual, the serving of the sacraments, or the graveside sentences. In these, pastors are carrying out the priestly aspect of their calling.

The blessing of God's people at the close of a service of worship is one more wonderful privilege covered in pastors' ordination.

A parting benediction is important because a local congregation does not cease to exist when it disperses. When a church is together for worship, it is a gathered community. When its people disperse to their many locations, it is a scattered one. In both cases it is still a station of the church. How appropriate it is, then, that before believers leave their place of assembly, they are sent forth with a promise that God will also be with them in their many and sometimes isolated locations.

CHAPTER 20

Serving Holy Communion

YOUNG pastors sometimes struggle over the use of rituals, especially the ritual for Holy Communion.

Their struggle may rise from an aversion to rituals because they seem dull and lifeless. Or the service may feel "unspiritual" to them because the words spoken are prescribed in advance.

I once heard of a young pastor's novel come-and-go Communion service. The elements were laid out on the Communion table and people were invited to come anytime Sunday afternoon and serve themselves, without benefit of ritual, pastor, or possibly even fellow believers. It was a communal meal with no community.

Or there was the pastor so opposed to rituals of any kind that after a few words he simply passed the elements around without any designated invitation, consecration, explanation, or prayer. Any unchurched person would be sure to go away asking, "What was that about?"

Whatever the cause for disinterest or aversion, here are some simple suggestions to help pastors conduct a Communion service. They may also be useful for laypersons who feel the need for fuller engagement with this sacrament.

1. **During the week prior to the service, live in the four brief New Testament passages that report our Lord's**

institution of this ordinance: Mathew 26:17-30, Mark 14:22-26, Luke 22:19-23, and 1 Corinthians 11:23-26. Let the scene set itself in your imagination and let the words sink in. If the truths seem wrapped in mystery, remember that in the early days of the Christian era, the Greek branch of the church often referred to the Lord's Supper as "the Mystery."

2. **Also, before the day the Lord's Supper is served, spend time with the ritual itself.** Read it aloud. Personalize its opening invitation to yourself. Think afresh what the sacrificial death of Jesus means and turn that understanding into prayer. It is sometimes the "savoring" of words – "putting them under your tongue and sucking them like a sweetie," as one Scottish divine advised – that releases their power.

3. **Practice reading the service out loud slowly and thoughtfully.** In doing so you may hear fresh truth for your own need. I mentioned above the advisability of reading the Bible in public services as though you are listening to it yourself, not as though you wrote it. The same advice fits the reading of the ritual of Holy Communion.

4. **If you have any impulse in your mind to diminish or neglect the serving of the Lord's Supper, remember that it has often been called throughout history "the central act of Christian worship."** Better to let that fact refashion your own understanding than to dismiss the fact and leave yourself burdened with a serious misunderstanding.

5. **Finally, when it comes to the service of the Lord's Supper, resist the tendency to make innovations, if you are a pastor, or to look for innovations, if you are a layperson.** Sometimes in our youth we are inclined

to diminish the value of constancy and repetition in the fundamental exercises of our spiritual lives in favor of new ways of saying or doing things. Innovation certainly has its place, but not with a staple ritual such as the Lord's Supper. Repetition is intended to fix its truths in believers' minds.

In his first letter to the Corinthians, written before the Gospels were written, Paul states that he got his instructions from the Lord, as a special revelation. We are arrested by the words that summarize the instruction he then relayed to the Corinthian church (11:23-32): "For whenever you eat this bread and drink this cup, you proclaim the Lord's death until he comes" (v. 26). What a summons we hear in those words, not just for then but for as long as time shall last!

Believers on every continent will meet to share in this Communion feast until our Lord returns and we are caught up to meet him in the air: surely this should prompt us to partake with humility, joy, and great expectation.

CHAPTER 21

What Makes a Funeral Christian?

I'VE been reading a book about funerals. That may sound morbid or melancholy, but it's a subject worth exploring because sooner or later we are all involved in a funeral – one for someone who is dear to us, or our own. Death breaks in to all families. When it does, for Christians one question should dominate: What will make this funeral thoroughly Christ-honoring while at the same time comforting to family and church community?

The book I've been reading is by Thomas G. Long, professor of preaching at Candler School of Theology, Emory University. It is the fruit of twelve years of research and reflection. His research took him throughout the entire United States, including Alaska, to get a clear sense of current funeral customs continent-wide.

Long registers with me as believing that baptism, rather than the new birth, is the key to heaven. At the same time, he appeals strongly for the centrality of the Christian gospel at a Christian funeral.

According to Long's findings, today's trend is to replace the funeral with a memorial service, a "celebration of life" event. Following this newer custom, the body of the deceased is buried separately in a private ceremony, attended typically by just the family. At the memorial service, stories are told by those who knew the deceased best. There is usually laughter.

On occasion, the microphone is made available to anyone who wishes to share memories spontaneously.

Long responds to this trend with two particularly helpful contributions.

First, he sets forth what is known about the early Christian way of dealing with death. In the early church, there was no effort to diminish death's reality. The body was washed, cared for lovingly, and prepared for burial by family members. In the service that followed, at one and the same time, human life was celebrated as sacred and death was recognized as irreversible and transitional, a towering reality.

Among the early Christians there was joy because of the deeply rooted conviction that resurrection, not death, has the last word. The body of a believer was carried to its grave with singing. Hence, the title of Long's book, *Accompany Them with Singing: The Christian Funeral*.

Second, Long argues that the central motif of a Christian funeral must be the gospel narrative of our Lord and Savior, Jesus Christ. That must mean that hymns and other songs sung, scriptures read, prayers offered, and sermons preached must glorify him. Long points out that the trend toward memorial services and the absence of the body diminishes the reality of death and tends to displace the great hope of the gospel.

The life of the departed should, for sure, be recognized in tributes, but this ought not to take center stage in a way that overshadows or even mutes the gospel story about the Christ who came to live, suffer, die, and rise again – the very ground of the Christian hope! The gospel is to be central to the event because death, according to the scriptures, has a penal aspect ("by sin came death"), but Jesus Christ defeated death when he "tasted death for every one."

Since physical death is our greatest certainty in life, every congregation should be prepared to help loved ones of the deceased to deal with death in Christian ways. For believers, grief is assuaged but not denied or minimized. Even if the deceased was not a believer, a funeral under the auspices of the church should reflect the great Christian certainties while speaking sensitively about God's mercies and his great love. A funeral is not a place at which to make points, but the gospel should be preached.

Every community has its funeral traditions. They are time-tested in respecting the dignity and worth of the deceased and in their customs for expressing comfort and value to those left behind. The trend toward memorial services with their emphasis on "the celebration of life" should be measured against long-standing traditional Christian practices: Do they give full recognition to the biblical understanding of death as well as celebrating the inestimable value and uniqueness of the departed? And is the balance between them what it should be? Most importantly: Is the gospel central or diminished or moved easily to one side?

Occasionally pastors are asked for elements in a funeral that do not fit the Christian motif. It may be a sentimental poem that says nothing concerning the Christian hope or may even offer an alternate point of view. Or the offered poem may even present a notion of the afterlife that distorts the Christian revelation.

These can be delicate moments for pastors. Some, out of tenderness for the family, may allow someone else to read or sing the piece. Others may apply a stronger measure as to its suitability but do so with grace. The only thing pastors need to be aware of in such a situation is that they are not mere functionaries. They are entrusted by the body that ordained them to apply a standard that is both biblical and aesthetically appropriate, all the while serving the grieving family as fully as possible.

Our culture is progressively secularizing all things Christian. But there should be some hard thinking and teaching in Christian circles to ensure that Christians continue to face the reality of death and at the same time keep the gospel of our Lord Jesus Christ central in any Christian event carried out in his name.

CHAPTER 22

Weddings: A Pastor's Great Privilege

IN this and coming chapters I turn to the topic of the wedding, covering topics that come to the fore when wedding bells are in the offing, and later, too, when their peals of joy may have died away. These topics include: the pastor's role in weddings; preparing couples for their wedding; various theological questions about marriage; the advisability, for churches, of having written wedding policies; the hallmarks of a Christian wedding; the need to speak up for marriage in the face of severe, society-wide challenges; the case for church weddings; and the art of the wedding rehearsal. My aim is to help pastors to prepare couples for marriage and to minister to them and their gathered family and friends through Christ-honoring services of joy. This chapter takes up the first four of the topics listed above.

THE PASTOR'S ROLE IN WEDDINGS

Pastors do not "perform" weddings as though they were dramas. To be sure, the wedding includes certain dramatic features, and the carrying out of its many parts should be well rehearsed and skillfully executed. However, a Christian wedding is more than a "production," and the role of the pastor is much more than the management of its fine points.

The pastor's role is fourfold:

1. To prepare the couple for their marriage and to direct them in the wedding ceremony itself so the wedding proceeds competently with beauty and grace.
2. To solemnize the event, administering the wedding vows as in the sight of God.
3. To draw the congregation in to celebration of the moment as a rite of passage, an event that is of interest and concern to the whole community.
4. To serve as an unofficial clerk of the state in registering the marriage.

In all of this, the function of pastors is both priestly and pastoral: priestly in the sense that they are set apart as God's intermediaries for such ministries as this; and pastoral in that they are personally concerned for the well being of the couple before them. To solemnize a wedding, however simple its proceedings, is therefore a sacred assignment.

The atmosphere of the wedding itself is to be both joyful and solemn. It will be joyful because a man and woman believe that, in the providence of God, they have found each other for lifelong marital union. It will be solemn because they are about to make vows of exclusive, unconditional love and loyalty to each other, whatever of good or ill life may bring thereafter. Pastors must approach such occasions prayerfully.

Two quick qualifications.

First, all of the above should in no way suggest that the interests of the wedding couple are ignored or diminished. It is understood that they will come to the pastor with their own set of expectations, and that during the visits preceding the wedding these concerns will be expressed and fully considered. Details concerning the wedding will be worked out carefully. But it must be assumed that the pastor is ultimately responsible for all that goes on during the wedding itself.

Second, pastoral approaches differ when it comes to preparing for and officiating at weddings. By way of analogy, Phillips Brooks forged a simple but unforgettable definition of preaching as truth mediated through human personality. But this definition is true of liturgy, too. Christian ceremonies, including weddings, are also truth mediated through human personality. That is, the essence of the service may be fixed in a certain ritual, but how the wedding ceremony is approached and conducted is somewhat affected by the personality of the pastor in charge.

Some pastors in training will adjust my approach to one that is more suited to their own temperament or ecclesiastical tradition. I only hope that they will find behind my approach a manner of officiating that truly honors God in the high moment of a wedding.

Preparing a Couple for Their Wedding

The pastor may receive notice of a couple's plan to marry in a number of ways. The prospective bride may linger after Sunday-morning service and say quietly, "Paul and I have set a date for our wedding and we would like to talk to you about next June 12." Or the bride's mother may make the approach by telephone. Or the affianced couple may drop by together to announce their intentions and reserve a date. Or total strangers may come knocking at the pastor's door applying for nuptial services. However the process begins, the pastor should arrange for a later meeting in a proper setting to discuss plans in detail.

What procedures should the pastor follow at that first meeting? Here are my suggestions. The pastor will lead in some light conversation to give the couple time to become comfortable. Then the pastor may produce a notepad or laptop to record basic information. This information should include the proposed date and time of the wedding, the couple's full names and phone numbers, names of likely attendants, preliminary information about prospective music, names of ushers and musicians, and any other details the couple may wish to share at that time and that bear on the pastor's role.

This fact-gathering procedure need not go on with great formality. It may be interspersed with friendly conversation. It is the pastor's first opportunity to get the larger picture of what the couple envisions and to become conversant with the names of the wedding attendants. Even if attendants are from out of town, the pastor will want to begin to know who they are so he will be able to deal with them with personal warmth. Information pastors gather at this meeting will serve as grist for the mill as they and the couple begin to work out details for the wedding. On some matters the pastor may need time to reflect, and may reserve final responses for a later meeting.

Brides and grooms come to the planning and execution of their weddings in a variety of ways. A bride may come with wedding plans that she's been dreaming about for years before she even met her fiancé. Another may come nervous about the details and in need of special guidance. Grooms often come with a low level of interest in the wedding itself. One couple may come with due respect for the pastor's role as they work out a satisfactory service. Another couple may come merely as consumers, seeing the pastor as little more than a clerk and expecting to be served exactly as they order. In a lifetime of ministry, a wide variety of expectations will turn up.

Accordingly, pastors should have in mind their own basic questions as the process develops:

1. How well will this couple respond to pastoral leadership?

2. Do they see the pastor's function as that of an official of the church to bring ecclesiastical resources to the table as they work out the details together? Or do they see the pastor as little more than hired hand to do their bidding?
3. Are the bride and groom of one mind regarding what their wedding should include? (I recall an angry explosion between a couple when they got to the subject of what music to use in their service.)
4. Are there rivalries between families playing in the background that the pastor should know about?
5. Whether Christian or not, does the couple have sympathies with Christian perspectives on weddings? Will they ask for things to be said or sung at the altar that don't really belong in the setting of a Christian wedding?

THE PASTOR'S PRIMARY DUTY

We are still in the pastor's study where the pastor is having a first scheduled meeting with the betrothed couple. There are some questions the pastor should ask before consenting to officiate at a wedding. These questions include: Is this the first marriage for both? If it is not a first marriage, pastors will have to respond in accordance with their understanding of scripture regarding divorce and the interpretations made by the Christian body that ordains them. What is the status of the preceding relationship? How long divorced? Who has the children? (Previous marriages with unfinished business make a new venture particularly risky.) At the same time, it should be remembered that in this divorce-afflicted society, people who have experienced the scourge of divorce are almost always deeply wounded people and should be treated truthfully but with understanding.

Other questions if appropriate, might include: Is there a pregnancy involved? Is the couple living together now? Often such questions are not necessary, but if they are, and if the answer is yes, the pastor has a right to know.

There are two reasons that pastors have a right to such information: First, officiating pastors should not be kept in the dark about facts that are likely to be known to those who attend the wedding. Second, pastors serve in a sense as a screening agent in society. Pastors have a right and duty to decide if they will officiate at a full-scale church wedding for a couple coming from a publicly known live-in relationship. But it is important for pastors to elicit this information without creating unnecessary hurt. We must never forget that the pastor is involved in the wedding as a pastor, not as a lawyer or corrections officer or even a psychologist.

What pastoral questions are ministers likely to have in mind as they move forward with the preparations? At some point as conversations develop the pastor may discuss with the couple the importance of setting long-established Christian practices in place in their home. They may commend to the couple the value of reading the Bible and praying together daily, even exploring with them how this can be incorporated into their busy schedules. At this point the pastor may give them a yearly Bible reading guide, produced by the Bible Society or the National Association of Evangelicals.

The pastor may even want to make them a gift of H. Norman Wright's *Quiet Times for Couples*, a daily devotional guide. If the response seems indifferent or resistant, pastors should not press but simply leave the thoughts with them, believing that they will not be lost. This line of discussion may open up the fact that one or both persons are professedly not Christians. Many faithful pastors have been able to lead one or both persons to a living faith in Christ as preparation for marriage, to their long-term benefit. At the very least, pastors should see this part of the dialogue as a main element in their ministrations to the couple.

Before this first fact-gathering meeting closes, the pastor

must determine whether he or she will see the couple again as a step in their preparation for the wedding. For what purpose? A pastor is likely to require the couple to go through a counseling program involving anywhere from two to five more visits. There are more and more instruments available to guide pastors and to outline the procedure for premarital conversations. One of the most useful ones at the present is Prepare/Enrich, an instrument that pastors may use in meeting with the couple (David Olson, Life Innovations Inc.). However, the pastor is required to be trained in the use of this program.

Pastors who use a book or books as a basis of instruction or a means of inciting discussion may look at *His Needs, Her Needs* by Willard F. Harley, Jr. Harley, a widely experienced counselor, has identified from his years of marriage counseling the five needs that all husbands have in marriage and the five needs of all wives. He regards these as universal needs that must be met in order to affair-proof a marriage. I suggest these resources as only two of many. The important thing is to help the couple to discover and discuss openly any areas of serious disagreement or lack of insight with regard to marriage.

The question of what guidance a pastor should offer in the area of sex is complex. It depends on the pastor's age, knowledge of the subject, personal wholeness in this area, and ability to be delicate but clear in communication. It also depends on the desire of the couple to receive instruction. The question is further complicated by the easy sexual mores of our culture. Two generations ago a couple might have come to the pastor's study with some sense of mystery about the subject. But our society has been so sexualized, and sexual practices have become so open and liberal, that any sense of mystery seems to have vanished.

My policy was to answer questions as they were asked, to recommend literature if needed, and to be ready for discussion if it developed. In my later ministry, I offered the CDs of Ed Wheat, M.D., for the couple's private listening shortly before or after the wedding. One such set is called *Intended for Pleasure*, by Dr. Wheat and his wife, Kate. The other is called *Love Life for Every Married Couple*. If there is need or desire for very specific information about sexual practices within marriage, one of the earlier Christian resources directed to that need is *The Act of Marriage* by Tim and Beverly LaHaye.

THEOLOGICAL QUESTIONS

Three theological questions are worthy of reflection.

First, should pastors officiate at the weddings of unbelievers? Some say no, but there is no support in the scriptures for such a response. Marriage is first a human, not a Christian, institution. It originates in the story of creation, not in the call of Abraham or the giving of the laws of Moses. By God's provision it is open to all humans so long as they meet basic conditions for successful union. However, when Christ is made the head of a marriage – that is, when he is honored and his wisdom sought from day to day – that marriage takes on a special quality and can be rightly called a Christian or Christianized marriage.

Second, should pastors officiate at the wedding of a believer to an unbeliever? That is a different issue. The Old Testament repeatedly commands that God's covenant people should not intermarry with unbelievers – with the Canaanites, for example. And when they did so, the idolatrous results are amply illustrated. Take the case of King Solomon. His career was illustrious, but he failed the Lord in this regard. For political reasons he married wives from surrounding pagan cultures. Was his great wisdom equal to the task? "As Solomon grew old, his wives turned his heart after other gods, and his heart was not fully devoted to the Lord his God…" (1 Kings 11:4). He ended up building pagan temples for some of them.

The New Testament speaks unequivocally against the

"unequal yoke" (2 Corinthians 6:14-18). A yoke was the wooden beam carved to fit over the necks of two oxen so that their energies were joined in drawing a common load. It is an apt analogy, showing that a believer and unbeliever cannot pull a common load. The apostle Paul uses strong arguments against the unequal yoke. He asks, "For what do righteousness and wickedness have in common?" And, "What fellowship can light have with darkness?" (2 Corinthians 6:14-15). Applying this truth will test a pastor's skill and will.

I once held a pastors' seminar on marriage, divorce, and remarriage. In advance of the seminar I asked a successful pastor to give us a brief paper describing his screening procedures. In his presentation he noted that, as a matter of conviction, he would not marry a believer to an unbeliever. He was a godly pastor, and I trusted his approach to the issue. I asked him what would he do if the person preparing to marry the unbeliever were the daughter of the chairman of the church board. This could raise a tough issue.

The question did not deter him. He explained that in the fall of each year he addressed the church board and explained his convictions on certain matters, this among them. He asked the board to stand with him if any such situation should arise. You can see the value of this approach. In the above case, the chairman of the board would know the pastor's conviction on the matter and the scripture it was based on. He would not then be shocked if the crisis should arise. And the bride-to-be, if a believer, would also have to understand that there was a biblical issue at hand.

All this compels me to drop a word here on what I call "blue sky teaching" from the pulpit. The term applies to addressing how the Bible deals with a particular issue at a time when no such issue is on the congregation's horizon. There are many issues that fit this category. For example, if a couple in the church is on the verge of divorce, the fact is known, and there are strained relationships between the families of the couple, that is not the time to preach a sermon on the subject of divorce. But such a teaching sermon could be of great value if preached when there is no divorce pending.

The third theological question that occasionally arises is whether the Lord's Supper should be served as integral to a wedding.

My view is that a wedding is a very specific event in the life of the congregation, having its own format. It is called a rite of passage. That is, it marks the movement of a man and woman from one state – singleness – to another – wedlock. It has its own prescribed rituals and procedures. Every element in this service is intended to convey meaning. At its core it is a covenanting service. All that precedes the exchanging of vows and all that follows are intended to give the service unitary wholeness. In other words, it is an event in and of itself.

In the same way, a service of Holy Communion is also a specific event in the life of the congregation. It is a communal meal. It is for all believers present as well as any who are not believers but who are seeking redemption. It is a service to celebrate the gift of salvation purchased through Christ's sacrificial death as well as his ongoing provision of spiritual nurture by providing the bread of life. In each Christian body, Communion has its own prescribed rituals and procedures. It, too, is an event in and of itself.

Since each ritual is what it is, it seems to me that properly merging the one – Communion – into the other – matrimony – is an exacting task. However, if it is attempted, it should be merged fully. Offering the bread and cup merely to the kneeling couple is not enough. Also, the elements should be consecrated. That requires a ritual that is not matrimonial in nature, and there should be enough of the ritual included to clarify the meaning of the ordinance. Otherwise, unbelievers attending the wedding may be left in the dark as to the meaning of the act as directed only to the kneeling couple and without explanation. It may seem to them as only a bit of magic. And because Communion is a communal meal, believers in the congregation should also be served.

All of this, it seems to me, speaks to the wisdom of making the wedding a full statement and rite of its own, without the involvement of Communion.

The Importance of a Church Policy Statement

Pastors will be greatly aided in their matrimonial services if the church has a printed policy statement to consult on weddings. These are secular times, and even Christians may have a surprisingly thin understanding of what is appropriate or inappropriate at a church wedding. A carefully written church policy can aid both pastor and couples in avoiding unexpected pitfalls and in ensuring pleasant experiences throughout the planning. Here are some of the questions such a statement can address:

1. Are there any restrictions on how church facilities are to be used? For example, may decorations be attached to pews, windows, walls, etc., and if so, by what means? May the platform furnishings be removed or rearranged?

2. Are there any times when the sanctuary is not available? For example, does the board disfavor Saturday-night or Sunday weddings?

3. What fees, if any, are levied for the use of church facilities?

4. Who cares for janitorial services after the wedding? Will it be a paid-for service or will family members agree in advance to care for it?

5. What musical instruments may be used – organ, piano, keyboard, flute, guitar, harp, or something else?

6. If the church organ is to be used, is the church organist to be engaged? This question may not be relevant in many cases, but where it is it should be addressed as a policy matter. Some churches where the organ is still a leading instrument require that it can be played only by trained and competent organists. An incompetent organist or player of any instrument can greatly detract from the beauty of a wedding.

7. Does the church require that only dripless candles be used? Wax on a carpet is hard to remove.

8. Are the guests to be notified by the wedding families that confetti or rice is not be thrown in the church or on church property? If thrown, the results may long be evident.

9. Even if an outside minister is to marry the couple, does the board require that a pastor of the church take part? There are little courtesies that should not be overlooked.

10. Will the policy statement note that wedding attire is to be modest? I heard recently of a wedding that was in every respect beautiful and Christian except that the attire of the bride and bridesmaids was embarrassingly immodest.

11. Does the church require that only Christ-honoring music be played or sung at the wedding? This policy governs the church's response if a bride wants a song out of her favorite movie, which has no Christian message whatsoever.

12. Will pastors charge a fee for officiating at weddings?

On that last point, historically, pastors have not done so. Officiating at a wedding is a pastoral service, just as a hospital visit or a prayer at a Kiwanis dinner is a service. In the case of the wedding, the couple is not "hiring" the pastor. The idea is that churches provide an income and dwelling for pastors and their families and then release them to minister without charge wherever needed in church and community. This is a long-standing practice and should not be replaced by a more money-based one. However, with regard to weddings this does not mean that pastors will not be rewarded for their good work. In most, if not all cases, the wedded couple will know to give the pastor a monetary thank-you gift in appreciation for services rendered. But this is a thank-you gift – it is unsolicited. The relationship has not been regulated by the thought of a fee.

Although I've set forth general suggestions here with regard to written church regulations, there is no one set that fits all churches and all situations. The above questions will be answered according to the values and needs of a particular congregation. For example, a little one-room church at a rural crossroads may not need to have anything in writing. The people just work things out as each event comes along. On the other hand, a suburban church, the building of which presents an attractive façade to the community and whose facilities are complex, will certainly need wedding regulations. Strangers to the church are likely to come knocking, drawn by the beauty of the building.

A pastor and church board will save themselves many headaches if regulations are defined in advance rather than being addressed when the issues present themselves.

How widespread and generous should a church's wedding ministries be? Of course, couples from the church family should be fully served. In addition, some church boards see services to persons unknown to the congregation as an opportunity to present the gospel and perhaps win a faith response. Others feel that such weddings on a regular basis can be resource-intensive and take pastors away from other pressing pastoral tasks. Weddings and all that goes with them do indeed take a lot of time, yet under certain circumstances they can have their allure for the pastor. Some pastors have been known to develop a reputation as "marrying Sams," supplementing their incomes handsomely.

In either case, the different points of view should bring in to existence a carefully worked out policy beforehand, one that is in keeping with the congregation's larger objectives.

A Special Bond

Officiating at a Christian wedding really is a great pastoral privilege. It is a challenge to excellence in leadership. It brings one close in a special way to other believers at a very important time in their lives. If the preparations and the wedding both go well, this creates a special bond. The pastor later begins to meet the couple's children as they arrive. And if pastors live to a ripe enough old age they learn of the grandchildren of people they married.

These days, pastors may not hold power positions in the community. And they may not draw down the salaries they know they are worth. But who will put a prestige or dollar value on this privilege of administering the vows of matrimony to special people in your life and thus launching them on the hope-wrought sea of matrimony?

CHAPTER 23

The Hallmarks of a Christian Wedding

I have known young couples who came to the planning of their weddings with a great desire that the wedding be memorable for them and thoroughly Christian for all to behold. That is, for it to be in every respect honoring to Christ. That was the case with Ken and Judi. They were seniors in college, nicely into their last semester, and anticipating a wedding on the Saturday after graduation. Their love for the Lord was genuine and deep. Ken had siblings who would come a great distance for the wedding. They were not Christians, and one of Ken and Judi's concerns was that their wedding clearly witness to them their strong faith in Christ. Everything had to meet that criterion.

As a matter of historical note, just one week before writing this material I received an e-mail from Judi, whom I had not seen or heard from in nearly half a century. She wrote to say that she and Ken had had forty-six years together before he was taken from her by death. Ken had left her with a great treasury of good memories as they had served the Lord and each other for that length of time together.

So, to continue our thoughts, what are the marks of a Christian wedding? That question can be answered at two levels.

In a broad sense, for a wedding to be Christian, the ritual and all of the wedding's elements must be in keeping with Christian truth, and in this Christ must be honored. A man and woman who have no personal faith in Christ but who in a general sense affirm what the church stands for may come to the church for a Christian wedding. After all, the event will not be a secular or Wiccan event.

In a more focused sense, however, a Christian wedding is one in which not only is Christian doctrine reflected throughout, but the man and woman making their vows are declared believers.

A beautiful Christian wedding has many elements, including the selected setting, chosen attire, flowers, candles, decorations, music, and programs. But the most important element is the ritual that is followed: the words spoken, the vows exchanged, and the symbolic actions.

THE SOURCE OF THE RITUAL

Should a bride and groom be encouraged to write their own vows? Are they free to vow anything that seems favorable to them? Even beyond that, should they prepare their own service?

Sometime back I learned of a pastor who had a looseleaf binder full of a variety of homilies, prayers, scriptures, poems, charges, and vows. This, I was told, was put into the hands of the couple to be married and they were permitted to mix and match, thus creating their own ritual, however short or long.

In another case, I heard of a groom who had strong interest in drama and wrote the ritual for his wedding in the form of a play. He and his bride were the two actors, and at the altar and before the audience (the congregation) they declaimed to each other with elevated voice and thespian gestures. The two ministers, I was told, stood mutely by except for the declaration of marriage.

It is true that such novel approaches to a wedding may launch a durable marriage, and that our culture encourages innovation. However, should not the content of a wedding service have a ritual that all who have gathered to witness the nuptials to some degree can identify with? Is not marriage "instituted by God" and do not the two who exchange vows enter the institution rather than create it? And should the church not be seen as a repository of that truth?

By my understanding, the church – any established church, whatever its tradition – should be more than a mere functionary to carry out whatever wishes it is confronted with. It will have understandings about marriage embedded in its theology, rituals, and practices. That does not mean that services cannot be worked out with a couple and personal requests cannot be honored. But it does mean that the church in such a situation should be seen as a teacher, and its pastor should bring a certain wisdom to the marriage altar that transcends particular trends or novelties of the hour.

Nevertheless, the Internet offers much assistance in this do-it-yourself approach to the ritual – which is the core of the wedding. How far should innovation and novelty go? How much input should the pastor have in regard to ritual?

In my early years as a college pastor a couple came to me for their wedding with the request that they write their own service. At first I was reservedly willing to go along with this, but the day before the wedding came and as yet no service had been brought to me. I learned that the bride had become so immersed in last-minute details that she and her groom had not had time to reflect on the task. They were happy to have an already prepared ritual to fall back on.

I have sometimes said half in jest that to write a good ritual, one needs to take three courses: one on the theology of marriage, one on English composition, and one on the nature of liturgy.

On another occasion, a prospective groom looked over

two rituals I had given him and his bride. One was traditional and the other contemporary, but both were Christian and thoughtfully written. The couple asked for the traditional one if one change could be made: where it said, "I pledge you my troth" (faith, faithfulness, fidelity), the groom wanted it to say, "I pledge you my love."

I commended him for wanting to speak publicly of the love he felt for his bride and she for him. But I explained that at that point in the service the issue was not their love. The church assumed their love for each other or they would not have been brought to the altar together. At that point, the church wanted to know if he, the groom, would vow to put his character – his truth, faith, fidelity – behind that love. That was what the vow was about. He was completely open to the explanation.

I favor a traditional ritual – one that is long-standing and well tested – for a variety of reasons. First, such rituals are durable. For example, consider the line that occurs in some major rituals that goes like this: "We are gathered together here in the sight of God and the presence of these witnesses …" That line first appeared in 1662 in The Book of Common Prayer. Its use and strength span four and a half centuries.

Second, when time-tested vows are repeated, they turn the sanctuary into a resonating chamber. Time-tested vows have been heard there often before.

A good, time-tested ritual locates the couple in the sequence of history. What they are doing at the marriage altar is more than merely an event of the moment; it is also an event in the flow of many generations. To repeat, if marriage is an "institution" created by God, as rituals regularly say, then the man and woman at the altar are not creating something new; they are entering something that has existed throughout history.

A good ritual also heightens the meaning of the event. It marks with well-chosen words a major life-changing transition. It states with an economy of words what the occasion really is. A good ritual tends to unify the congregation around basic Christian understandings. For a memorable wedding, the minister and betrothed couple don't need to say a great number of words; they simply need to say the right words, which a well-crafted ritual provides.

WEDDINGS AND WORSHIP

One more issue: Is there a trend toward setting the wedding proper into the context of worship? I believe there is. To begin the service with prayer and a congregational hymn invites the presence of God and engages the congregation. They are not there merely as observers. A homily by the pastor, though brief and given before the ritual begins, also adds to the worshipful nature of the event. The offering of a pastoral prayer while the newlywed couple kneels after exchanging their vows adds to the spiritual vintage of what has gone on and reinforces the vows made.

CHAPTER 24

Speaking Up for Marriage

SOME time ago, a constitutional struggle in California brought the subject of same-sex marriage to the fore. The public had voted against making it legal. A judge, himself reputed to be gay, seemed on the way to overturning the will of the people on the pretext that the vote was unconstitutional. According to news reports, emotions were running high.

A young Christian woman I encountered at the time responded to the issue in a way that troubled me. She seemed comfortable with the probability that same-sex marriage would become a viable option throughout the land, because the oncoming generation was showing increasing acceptance of the trend. It seemed to me that for her the issue was just a matter of sociology.

Our conversation was serious but pleasant. I was talking with someone who appeared to be committed to Jesus Christ and who subscribed in theory to the wholeness of Biblical truth. Her response seemed sincere, but she was unaware of the scripture's teaching that marriage as God planned it was for one man and one woman (Genesis 2), a restriction pronounced to be true by Jesus, her Lord (Matthew 19:4-6). Nor did she know that this was believed to have been a workable practice from the beginning of history.

In my heart I wanted from a "Christian" a "Christian"

response that was more perceptive of the negative consequences should the judge's interpretation win. I wanted her to be willing to speak up in defense of marriage as a covenant between one man and one woman for life, supported not only by scripture but also by the long-standing traditions of society.

Christian concern about standing for traditional marriage need not be rooted in any disrespect for homosexual men and women. I myself have had numerous respectful contacts with homosexuals and lesbians whom I could affirm fully as God's valued creatures, while at the same time upholding the biblical prohibition of homosexual practices.

Christians believe in traditional marriage as the God-ordained union for bringing children in to the world, and for preserving and stabilizing family, community, and society as a whole.

I don't know how much is being done in evangelical churches to lead young believers in to serious dialogue on this and related subjects dealing with the nature of marriage plus the sins that violate this bonded union. I hope that marriage is being defended on scriptural grounds again and again in response to the frequent assaults in academy and media.

Christian young are going to be deeply affected by outcomes of the struggle over the standards of society. Therefore, piety, even evangelical warmth, will not be enough. Young Christians must be helped to shape their thinking in terms of Christian morality, embracing and defending standards of right and wrong as discovered in the Bible.

A Scriptural View of Marriage

There are several viewpoints swirling about these days concerning "marriage," all attempting to speak to the question: How should humans be linked in a union that is both intimate and permanent? Is it one male/one female; or same-sex union; or living common law; or a binding union involving more than two? To which arrangement should we attach the word "marriage"?

The subject is contentious and the debate goes on. While respecting the worth of all contenders, I want to pare the question down to a fine point: From a Christian point of view, what constitutes marriage?

The reason I raise the question is that although most Christians know the answer in a sort of intuitive way, all too few can give a scripturally structured response. As a result, in this ongoing critical debate about what constitutes marriage, the Christian voice is more muted than it needs to be.

I realize that what I write here will not be convincing to those who reject the Christian scriptures. But there is a vast reservoir of people in western culture – inside and outside the church – who still believe to some degree that the Bible is authoritative and contains the word of truth on the subject of what constitutes marriage.

For the latter group, here is a three-part answer: First we look at the Genesis account of creation, where marriage was established. Next we look at the words of Jesus, who validated the creation account. Finally, we consult the apostles, who together with our Lord put the creation account before the developing church.

The Genesis Account of Creation

The first chapter of the Bible tells us that God created everything that exists. The account climaxes with the forceful word "creation" repeated three times: "So God created man in his own image, in the image of God he created him; male and female he created them" (Genesis 1:27).

The very next verse commands, "Be fruitful and multiply," indicating that males and females in God-ordained union have a special assignment in life, the procreation (creating on God's behalf) of all human life.

The second chapter of Genesis follows with the well-known story of Adam and Eve. The Lord God sees that Adam is lonely and so Eve is his special provision to meet that need, while providing companionship for both.

This incomparable story ends with what seems like an editorial conclusion: "For this reason a man will leave his father and mother and be united to his wife and they will become one flesh" (Genesis 2:24).

Clearly, marriage is the "one flesh" union of the two genders: one man and one woman. Only by that union can new life be brought into being in full accordance with the Creator's will.

Thus, marriage belongs to the order of creation, a point that Christians dare not brush lightly aside.

The Words of Jesus

The New Testament gives us the response Jesus gave to questions thrown at him by some Pharisees. They wanted him to respond to the conflicted teachings of earlier rabbis on the divorce issue. Instead, Jesus pointed them back to the marriage issue as presented in the story of creation given in the Bible's opening book (Matthew 19:3-9).

"Haven't you read," he asked, "that at the beginning the Creator 'made them male and female'?" (19:4). To this he added, "For this reason a man will leave his father and mother and be united to his wife, and the two will become one flesh" (19:5).

The Words of the Apostles

Besides the words of the creation account and the words of Jesus, we have the words of the apostles written to the developing New Testament church. In speaking of domestic order as one of the fruits of the gospel, Paul adds the same verse from Genesis 2:24: "For this reason a man will leave his father and mother and be united to his wife, and the two will become one flesh" (Ephesians 5:31).

In defining the essential nature of marriage, the term "one flesh" is unchanged in these passages of scripture from Genesis, the Gospels, and the apostle Paul. Marriage involves a conjugal relationship, a relationship that is humanly and physically complementary. Thus, in human experience, "one flesh" in all its dimensions can be fully experienced only in the union of one man and one woman.

So, in Christian circles, believers young and old, single and married, must ask as though for the first time: Does marriage have God-ordained boundaries? Must it be exclusively a union between one man and one woman? If so, by extension, it cannot be adaptable to any other humanly devised joining.

If all Bible believers on this continent would embrace afresh this revealed truth and then speak up for it with confidence but without rancor, that would be the most powerful influence imaginable in winning the debate and sustaining the definition of marriage as the union of one man and one woman.

GENESIS ON DEVIATIONS TO MARRIAGE

In the book of Genesis, the narrative darkens after the early passages on creation and marriage as a part of the created order. I dealt above with the passages that show marriage to be part of the order of creation. From there, however, the narrative takes on a tragic element.

The third chapter of Genesis reports the sin of Adam and Eve in disobeying God's command, and the dire consequences that follow. They and their descendants must live under the penalty of their sin.

Chapter 4 reports that their descendant, Lamech, "married two women" (v. 19). He veers from God's order of creation. And with the introduction of bigamy the distortion of marriage is shown to invade ancient beginnings. Later, even Abraham, the "father of the faithful," had children by two women, his wife, Sarah, and her maidservant, Hagar (Genesis 16).

And Abraham's grandson, Jacob, in accommodation to the practices of a fallen culture, was tricked into marrying two sisters, and he eventually had children by them and their two maidservants (Genesis 29:31-30:23). The stories report this as fact, but they also tell of the hurtful consequences: family strife, jealousy, and bargaining for sleeping rights.

All the while, Genesis repeatedly holds up the standard of one man and one woman for life. For example, although Pharaoh of Egypt did not belong to the chosen people, and thus was not blessed with their special revelation, he was nonetheless aware that it was wrong for a man to invade the sanctity of another man's marriage (Genesis 12:10-20). Call this the result of "general revelation," God's gift to all humankind.

Then, Abimelech was a heathen ruler in the southern regions of Philistia where Abraham and his retinue had settled for a period of time (Genesis 20). Yet he had the same inner warning against the consequences when one man invades another man's marriage.

Through the story of Sodom, the Genesis account speaks against homosexual practice whereby heterosexual marriage not only was disregarded but the very idea of heterosexual love was perverted: men, with no interest in women, sought sexual satisfaction with men – and did so violently. The cost of this abandonment to sexual perversion was an eventual divine judgment by fire (Genesis 19:1-28).

Genesis closes, however, with the story of Joseph, a Hebrew alien in Egypt. He had no family there to support him and no faith community to guide him. No written commandments had been given. Yet when his master's wife tried repeatedly to draw him in to a sexual liaison, he steadfastly refused, asking his temptress, "How then could I do such a wicked thing and sin against God?" (Genesis 39:9b).

Thus, this opening book of the Bible portrays the divine standard at the outset and then the distorting influence of sin on God's provision for monogamous marriage. It is true that polygamy, adultery, incest, promiscuity, and homosexuality appear throughout Genesis in a variety of ways, but as reported fact, not as something affirmed by God. From chapter 1 forward, and against all distortions, Genesis affirms marriage as the union of one man and one woman.

CHAPTER 25

Preventing Shaky Marriages

DIVORCES among evangelicals are far too common. In fact, their frequency has been referred to as the scandal of the movement. The causes of this painful state of affairs are probably many, but I refer to one likely cause that is rarely, if ever, discussed.

From a surprising number of Christians who have talked with me concerning their failed or dismally marred marriages I have heard the same confession, though told to me in different ways. They have said that, in one way or another, as they approached their wedding date, they knew at some level that they were not doing the right thing but forged ahead anyway.

I first heard this when I was nineteen years old and had just graduated from Bible college. A businessman I knew asked me to spend some time with him. He was suffering "emotional exhaustion" and had been advised by his doctor to get away from his work.

I didn't know what was troubling him, until he said, in a reflective moment, "I knew the day after I was married that I had made a mistake."

The day after? He had learned immediately that the girl he had married had no interest in really being a wife to him, and his situation had not changed in more than a decade.

My nineteen-year-old innocence about such things was

shattered. I carried that confession in my heart for a long while. Now I wonder, surely there were signals before he was married that should have been heeded.

Warning Flags

I have encountered many similar stories since that shocking moment. In each case it appears that warning flags were ignored during courtship. For example, I was conducting a family life weekend and after the final service, a believer said to me in the church foyer, "Back there, before my first marriage, I stood at the altar saying to myself, 'I'm not going to keep these vows.'"

A woman at a Bible conference lamented the emptiness of a forty-year-long loveless marriage. Then she explained that, as she was approaching her wedding, she knew she didn't really love the man she was marrying. She saw him as immature, even kiddish, and couldn't respect him. But she had played the romance game for too long. And, she said, the invitations had gone out and gifts had been coming in, so she avoided the embarrassment of canceling the wedding by stiffening her resolve and playing out the sham romance to the end.

A friend of ours whose marriage had collapsed said that both he and his fiancée admitted to each other as their wedding approached that there were grave problems in going forward. But instead of facing them realistically, even to the extent of calling their wedding off, they decided that "the chemistry was good" so they carried on. The resulting years of distress were noble but painful.

During thirteen years as a college pastor, I heard other versions several times. For instance, a newly married young woman, of Pentecostal background, told me that a few weeks before her wedding her fiancé had turned up at her home drunk, causing a noisy disturbance. But she and her parents had planned a wedding and they weren't about to call it off. The marriage lasted two months.

In all the above cases but one, the people professed Christian faith at the time of their wedding. And all of them admitted to having received signals that should have turned them back.

A Casualness About Marriage

How do we explain such marital disasters in the ranks of those who profess faith in the living presence of the Holy Spirit and his willingness to guide us into all truth? Is it the tyranny of hormones? The irrationality of falling in love? Can it be blamed on bad modeling in a society that is in poor domestic repair? Or perhaps on societal pressures or anxieties that push the young to seize the moment because "this may be my only chance"? All these deceptive notions may come in for some blame.

I suspect instead that behind many such cases lurks a casualness about marriage. Some may protest that at the time they in fact held marriage to be forever, and believed that love would conquer all. But they admit now that they were playing out a game and felt trapped or didn't know how to get out of their situation. It is likely that somewhere in the brain the culture-wide notion may have been lodged that says, "if it doesn't work, we'll just try again; nothing is forever."

If casualness is not the explanation, naïveté may be. I recall the case of a young woman who forged ahead into a marriage with a homosexual, believing that she would change him. She was a "rescuer." Family and friends saw trouble ahead, but she was confident of her powers. Her decision was unfair both to her and her fiancé, and the short-lived marriage ended in a harrowing divorce.

Signals of caution sent by relatives and friends are often ignored – even indignantly resisted – because in our culture most insist that the choice of a mate is a highly personal, even private, matter. Also, in this culture, romance tends to rule all, so when it takes over, the mind doesn't stand a chance. To be sure, this flowering of misty-eyed idealism with its elevated heart rate and blind confidence about the future is a thrilling part of the process. Romance is a precious gift! But if it overwhelms judgment and resists the guidance of the Holy Spirit there is often a stiff price to be paid.

Insights to Counteract Impediments to Wisdom

But are there Christian insights to counteract irrational impediments to wisdom?

For starters, there is the simple biblical prohibition against the "unequal yoke." From evangelical pulpits is it taught clearly and urgently that Christians should marry only Christians (2 Corinthians 6:14)? And in the pew is it truly believed? This in itself requires the serious exercise of God-given discernment. In the mate pool, not even all who claim saving faith have saving faith.

Add to the above the common-sense dictate that courtship needs time for a couple to experience each other in a great variety of social situations. This includes family times when each becomes well acquainted with the family of the other. The old adage should be heeded that when one marries, one not only marries a mate; one marries a family.

Add to these the hard questions anyone should ask before any talk of an engagement even begins: Does this person have a Christian faith that is at least as vital as mine? And, since past performance is the best predictor of future results, has this person shown a basic competence in life – with regard to work, or school, or even play? Is this person kind to animals, children, the elderly, family? In tight situations, does he or she tell the truth? Since money is a major stress point in almost all marriage failures, one should be aware that a partner with a bad history in earning and spending money is a poor risk if significant change cannot be expected.

One value of such questions is that those asking them of others must apply them to themselves as well. That is only fair, and it may turn up some arresting bits of self-knowledge.

The scriptures say personal judgment can be enhanced by seeking counsel: "Plans fail for lack of counsel, but with many advisers they succeed" (Proverbs 15:22). There are sure to be mature, godly people who can stand back from the emotions of the situation and, after prayer and reflection, offer helpful advice. Often the counselor is someone who knows or can experience the prospective mate in more objective ways. Well-trained pastoral counselors can help by administering personality tests to both parties, or by asking questions that open doors for discussion.

We Are Held Accountable

Whatever procedures are followed, it is important to remember that God holds us accountable for our decisions in this as in every other area of our lives. One engaged couple of my acquaintance spent a year apart, one serving overseas during that time, to seek the mind of the Lord and test their love was genuine. This will seem extreme to many of us, but it led to a stable marriage and may suggest other ways of "waiting on the Lord."

Our culture has a poor record with regard to being supportive of enduring marriages. This makes the earnest seeking of divine guidance all the more important for those thinking about marriage. The apostle Paul wrote to the Ephesian church: "Find out what pleases the Lord" (Ephesians 5:10). The idea behind this exhortation is, "find out by careful trial or by proving and testing." The Proverbs teach that God gives the gift of judgment and expects us to use it: "The heart of the discerning acquires knowledge" (Proverbs 18:15).

Laying the issues before the Lord in earnest prayer, seeking godly advice, counseling with a qualified pastor, and taking seriously the signals from friends and relatives who know both parties – all this greatly reduces the possibility of failure in one of life's most important enterprises.

There is really no need for anyone to overlook or disregard the red flags warning that a marriage, if contracted, is likely to end in failure. The issue is not as mysterious as we may wish to make it. As the Psalmist promises, "The fear of the Lord is the beginning of wisdom; all who follow his precepts have good understanding" (111:10). A widespread embracing of this biblical counsel and a willingness to tell ourselves the truth about the genuineness of the love that points us toward the altar would change weddings among evangelicals for better and not for worse.

CHAPTER 26

The Case for Church Weddings

TO many moderns, a church building is only one of many possible sites for a wedding with no other significance than its convenience. There are more novel settings. For example, two skydivers go aloft with an officer authorized to marry, exchange vows in their plane high in the sky, and then jump together. How symbolic! Two snorkelers underwater pledge unending faithfulness to each other, bubbles rising while underwater cameras roll. The less venturesome may choose a city park or museum or an orchard. Only imagination limits the choices.

So, why resist these unusual ideas and hold the wedding in a church?

Consider the present understanding of marriage in our culture. Over the space of four hundred years, marriage in the popular mind has shifted from a covenant involving God and community to a contract between two lone individuals.

This shift is increasingly reflected today in the framing of laws redefining marriage. And, for growing numbers, the importance is even further diminished. They see marriage as only one of several options, and as not really required for cohabitation. Even more revolutionary voices call for a radical redefinition of the relationship to include same-sex marriages. The Christian consensus that was firmly established during the Reformation of the sixteenth century may be fading.

In reply to all this, since we are called to give witness to our faith at every opportunity, how can we frame the Christian response? A wedding in a church gives one more opportunity to make a Christian statement to friends and community in a setting rich in Christian meaning. But that is only one reason. There are several more.

A Moment for Covenant

The wedding for Christians is a covenanting event. That is as it should be since we Christians are bound together by covenant. The God and Father of our Lord Jesus Christ has called us into covenant with him, and that solemn relationship is formally sealed by nothing less than the sacrificial blood of his dear Son. We gather to worship Sunday after Sunday to celebrate this covenantal relationship.

At the same time, the scriptures treat marriage as a relationship sealed by covenant: a solemn pledge to a lifetime of faithfulness between a man and woman, made in the presence of God. If, then, marriage for Christians is a covenant within a covenant, what could be more appropriate than to come to the same place of worship to exchange vows "in the sight of God and the presence of his people"?

A Rite of Passage

A wedding is a "rite of passage." Across two thousand years, the church has considered certain events in life to be epochal moments in our life journey: marriage, birth, baptism, conversion, death. These have not always come in the same sequence or been given the same weight. But such events are so momentous that they deserve appropriate celebration.

When a couple comes to the altar, what happens there in a few minutes changes them forever. They approach the altar as two single persons, legally unrelated; they leave as a married couple: a new unit in society. Their status will be forever altered, and so will the church community of which they are a part. Should not anything so crucial deserve appropriate celebration in the setting of Christian worship? The event is more than a legal moment; it is a sacred moment of life-changing significance.

A Community Event

For a Christian couple, a wedding may be a very personal matter, but it cannot be a private one. It is the couple's wedding, to be sure, but it is also the church's, meaning it also belongs in the context of a particular unit of the body of Christ. So, the Christian church has a large stake in the wedding: its sanctuary provides the setting; its congregation provides the witnessing community; its ministers provide the authorized officers; and its rituals provide the theological content concerning what the event means. It can be argued that all of this is brought together best and most coherently when the couple meet at a Christian altar and the people gather with them in a setting conducive to the worship of the God who is the creator of marriage.

A Pledge of Ongoing Support

Also, at a church wedding the gathering of the people looks beyond the event itself. Obviously, the congregation is there to give the couple a grand sendoff in their new venture. But they are also there to betoken their ongoing support in the following months as the couple is established as a new unit in society.

While every marriage is expected to go forward without a serious snag, this often is not the case. Unforeseen stresses surface. In many cases, when unexpected storms of misunderstanding or conflict have blown up, marriages have been saved and gone on to become successful unions by the support and nurture of the community of believers. Should not the presence of the community in a setting of worship be a forecast of that support?

An Occasion for Joy in a Setting of Divine Worship

At a Christian wedding, the worshiping community gathers to share in the couple's joy. The wedding itself is an occasion for celebration, and this ought to be shared. Joy spills over at the reception that follows, especially if it is also ordered to exalt Jesus Christ. In all, it is a memorable day. In a world where there is so little joy, this should be maximized whenever possible. Consider that everything about a church wedding – its setting, its long-established ritual, its traditions, its very mood, and the reception to follow – should prompt believers to rejoice in God.

A Christian Witness

A church wedding is an occasion for Christian witness. This is important because marriage has been diminished in the minds of many in our postmodern world. Thus the celebration of marriage as a profoundly spiritual as well as physical union has fallen off. Some choose to live together without ever being formally wed. Some couples marry carrying unspoken anxiety that the union will not last. Others go even beyond that, throwing a wedding but all the while thinking skeptically of its meaning. They say to themselves, "I'll give this a go, but I'm certainly sophisticated enough to know that I'm bigger than the ceremony, and it doesn't fundamentally hold any sway over me; if this doesn't work out I'll try something else." And some couples marry out of sequence, perhaps after long months of cohabiting and even the birth of children. To all this, in quiet ways, a fully Christian wedding speaks as a witness to a better way – God's way.

A Time to Reflect

Finally, a Christian wedding is an occasion for all worshipers to review the sacredness of marriage. As a minister reads well-known vows at the altar, and the covenanting couple affirm them, married couples witnessing the event remember their own vows, sometimes made decades earlier.

A friend tells me that every time he and his wife attend a wedding, they renew their own vows as the wedding vows are administered to the couple, and they've done so for more than half a century. At the same time, single people may clarify their understanding and deepen their resolve to remain chaste as singles, reserving their deepest intimacies for possible marriage. The very words of the ritual set up a resonance in a worshipful atmosphere. Does a Christian wedding ever take place when couples in the congregation do not renew their vows, refresh their memories, and sense afresh the romance of their relationship?

As I stood before two couples on different occasions recently, administering the vows, my prayers were with them, but my prayers went beyond the two to the gathered congregation. In their hearts the worshipers gathered may have found themselves praying for troubled marriages, for widows for whom marriage is only a memory, for singles whose idealism may be under attack. When God's people gather to look on prayerfully as a man and woman exchange wedding vows in a sanctuary dedicated to worship, God's grace flows in the midst of mixed joy and sorrow.

I am aware that there are pastors everywhere who are trying to bring healing to relationships that are far from the ideal. For them, church weddings are not the only concern. I am aware also that in some cases pastors are up against stiff cultural odds, dealing with couples and families that have lost any contact with Christian ideals. I have been in touch with such situations myself. Is it not possible that a commitment to weddings solemnized in a church will help pastors, churches, and marrying couples to keep their bearings, a way of navigating by the North Star when the ocean is heaving?

CHAPTER 27

Conducting a Wedding Rehearsal

BEFORE we discuss the wedding rehearsal, consider the case for a wedding coordinator, who plays a major role in the rehearsal and the ceremony itself.

The Case for a Wedding Coordinator

For many years in my pastoral ministry my wife served as a wedding coordinator. This arrangement came into being at first to meet a specific need having to do with the size of the sanctuary. The center aisle of the church was very long, and it was difficult during both the rehearsal and wedding for me to be in touch with the bridal party while they were assembled in the foyer of the church.

My wife, Kathleen, relieved me of this problem by working from the foyer of the church and giving her special attention to the bride and her attendants. This reduced their stress. As intended, she was able to start the bridal party down the aisle at the right time with the right spacing, thus keeping them composed. But it turned out that from her position she could also unobtrusively oversee inexperienced ushers, who sometimes needed a bit of extra help in getting people seated so that the foyer did not become crowded. She could also inform an usher when it was time for the groom's mother and father to be seated (five minutes before the hour for the wedding to begin). And she could also be counted on to give the signal when it was time for the bride's mother to be seated (at the hour set for the wedding). All of this lowered stress levels for several participants and greatly improved the aesthetics of the wedding itself, helping things to progress smoothly.

All this is to say nothing about her availability to deal with emergencies. On one occasion, as the first bridesmaid was about to start down the aisle, the little ring bearer whispered, "I have to go to the bathroom." Kathleen quickly assigned the duty to the father of the bride, pointing the direction to the nearest bathroom. She chose the bride's father because he would be the last to come down the aisle, bringing the bride. With only a slight delay, they were back in time to join the procession.

On another occasion, a best man turned up from the side room in panic because a button had come off his coat. Kathleen ingeniously pinned him together, and there was no delay. On yet another, ten minutes before the wedding was to begin, the groom came to her and reported that he had left the ring at his place of lodging. My wife said, "Go quickly," then sent a message to the minister and the organist that the wedding would be delayed for ten or so minutes.

The congregation never knew about these small glitches. Without a wedding coordinator, situations like these might have been much more unnerving.

On a recent occasion, just after the bride's mother had been seated, she immediately reappeared at the back of the sanctuary standing before Kathleen in tears. Apparently when she sat down in the pew, the zipper at the back of her dress had given way, top to bottom. Kathleen quickly commandeered some pins, and in moments the bride's mother was back in her place, the bride was composed, and the wedding carried on as scheduled.

It was not surprising that, again and again, it was the

mothers of the bride who expressed the greatest appreciation to her for her services. They themselves experienced greater composure because they had been at the rehearsal the night before and had seen the value of the coordinator's work. We highly recommend this practice to any pastor.

THE REHEARSAL

The wedding rehearsal is a good test of the pastor's leadership skills. A grandson of mine reports that at a series of weddings in which he had been an attendant the rehearsal the night before was chaotic. Whether a rehearsal is chaotic or well ordered largely depends on the minister's skill.

Imagine: The parents of the groom have provided the wedding party with a dinner, and the party is now arriving in the sanctuary of the church. They are mostly young people, long associates of the bride and groom, and they're full of youthful excitement over the wedding soon to take place. Weddings awaken such enthusiasm. How do pastors meld this zestful company into an attentive and cooperative group? Or what do they do if an aggressive relative of the bride or groom tries to manage the event from the sidelines? Let me summarize what I believe are the steps of an effective wedding rehearsal.

1. Ask the whole group to take seats together in one section of the church where they can receive preliminary instructions. Invite them to join you in prayer for God's blessing on this rehearsal and the wedding to follow.

2. Make a summary statement. Explain that weddings are elevated moments because they launch a man and woman on a lifetime venture from which we pray they will never turn aside. To make that venture successful, both will join in a covenant that they will be true and

loyal to each other for a lifetime, whatever of good or ill may fall across their path. Tell the group that they have been invited to join in making this rite of passage memorable and, in order to accomplish this, all must do their parts well.

Explain that you're asking all of them to be attentive to every aspect of the rehearsal, not just their own part, because you want them to understand not only their part in the wedding but also that of every other member of the party.

When each participant understands the big picture, the event takes on deeper meaning for everyone. Tell them that the rehearsal will not last longer than an hour or an hour and a quarter.

3. Phase 1: Start with the ushers. They are usually the least trained for the event. But their part is very important. Let the whole group hear what you say to them.

Tell ushers that they will bring guests in on their right arm. This is not some ancient custom to follow but sets a standard and gives uniformity to the ushering. Explain that when they offer their arm to a woman, they must bend their arm across their chest. Demonstrate. Show them that if they let their arm hang limp or only slightly bent as they offer it, this will be like offering a woman a piece of rope to hold.

Let them know that guests of the bride are to be seated in the left half of the sanctuary, looking from the back, and guests of the groom in the right half.

Explain that their task is important because they are actually in charge of the sanctuary, and how well and uniformly they seat the congregation will determine its balance when all the guests have arrived and been seated.

Then take one of the ushers into the aisle and

demonstrate how they are to indicate with their free arm the seat they are offering, whether on the right or the left of the aisle.

Young ushers especially tend to be self-conscious and even diffident. They should be encouraged to carry out the task with confidence. Have them practice taking a couple to their seat.

Instruct them that the groom's parents are to be seated five minutes before the time set for the wedding to begin and the bride's mother is to be brought in at the moment it is to begin. Custom is that she is the last to be seated, both as an indication of honor and the signal that the wedding may now begin. If guests are still arriving, she must be held back until they are all seated, with the ceremony accordingly delayed.

4. Phase 2: At this point, take the wedding party to the front of the sanctuary where they are to stand for the ceremony. With their backs to the congregation, help them to form a slightly curved line in which they are at least one good step apart from one another.

Have the bride's father or the person to give her away stand one step behind her and slightly to her left. If there is a ring bearer, he will be between the groom and the best man. If a flower girl, she will be between the bride and her maid or matron of honor.

All this is for aesthetic reasons. Bridesmaids don't look good bunched up against the bride. So also with the groom's attendants. This is where the aesthetics of the wedding come in. As a pastor, you are set on making the wedding not only sacred but also beautiful, with appropriate symmetry.

While you have the wedding party at the altar, give these bits of construction.

First, explain to the bride and groom that the ritual

will be followed at a deliberate pace so they don't have to worry about forgetting something. They often display some nervousness because they want to do their part well. Assure them that they will have time to think. Also, assure them that if it should appear that one or the other has missed a cue, you will give voice or hand signals to prompt their memory. The idea is that you will carry enough of the weight at the altar to reduce the nervousness of the couple so they, in some measure, can enjoy their wedding.

Second, tell the bride that the first thing she will do when she is brought to the altar is to pass her bouquet to her maid or matron of honor.

Third, tell the best man and bride's attendant to hand the ring to you cupped in one hand so you can pick it out without dropping it. Have them practice this move. No one wants a ring to fall and roll under the piano, which then has to be moved in order to retrieve it!

Fourth, ask each member, before leaving their positions, to take note of where they are standing and to stand there when the wedding is in progress.

5. Phase 3: Have the wedding party divide and let the bride and her attendants leave for the foyer, where they will be ready to rehearse the processional. Let the groom and his attendants stand just inside the door through which they and you are to enter. Of course they will be out of sight at this point for the wedding itself, but in the rehearsal they should see their part in reference to the whole.

The next step is to rehearse the entrance of the wedding party. With the groom and attendants, take up your positions at the altar. (I refer to the altar whether there is one physically or not, because I assume an altar as a center of worship.) Have the groomsmen stand facing the sidewall opposite them rather than looking out directly at the congregation. This will enable them to turn their heads slightly to watch the bridal party and then the bride enter.

Ask the bridal party to take their places; have them, also, stand facing the side wall opposite them. When the bride has arrived and they are all in place, have all attendants turn slightly so their attention is directed toward you, the minister.

In Canada it is still common for the signing of the register to be included as an element in the service. Let everyone know that after that, after you introduce the bride and groom for the first time as a married couple, the instrumentalist will begin the recessional and everyone is to proceed down the aisle to the joy of the congregation. Point out that the bride comes to the altar on her father's right arm, stands to her groom's left, and then, when she and the groom turn to leave the altar, she is on her husband's right arm. Indicate that it is customary for the bridal party to come in at a deliberate pace but for the wedding party to leave the altar at a more lively pace, with joy.

6. Phase 4: Have the wedding party take up positions at the back and side once again so that you can go through the whole event from beginning to end with musical accompaniment. It's good to have the bride and bridesmaids carry a scarf or book to substitute for their bouquets. This time at the altar, review with the bride and groom – but so all can hear – each part of the ceremony, but without reading the vows.

It is interesting that, in some traditional services, the vows appear twice. The first set asks bride and groom only to respond "I do" or "I will." The second time they are asked to repeat after the minister each phrase of the vow. This practice, it appears, comes to us from a time when there were two separate ceremonies. The first was for a betrothal, or engagement, ceremony for which the couple came to the church. They announced their intention to marry. The second set was the vows of marriage proper, also exchanged in a ceremony at the church.

Show the bride and groom how, in the second time of pledging at the altar, you will ask them to face each other squarely and, each in turn, to take the other's right hand for their vows, and to repeat the vows after you. Explain that they are not making their vows to you; they are not even making them to God; they are making them to each other, "in the sight of God and the presence of these witnesses."

After practicing the recessional, ask everyone to come together again at one place in the church so opportunity can be given for questions. You can expect several questions seeking clarification or added details.

Although on occasion a wedding can bring unforeseen stresses into the open – an interfering relative has to be worked with, or music is proposed that doesn't belong in a Christian setting, or a principal to the event attempts to commandeer the proceedings – it is nevertheless one of the most pleasant and challenging assignments a minister can have. And a well-run rehearsal makes it all the more so, ensuring that the big day is a truly wonderful day.

PART IV

THE PASTOR AS PROFESSIONAL

CHAPTER 28

Ministerial Ethics

ETHICS has been called the science of conduct. Each profession develops its own ethical code. The Christian ethic is based on Jesus' words "do to others as you would have others do to you." In a sense, all of life is ethical.

Here are ten time-tested norms of pastoral ethics for pastors to ponder from time to time.

1. **Give love and leadership to your family.** If married, let the welfare of your home be a priority. Make time for spouse and children. Speak affirmatively of them in public, but not often. If stresses in the family are exceptional and prolonged, seek professional help. Pray daily with those under your roof.

2. **Be accountable and submissive to your overseers.** Seek their advice. Notify them of long-range plans. Receive their compliments or admonitions with humility. If you have complaints against them, speak to them directly. Play by the rules.

3. **Guard your tongue. Avoid tale bearing.** Your words carry weight; they can wound or heal. Make complaints against people to the people themselves, or say nothing. Keep confidences. Teach your spouse and children to keep confidences. In discussing personal problems with

cabinet or committees, speak with respect about people absent.

4. **Speak well of your predecessors. Build on their labors. Commend their strength.** Keep their weaknesses to yourself. When they visit, greet them graciously. Rejoice that the congregation loves them; in time they will love you in the same way.

5. **Respect your successor.** When you leave the community, leave behind a clean and vacant house and study, and up-to-date membership and calling lists. If you return to the community to visit, notify your successor and, as a courtesy, ask permission. If you are asked to return for weddings or funerals, insist that the present pastor be notified and have a part in the service. Never return to do pastoral work unless the current pastor agrees.

6. **Show regard for everyone in the flock.** Have no favorites. Always see yourself as the pastor of the whole flock. Respect those who oppose you or disagree with you.

7. **Be scrupulous in matters regarding money.** Live by a realistic budget. Insofar as possible, avoid debt. Beware of greed. Always put ministry matters first, money matters second. Set an example of generous giving. Pay accounts promptly. Never ask to borrow from your members. Treat church property, right down to postage stamps, as not belonging to you. Seek not only to be honest but also to be perceived as being honest.

8. **Be a good citizen.** Introduce yourself (or be introduced) to community leaders. Support worthy community projects. Keep property neat and tidy. Obey the laws.

9. **Give full energy to your work.** However meager your income, spend yourself without reserve for the Lord's

work. Beware of wasting time, even in the study. Perform a time check on yourself periodically. Work as in the Master's sight.

10. **Be circumspect with the opposite sex.** Be friendly but not overly friendly. Use physical gestures (handshakes, shoulder pats, etc.) only in keeping with culturally accepted norms. Avoid compromising situations. If married, listen to the counsel of your spouse. Pay strict attention to the signals of your conscience. "… set an example for the believers in speech, in life, in love, and faith and in purity" (1 Timothy 4:12).

A Code of Ministerial Ethics

Choosing from among several codes of ministerial ethics, here is the Presbyterian code of ethics adopted by the New York Presbytery three quarters of a century ago. In the realm of ethics, has anything changed? (Note that all is written in the masculine.)

I. Personal Standards

1. As a minister controls his own time, he should make it a point of honor to give full service to his parish.

2. Part of the minister's service as a leader of his people is to reserve sufficient time for serious study in order to apprehend thoroughly his message, to keep abreast of current thought, and to develop his intellectual and spiritual capacities.

3. It is equally the minister's duty to keep physically fit. A weekly day off and an annual vacation should be taken and used for rest and improvement.

4. It is unethical for a minister to use sermon material prepared by another, without acknowledging the source from which it comes.

5. As an ethical leader in the community, it is incumbent on the minister to be scrupulously honest, avoid debts, and meet bills promptly.

II. Relations with the Parish

1. In accepting the pastorate, the minister assumes obligations which he should faithfully perform until released in the constitutional manner.
2. As a professional man, the minister should make his service primary and the remuneration secondary.
3. The minister should not regularly engage in other kinds of remunerative work, except with the knowledge and consent of the official board of the church.
4. The confidential statements made to a minister by his parishioners are sacred and not to be disclosed.
5. As a minister is especially charged to study the peace and unity of the church, it is unwise as well as unethical for a minister to take sides with any faction in his church, in any but exceptional cases.
6. The minister is the servant of the community and not only of his church, and should find in the opportunity for general ministerial service a means of evidencing the Christian spirit.

III. Relations with the Profession

1. It is unethical for a minister to interfere directly or indirectly with the parish work of another minister; especially should he be careful to avoid the charge of proselytizing from a sister church.
2. Except in emergencies, ministerial service should not be rendered to the members of another parish without the knowledge of the minister of the parish.

3. The minister should not make overtures or consider overtures from a church whose pastor has not yet resigned.

4. It is unethical for a minister to speak ill of the character or work of another minister, especially of his predecessor or successor. It is the duty of the minister, however, in cases of flagrant misconduct, to bring the matter before the proper body.

5. The minister should be very careful to protect his brother minister from imposition by unworthy applicants for aid, and should refer such cases to established charitable agencies rather than to send them to other churches.

6. The minister should be scrupulously careful in giving endorsements to agencies or individuals unless he has a thorough knowledge and approval of their work lest such endorsements be used to influence others unduly.

7. As members of the same profession and brothers in the service of a common master, the relation between ministers should be one of frankness and cooperation.

Advice to Ministers

And here are excerpts from the Book of Discipline of the Free Methodist Church, under "Advice to Ministers":

> Devotional life: Practice family, private and public prayers. Include adoration, confession, petition, intercession and thanksgiving. Make prayer a daily means of grace. Fast as health permits. Search the scriptures. Read the Bible systematically, using commentaries. Meditate upon what you read. Seek to put what you learn into practice. Take every opportunity to partake of the Lord's Supper.

Family life: Be faithful to your marriage vows (1 Timothy 3:2). Show honor to your spouse in private and in public. Take time for your family. Manage children with loving discipline (1 Timothy 3:4, 5). If not married, consult with your leaders before taking steps toward marriage.

Use of time: Be disciplined. Live an orderly and balanced life. Exercise the stewardship of time. Resist both laziness and compulsive work.

Personal ethics: Love your neighbor as yourself. Speak evil of no one. Manage money as a stewardship. Keep debts within bounds and model wise and disciplined spending. Take tithing as the starting point for the generous giving of your means. Be discreet with the opposite sex. Respect your peers in ministry. Honor the work of your predecessors. Keep your ordination vows.

Personal health: Master and apply the rules of healthful living, especially with regard to eating, rest, and exercise. Set an example for those you lead.

CHAPTER 29

Honesty in the Pulpit

SEVERAL years ago I received a letter from a woman who said she had heard me speak when I was a college student and was sure I had used a sermon outline of her father's. She said she had remembered this ever since.

I replied that I did not recall the incident but that it may well have happened. I asked for mercy because at the time I was not yet a college graduate, I had not been to seminary, and I was not ordained. I was, so to speak, a freelance preacher, without training in the ethics of the calling. I may not have even known the meaning of the word "plagiarism." Our letter exchange was reconciling.

~

I read a story quite some time ago about a bishop who slipped into the back pew of the church to hear a young man preach. After the service, listeners gathered around the young preacher and thanked him warmly.

Then the bishop approached him and asked, "How long did it take you to prepare that sermon?"

"Only a few hours," the young man replied confidently.

"It took me twenty years," the bishop responded.

~

I attended a service of worship where the preacher's words seemed to me too smooth, much different from his normal way of speaking, too finely tuned in their theological insights. I was ill at ease but had no way of knowing his sources. However, one man in the congregation did. He went home and googled the sermon's title. Lo and behold, the search yielded a seminary professor's article. The preacher had used it, word for word. The trust between that man and his pastor was badly damaged. The pastor had committed a fraud on his whole congregation. The very notion of preaching the Word of God was violated.

A Serious Matter

When an untrained speaker plagiarizes another person's work, you might call it a blunder of ignorance. But for an ordained minister, it's a more serious matter. Ordination must mean, among other things, that preachers are certified to be honest in their dealings, including their dealings from the pulpit. That is, they must not pass off another person's work as their own. That's what plagiarism is. Coming from the Latin, a *plagiary* is one who abducts the child or slave of another – thus a kidnapper or seducer. Passing into the intellectual realm, to plagiarize, says the 1987 edition of the Oxford English Dictionary, is "to take and use as one's own the thoughts, writings, or inventions of others." It is a very real kind of theft.

We have been beset by a flurry of complaints about plagiarism in the pulpit in recent years. An Episcopal rector in a suburb of Detroit was given a ninety-day suspension while reports that he had plagiarized were being investigated. He has since apologized to his congregation and been returned to his pulpit. A Presbyterian minister in Clayton, Missouri, resigned after admitting that his sermons had been plagiarized. Laypersons are becoming suspicious that what they hear from the pulpit has been abducted from the Internet and is being presented as the preacher's own child.

Plagiarism is epidemic at the university these days. One estimate has it that 30 percent of university students plagiarize. The estimate may be low. The Internet is seen as the main source of kidnapped material, but it may also come from a book or journal or term paper of another student or the course of another year. Paper mills abound: a student can get a paper customized to meet the needs of almost any course.

Indeed, plagiarism ought to be an issue at universities; the very idea behind those institutions is that students are there to learn to think for themselves, to base their views on their own honest research and reflection, to express their conclusions articulately. And universities are trying to deal severely with the practice of plagiarism whenever it is discovered. In 1982, a graduate student at New Mexico State University was awarded a PhD in psychology. In 1987 an anonymous tip came to the university that his dissertation contained plagiarized material. After checking, the university rescinded his degree.

If plagiarism matters at the university, should it not matter even more in the church? A sermon is supposed to be a message from God received by a speaker through diligent study and prayer. In its human aspect, it is the result of personal hard work. If preachers pull a sermon from the Internet and pass it off as their own work, is this not both larceny and a massive deception? To such a ruse, the apostle Paul might counter, in Christ "we speak before God with sincerity, like men sent from God" (2 Corinthians 2:17b), and "… We do not use deception nor do we distort the word of God" (4:2b).

All this does not mean that we preachers are barred from getting help from the work of others. Indeed, there is no copyright on ideas; it is how an idea is fixed in form that is not to be copied without citation of the source – and without permission of the copyright holder when a large portion of material is used. There are ways to draw on sources with integrity. We may tell our congregation that the sermon we are about to preach is from a favorite preacher who has been an inspiration. If the sermon is then preached with appropriate divine unction, it will bless, and we will be respected for our honesty. The same is true if we are following an outline from a sermon heard at a recent preaching seminar.

It's true that after we have combed the commentaries and sought help from other sources to prepare a message, we can't footnote every idea we set forth. A sermon sounding like a term paper or professional lecture filled with citations will not rouse the sleepy in our congregation. Perhaps this is why E. Stanley Jones said, in humor, "All work and no plagiarism makes a dull sermon." Preachers who have dealt with a biblical text for twenty years aren't likely to remember the source of every idea they hold.

But there are three questions that we preachers can ask.

First, we can ask if what we are giving our people over the pulpit has on it the marks of our own hard work. For example, even if we have read Chuck Swindoll on the text we are preaching from, there still ought to be evidence that what we got there has been put through the studious processes of our own mind, supported by prayer.

Second, we can ask if what we are giving our people has on it traces of originality. Is what we are preaching a prefab structure erected quickly from a book of sermons or from an Internet site? Is it fresh? Creative?

Third, if we are using another preacher's outline, or illustrations, or unusual insights, or if we otherwise quote that preacher, we can ask whether we are giving due recognition to the source of the hard work of another.

Victor Shepherd, a friend and seasoned pastor, tells me that early in one of his pastorates he told his congregation, "If you lie to me, I'll not stop loving you, but I'll stop trusting you." If plagiarism prevails, parishioners could end up saying the same thing of their pastors. Trust is fundamental to the relationship between us and our people. If we lose their trust through any kind of deception, we are scuttling the very resource we need to do the Lord's work among them well.

A Conspiracy of Silence

We would agree that lazy doctors are dangerous because they have ceased to care deeply for the welfare of their patients. Are lazy pastors dangerous, too? In the life of ministers, a lack of concern for our parishioners begins to form when we no longer address the task of preaching with hard work. Dr. W.C. Mavis, a professor of pastoral care, told us seminary students more than half a century ago that when ministers are careless about doing honest work in their twenties and thirties, a form of neuroticism will likely set up in their forties. The joy of service will fade, and a repressed guilt may become constant in their lives.

This is to say nothing of the atrophy of the mind. We Protestant preachers are expected to be thinking as well as caring people. This requires daily study, the courting of new ideas, the search for fresh insights. We are to be "shirtsleeve theologians." That is, we are to wrestle with the issues of life among our people by seeking God-ordained understandings. This is no small assignment. We will do it well if we continue to have regular first-hand encounters with the sources of our calling.

The problem needs to be addressed. Otherwise, in this age in which meticulous honesty seems to be a low priority, plagiarism could become an accepted practice for busy and harried pastors. In fact, pastors and parishioners could enter into a conspiracy of silence, ignoring from both sides of the pulpit the plagiarism that is a regular part of weekly fare. If that should happen, the authenticity of the church would suffer seriously. So, it's time for overseers, supervisory boards, pastors' seminars, and parsonage families themselves to get the matter out on the table, agree to whatever time adjustments must be made, and in so doing to maintain or recover the integrity of the Protestant pulpit.

Protecting Integrity

How can the integrity of preaching be guaranteed, or if need be, restored? How can both pulpit and pew join forces to make sure the Word of God is expounded with integrity?

The starting place for the congregation is the church board. I do not mean to encourage an undercurrent of suspicion in congregational life, but if verifiable cases of plagiarism surface they should be reported to the board. The board will check the reports it receives because it is the body that carries responsibility for the wholesomeness of all that goes on in the church.

And the starting place for us preachers is a renewed vision of what preaching really is: the delivery of a message from God to a gathering of his people, forged out of hard study and prayer and confirmed in its delivery by the Holy Spirit. With that renewed vision, both pulpit and pew will have joy in work well done. In turn, this will put plagiarism forever in its place as a sham and a cheap substitute for real preaching.

CHAPTER 30

Sexual Integrity in the Ministry

FOLLOWING is an edited letter that I sent to all of the pastors in my denomination in Canada when I served as their bishop, to help them understand, and withstand, that most destructive arrow in the tempter's quiver: sexual failure.

Dear Pastors:
At our family altar this morning, I heard Kathleen praying for "all our dear pastors across Canada." It was not an unusual petition and certainly not prayed for the first time in our home, but it carried a special urgency because of recent events.

Here is some background.

Across nineteen years I have served as overseer to the Free Methodist Church, at first in the United States and Canada and for the last three of those years primarily in Canada, though for both periods my assignment took me annually to overseas conferences as well.

While serving in this office it has been a joy to meet our Free Methodist people in their home churches, at special functions, and on an annual basis in their annual conferences. I have also experienced fellow pastors in many places as persons of integrity who were faithful to their assignments, sometimes laboring in hard fields.

But my wife's prayer this morning was on behalf of a

brother pastor who had fallen to sexual temptation and whose fall had sent shock waves through the ranks. His credentials had to be lifted while the circumstances were carefully reviewed. The news had been disquieting to colleagues because the work ministers do is grounded not only in the grace of God bestowed on his people directly but in that grace as reflected through the integrity of their character and work.

I am using this letter to share with you the insights that we all need as to the cost of a minister's fall, not only the cost to the fallen one but the cost to a pastor's family, the congregation, and the church at large. Our brother's fall resulted from a failure to maintain integrity in his own life and that of his marriage. Discipline was for "conduct unbecoming a Christian minister." You are receiving this because when a soldier falls in battle, every other soldier is reminded of his or her vulnerability.

There are questions that should be considered and answers that deserve to be set forth. For example, how serious is a sexual failure in the parsonage? What are its ramifications? Though we all live in parsonages, we may have never considered the question in detail. We should do so now. Then, what are the conditions in society that should make us especially careful in our conduct with the opposite sex? Finally, is there a checklist anyone of us may review for our own instruction in these matters?

I should note here that I write as a man to a company of ministers almost all of whom are men. These facts will be reflected in the perspective from which I consider the issue. But perils as reviewed and instructions on the issue are equally applicable to ministers of both genders.

Pride, Money, Sex

I begin with the reminder that ministers' three primary areas of vulnerability are pride, money, and sex.

We are all most vulnerable at the point of pride, the root of all sin. Pride is "the darling sin," the "sin that apes humility." It is therefore, the hardest to detect in ourselves. Yet there are signs if we are open to recognize them. Signs include an undue fondness for adulation and a near complete unwillingness to hear reproof – from a caring church member, an overseer, or a spouse.

Then there is money. We can get in trouble with money by overspending, over borrowing, or getting careless about keeping our accounts with spouse or the church. Even such seemingly insignificant matters as taking church stamps for personal use, using the church phone for personal long-distance calls, or failing to meet financial obligations on time can chip away at our reputation for honesty. It's hard to stay honest in these areas. Only consistent vigilance will keep us there.

But, pride and money notwithstanding, sex seems to be the major area of vulnerability for the modern minister. A generation ago we learned with dismay and revulsion about the sexual antics of the Jim Bakers, the Jimmy Swaggarts, the John Wesley Fletchers, and others. These were flamboyant ministers connected with flamboyant "ministries." Yet there are indications that the more sedate old-line churches are also plagued with sexual failures – at the top. It is true that without vigilance, the church can catch the world's diseases. That is obviously what may have happened in the case I reference.

THE COST OF SEXUAL FAILURE

Let me begin by giving you an inside look at the cost of a sexual failure in the parsonage. This may prove painful, but its result can be health giving.

For the spouse and family, sexual failure is more devastating than an earthquake. There are tears, sleepless nights, anger, and a great sense of disillusionment. For all those closely involved, the world seems to come apart. Sometimes it takes months or even years to recover trust and equilibrium. Unless the failed minister's spouse earnestly seeks God's help and has a large capacity to forgive and start again, trust may never be fully restored.

Failure is like an earthquake to the church, as well. Some members forgive easily, some are vengeful, some leave the church never to return. Gentle, trusting people are hurt by the experience and take months or even years to heal. Others who are inclined toward hostility aim their hostilities at one or the other of the parsonage couple, or the board, or conference officers who must deal with the issue, or even at general overseers. Meanwhile, a pulpit has to be filled on short notice for a crestfallen congregation and there are eventual moves to be arranged.

As well, there are costly unscheduled expenses: special meetings of the board of ministerial education and guidance, special trips on the part of the superintendent and often the bishop; special meetings of the local board; and a flurry of long-distance telephone calls and letters that require a great expenditure of time. All those leaders who must deal with the matter are faced with the misunderstandings that may arise and the damaged or lost friendships they may suffer.

Ministers who lose their credentials for sexual "conduct unbecoming of a Christian minister" discover that their conduct was attractive and enticing while it was kept at the level of fantasy and secret meetings but came to appear shameful and humiliating when it was brought to public gaze. In fact, ministers who have the humility and penitence to acknowledge their wrong are devastated beyond description. Sometimes a long period of depression sets in. Such is the deceptive power of sin. Church leaders always labor for restoration, but the road back is long and lonely, as those who travel it will tell you.

The greatest peril of all is that the minister who involves

himself in sexual wrongdoing may lack the humility or penitence to face his wrongdoing and accept the discipline of the church to restore him to fellowship. That is, his pride may do him in. While we believe in the never failing mercies of God and continue to pray regularly for the unrepentant, we at the same time are awed by the reminders the scriptures give us, that unrepented sin brings judgment and that "it is a dreadful thing to fall into the hands of the living God" (Hebrews 10:31).

The Sexual Fashions of Our Times

The sexual fashions of our times appear to make sexual failure easier for everyone than in earlier times. This includes both ministers and spouses. Consider some aspects of our times that make us all more vulnerable to sin in this area.

1. **Marriage has become an institution subject to easier collapse.** The increased shakiness of marriage seems to be a worldwide phenomenon. I even heard church officials in Estonia, before the Iron Curtain fell, lament the trend. As a result, in times of conflict couples may talk more easily of "splitting up" than would have been thought of a half century ago. Parsonage couples need to be alert to the fact that commitment to marriage has diminished generally and that the parsonage is not exempt from the trend. Once a minister or spouse allow themselves to threaten walking out or separating because an argument is not going well, they should be aware how far this is from the Christian ideal of lifetime covenant. Such threats put us on the side of the world, not of the covenant-keeping God. They may do grave damage to our marriage relationships.

2. **Sex has come to be accepted as no more than a natural appetite, to be satisfied as we satisfy our**

other appetites. The repeated call for "safe sex" in the face of the peril of the spread of AIDS is only one of the glaring testimonies to this viewpoint. Abstinence for the single and chastity for the married are regarded by many as out of date. The Christian belief is widely repudiated that sex has both a physical and a spiritual aspect and its fullest expression belongs only within marriage.

Television, with its explicit sex scenes and suggestive humor, is the most immediate promoter of the naturalistic view. A recent study established that during a recent television season, there were 65,000 allusions to sex, many of them shockingly explicit. We all have television sets and, without care, the spell can gradually be cast over any of us. Even more enticing are the suggestive offerings on the nearly limitless menu of the Internet, plus the alluring market for compromising videos, DVDs, etc.

3. **Male/female relationships are no longer carefully regulated by socially accepted standards and restraints.** It seems almost beyond belief that as recently as 1925, a young couple did not date without a chaperone. And as recently as 1945, Bible schools regulated couples (or tried to) concerning when they could talk to each other. Such social expectations have been dissolving for a long while.

The Second World War sped up the process. The sexual revolution of the 1960s made social norms largely a matter of personal preference. Coed dorms became common at colleges and universities. Male and female executives, married or not, on occasion take business trips together. In two thirds of a century, we have moved from repressive regulations to a libertarian view that says almost anything goes. We would be wise to acknowledge that ministers can get caught up in this looseness with less than wholesome results to their marriages and their callings.

4. **The number of sexually damaged and confused people appears to have increased.** I know from firsthand experience as a counselor that incest and rape, especially when perpetrated against the very young, can do lifelong damage. It often leaves women with an ambivalence toward men – they both love and hate them – and this is often the motivation for promiscuous impulses and seductive moves. No one can count how many ministers have foolishly, and perhaps naïvely, walked into sexual traps set by sexually confused or ambivalent people, or aggressively taken advantage of the confusion.

In spite of our culture's openness to "safe sex" and its assumption that chastity and fidelity are unrealistic expectations for moderns, the free practice of sex is leaving growing numbers of people confused and dangerous. I recall a single young woman who left our community to have a baby and put it up for adoption several states away. However, she returned to the community armed with birth control pills that her doctor had urged upon her and became compulsively sexually active. This was not normal youthful passion. It was a sign of sexual confusion, perhaps the working out of guilt. I also recall the respected young professional woman who confided to me that she was seriously considering cutting out of the church and getting involved in an affair. She later did what she had threatened to do. I had the strong impression that she confided in me to test me on the way out.

I don't mean to imply that our world is filled with designing women out to seduce male ministers. It has its share of designing men, too. There are plenty of male predators out there. But recall that I write as a man to a company of ministers the most of whom are men. Female ministers have their own vulnerabilities and need to be equally aware of the sexual confusion that abounds in our times. This should be addressed in a separate statement.

Perils That Lurk in Counseling

What is important is that ministers be savvy enough to know when peril is near. It often occurs in the context of counseling, especially if counselors are untrained and naïve, and ministers need to be alert to detect situations that call for caution and perhaps referral. Let me list some of these.

1. An alert male ministerial counselor may notice that a woman counselee begins to dress for an appointment much as she might for a date.

2. Sessions may begin to go well beyond the hour allotted and involve chitchat rather than careful counseling procedures.

3. Both minister and counselee begin to anticipate with pleasure the next session.

4. The number of appointments goes well beyond the minister's skills, so there is no movement in the therapeutic process, only emotional entanglement.

5. The counselee shares intimacies out of her life and the minister is tempted to respond in kind, thus dropping the sacred veil from his own marriage.

6. An element of secrecy develops that is different from confidentiality. Meetings may take place in odd places or at odd times. Or the minister may begin to ask the counselee to leave from the session unnoticed, a sign his conscience is trying to signal him.

7. A minister begins to allow a counselee to dominate his time, responding to calls late at night or even in the middle of the night. Late-night calls should be rare and truly of an emergency nature.

8. The counselee may begin to make excessively complimentary remarks about the minister. When this happens, a minister is in danger of being seduced by his own ego.

9. If complimentary remarks begin to go both ways, every red light in the conscience should be flashing. If they are not, the peril is doubly great.

10. A counselee talks of her sexual needs, or she asks for hugs, or gives them. This is likely to be a step on the road to seduction.

11. The counselee gives gifts. Gifts are inappropriate and always threaten the professionalism of the counseling process.

12. A minister's God-given sense of propriety may be offended in any other of a score of ways. Or he may feel an uneasy sense of disloyalty to his wife.

At this point we should note that it is never appropriate for a minister to respond with scolding to what may be judged inappropriate or seductive signals. Here are some reasons: The counselee may not be alert to what she is doing and so in her vulnerability may be deeply shocked; or, the minister's inference could be entirely wrong and a serious offense is thus committed against the counselee; or, if the minister is right, a scolding could arouse anger that will fuel reprisal over the coming weeks. But these cautions notwithstanding, the minister needs to bring the contacts to a clear close by referral to a woman in the congregation or to his wife. Or he may ask permission to discuss the case with another professional.

Or he may simply give notice that he does not have the skills to continue the counseling.

Ways to Keep Relationships Wholesome

But there is something more important than learning how to get out of a perilous situation, and that is to learn how to regulate one's life so that one can carry on a broad range of ministries to troubled people while minimizing the perils. I turn to this matter now. There are several things any minister can do daily that will keep his life wholesome in the midst of "a sinful and adulterous generation." And this without becoming prudish or cutting out legitimate opportunities to minister. To neglect any of these is at least to ensure a flat and largely ineffectual ministry and at most to imperil integrity, thus inviting public embarrassment or even the loss of ministerial credentials. Here they are:

1. **Keep in daily communion with Christ.** Throughout one's whole lifetime. love for Christ must remain the pastor's first love. Peruse the language of the New Testament relative to the Christian life and you'll see how central this idea is. Paul's prayer for the Ephesians is that "Christ may dwell in your hearts through faith" (Ephesians 3:17). To the Colossians, he writes, "So then, just as you received Christ Jesus as Lord, continue to live in him, rooted and built up in him, strengthened in the faith as you were taught, and overflowing with thankfulness" (Colossians 2:6-7). He also wrote, "Let the word of Christ dwell in you richly as you teach and admonish one another with all wisdom ..." (Colossians 3:16).

   If exhortations like these are for all Christians, should they not be doubly heeded by those of us who are assigned leadership roles in the church? Being a pastor is more than preaching sermons, leading board meetings, and making hospital calls. It is doing all these and more out of a fresh and richly endowed life of devotion to Christ, our Lord. What a blessing it is to step to the pulpit to preach, nourished by a deep inner awareness of the presence of Christ, a presence we have cultivated during the week.

Yet, as urgent as the New Testament is in exhorting us to keep our hearts as Christ's home, we ministers may easily neglect to do so and then cover over our neglect by a professional manner we have learned or a facility with "God talk." One minister who fell into sexual sin confided to me that before his fall he had come to read the Bible only in search of sermon texts. It had ceased to be the source that nourished his own spiritual life.

The late E. Stanley Jones said he believed most failures in the ministry begin with failure in the devotional life. No one thing is more important to our integrity than the cultivation of an inner life that is ruled by Jesus Christ.

2. **Give attention to the nurture of your marriage.** More than twenty years ago, a young niece and nephew of mine, both graduates of an interdenominational Bible college, told me of their visit with two of their former classmates in a midwestern American city. The classmates were a parsonage team. The congregation was throbbing with activity and growing rapidly. To most observers it would be considered a modern success story. However, my niece and nephew discovered, in the midst of it all, that the successful pastor was sleeping regularly in his church study while his wife occupied their bedroom in the parsonage. Some kind of alienation had developed between them. Whether success had gone to his head or not, I do not know. But I do note that any situation even vaguely resembling this is a ticking time bomb for moral failure.

Parsonage life can be busy and, at times, hectic. Situations arise that preoccupy the minister's mind. Emergencies are time-consuming. The fact that the spouse is working outside the home adds to the already great pressure. Yet, no parsonage life need be so busy that there is not time for minister and wife to keep the relationship rich and growing. When it gets that busy, it is too busy, and things need to come to a halt for a period of reassessment. It may be that a third party must be called in for counseling. The security of a parsonage marriage is immeasurably important!

I recall spending a week in a parsonage several years ago during a preaching mission. I was still a local pastor. The pace of things seemed dizzying in that home. Both the minister and his wife were fully occupied outside the home. There were two high schoolers in the family running on separate schedules. There seemed to be no face-to-face meetings of the family during the day except over breakfast, which itself was too hasty to allow for any family sharing.

I didn't feel critical of the situation; I considered it to be quite normal for a modern North American family. But when I learned two years later that the minister had become sexually involved with a woman and had had to leave his community in disgrace, taking his family with him, I remembered that fast-paced week.

Please do not misunderstand: Both minister and wife were honorable people. And their marriage would have been judged by most people to be stable. I am sure no illicit sexual relationship was carefully planned. My surmise is that husband and wife, in their well-intentioned busyness, had lost contact with each other, and the serious deficiency in the marriage had rendered him vulnerable to the temptation to flirt with another relationship or vulnerable to a seductive woman.

Companionship is at the heart of any good marriage. But companionship must be regularly cultivated. With fair regularity, husband and wife must come home to each other. When they strike a pace that makes this difficult or impossible, even the finest may fall.

In our helter-skelter world, the nourishment of a marriage is not easy. But smart – not to say Christian – couples pay the price to achieve it. Consider some ways successful couples have devised to do so.

A minister whose children were old enough to take care of themselves told me of one technique he and his wife used to keep in touch. She worked outside the home and he carried heavy responsibilities. But often, after 10 p.m., they slipped out to a nearby coffee shop where, for the price of a doughnut and coffee, they could talk and keep up to date with each other. This sort of liaison satisfied a soul-deep need on the part of both partners. Call it communion.

A minister and his wife in Michigan shared with me that, at one point in their married life, when their children were still at home, they went for a long walk early every morning, praying together aloud as they walked.

Our friends, the late Wilson and Mary LaDue, both professors at Greenville College a generation ago, observed a 4 p.m. ritual faithfully. At that hour, everything came to a standstill as they took time out to light a candle and have coffee together.

Someone once took the well-known saying, "Where there's a will, there's a way," and revised it to say, "Where there's a will, there are twenty ways." The latter is demonstrably true in the case of the need to keep a marriage nourished. Couples who have a heart for it will find ways aplenty.

What if the marriage has become so prosaic and uninteresting that neither minister nor wife has any desire to find a way? This lack should be taken as a danger signal. A marriage that started with starry-eyed idealism but has degenerated to boredom is in trouble, however appropriately the two conduct themselves in public. Either party may be vulnerable to illicit opportunities that promise to add spice to a dull existence. They should acknowledge their need and seek counseling from a qualified Christian, paying any price necessary to get their marriage onto a more solid footing.

Our own experiences as a husband and wife in a big city, and separated often by my travels, is that, however busy life becomes, we take time to share our experiences, renew our dreams, exchange news of the family, and basically enjoy each other. We both understand that neglected marriages are like neglected gardens. The weeds of discontent soon crop up and start to do their damage. Spouses who feel neglected, whether male or female, are vulnerable to some attentive, caring person who may come along. All spouses should get the greatest attention and caring from their life partner.

3. **Live orderly, disciplined lives.** We bristle slightly at the often-heard charge that ministers are among the greatest of time wasters. Yet, when we run a check on ourselves, we see that it is a charge not completely wide of the mark. If we get to our study by 9 in the morning instead of 8 and leave by 11:30, that's a short work morning. If, in addition, what we do in the morning hours is low priority – looking at the mail, thumbing through a magazine, balancing a checkbook – then we are not really working when we are there. And if lunch hour runs to one and a half hours and we're around the house for two all told, that's another hour wasted. As a result, we can go through the week feeling busy, even harried, but accomplish little.

The temptation to waste time has increased with the coming of computers and the Internet. Computers are at arm's reach and are private to us. Pastors need to engage with other pastors and to become accountable to avoid the lure of these potential time-wasters.

This matter of living a disciplined life is important, because an undisciplined life is more vulnerable to moral failure than a disciplined one. Bishop Leslie R. Marston told me when I was his pastor that he worried very little over the moral rectitude of pastors who lived with a clear sense of purpose, had well-defined goals, and went about the Lord's business with enthusiasm. You may say that this is not a totally dependable measure, as he would agree, but it is true enough to be seriously considered.

4. **Work like a professional.** To be a professional does not mean to be stiff and formal and slightly affected in manner. It means to take our task seriously, to buy in to the collective wisdom of the past regarding our calling, and to take full advantage of our training. It involves how we conduct ourselves in a hospital room, a member's home, our study, or the pulpit. In this case being a professional is the opposite of being an amateur.

    I'm convinced that the relaxing of social norms in society at large and the resulting easy-going ways we have developed for relating sometimes contribute to moral failures that touch the ministry. Ministers who want to be "chums" instead of "shepherds" lose much more than they gain. The egalitarian influences of the 1960s have not served us entirely well. Parishioners may accept us as a chum on the tennis court, but when they are hours away from a serious surgery, they want a pastor who is a professional.

    One thing a professional minister does not do is take

a female parishioner to lunch for a counseling session. I've known this practice to be a source of serious complaint several times. In one case, it was the jealous husband of a parishioner who complained with feeling; in another it was the offended wife of the pastor. Does a highly skilled surgeon take a female patient to lunch to discuss next week's gallbladder surgery? Pastoral counseling that is done "anytime, anywhere" is flippant and is rightly called "curbside counseling." It is done by amateurs. A professional minister has a properly equipped room for counseling. It is usually open in some way to the outside, next to a secretary's office, and is furnished for serious business.

Nor does a professional male pastor close a counseling session by hugging a female counselee. Admittedly, hugging is becoming a more frequent social greeting. Someday hugging may fit our social practices as a handshake does now. But at present, it is not an established custom whose meaning is well defined socially. And it is particularly dangerous in a counseling session because the counselee may misunderstand what it means. Pastors themselves may find familiarity overtaking them, thus canceling out their professional usefulness.

The practice of hugging in social settings is affected by the temperament of the pastor (some ministers are more "huggy" than others). It is affected also by his age (a sixty-five-year-old pastor may be excused for offering a hug when a thirty-five-year-old is not). It is regulated somewhat by the expectations of a parishioner (a warm, loving person may initiate a hug to which a pastor must respond courteously). However, pastors who promote this practice in public settings need to know that in every group of a dozen people there are men and women who secretly disapprove. It shocks their sense of propriety.

Furthermore, a professional pastor is confidential but not secretive. He does not meet women in out-of-the-way places "to help them." He keeps someone – his wife or secretary – informed about where he is to be at all times. He may announce that he is going to the hospital or to visit a shut-in or to a restaurant to have lunch with a businessman and will stop off at the post office at five on his way back.

This practice is for his own protection as well as to keep himself within reach by telephone in case of an emergency. I can think of three ministers who might have found it harder to fall into sexual sin if they had held themselves to this practice of making their location known at all times.

5. **Be accountable.** A minister friend shared with me how making himself accountable saved him from possible trouble. He was involved in Christian work with a female colleague. He became aware that he was developing feelings for her. He went immediately to a fellow minister of stature and reported what he was experiencing, asking to be held accountable.

In a nutshell, he had heeded the alarm bells that were beginning to ring inside his being. His conscience was functioning well, alerting him to the beginning of a perilous temptation. Had he shunned the signals, keeping the knowledge of what was happening to himself alone, he very well could have become involved in an infatuation leading to dire consequences.

Making ourselves accountable in a situation like this requires that we turn to someone who has the leverage to call us to account. During the 1960s, I watched as teenagers sought counsel from one another concerning their sexual temptations. It seldom helped because the leverage was not there. Ministers in the early stages of sexual temptation should turn to a senior minister (one nearby) or a superintendent. Often the shock of self-disclosure is enough to break the spell.

This may seem like strong counsel. Not many of us will find it easy to acknowledge to a fellow minister that we are vulnerable to sexual temptation. Nor should we feel the need to report every erotic feeling that touches our beings. But when the alarm bells begin to ring they should be heeded. It is a loving God who sets them off, through the medium of our conscience. Better that we should experience the embarrassment of confessing to a weakness than to wait and suffer the shame of experiencing a humiliating fall.

We all have built-in relationships of accountability. There is accountability to spouse and family. I know a great deal about this. My wife loves me deeply, but across more than sixty-five years of marriage, she has never failed to alert me to any public word or manner that she thought inappropriate. My children love and respect me, but none of them would fail to offer help over some social issue if they thought I needed it.

There is also accountability to the denomination. This includes taking our ordination vows seriously, being a team player in the conference, taking the requests of the superintendent seriously (for reports, etc.), making attendance at annual conference a top-priority matter, and otherwise reciprocating the trust the denomination has placed in us.

Consider also the matter of accountability to the local church that pays our salary and gives us a field in which to minister. If the congregation is two hundred strong, accountability to every one of them in a personal way is too much to ask. Two hundred bosses are more than any one of us can handle. But the official board deserves a monthly report on how we spend our time and what special goals we are pursuing. And the cabinet should have a regular opportunity to dialogue with us on how the work of the church is progressing. The word "dialogue" means input from both sides.

6. **A final caution: We must keep in touch with our falling and rising emotions especially in times when circumstances in any way threaten our sense of worth: when we experience setbacks in our work, colleagues get promotions that appear to leave us behind, things may be said to us that cut at our sense of significance.** I read recently of a very simple experiment that showed that men thrown into a state of insecurity become more susceptible to the blandishments of attractive women. I was not surprised. In times of war, divorce, even social dislocation, people otherwise inclined to be moral find it easier to fall from their own ideals.

There are times of insecurity in a minister's life. The work may not be going well and, though he may not talk about it, the minister may have a visceral feeling that he is not succeeding. A clique in the congregation may be mounting resistance. The board may be unresponsive to the minister's proposals for the future. At the same time, a nearby minister may appear to be flying high. A series of experiences like this can generate a very threatening sense of insecurity.

Character is really tested in such a time and should prompt us to schedule time for more concentrated prayer. It is also time to keep marriage communications open. Blessed is the minister whose spouse understands the special need for compassion and support in such an hour. It should, above all else, be seen as a time of the Lord's testing and therefore a call to put on the whole armor of God (Galatians 6:10-20).

Let any minister take seriously these counsels and his chances of falling into sexual sin are minimal:

(1) Keep in daily communion with Christ. (2) Nurture your marriage. (3) Live an orderly, disciplined life. (4) Work like a professional. (5) Be accountable. (6) Keep in touch with yourself during insecure times.

TIMES OF CHALLENGE

My wife and I do pray for you, and I know you pray for us. Times like ours, to quote Charles Dickens, are not only the best of times; they are also the worst of times. They are times of challenge to live before the Lord and his people as persons of integrity. But we cannot do this in our own strength. So, I close with a strengthening benediction, from Hebrews 13:20-21: "May the God of peace, who through the blood of the eternal covenant brought back from the dead our Lord Jesus, that great Shepherd of the sheep, equip you with everything good for doing his will, and may he work in us what is pleasing to him, through Jesus Christ, to whom be glory for ever and ever. Amen."

CHAPTER 31

What Do Table Manners Have to Do with It?

WE have been considering the professionalism of the pastor, looking at such matters as scriptural, ethical, and professional codes, sexual integrity, and honesty in the pulpit. I end this section with some thoughts about table manners.

You may well wonder what table manners, or any other type of manners, have to do with the pastoral life. I would argue that there is a profound connection between manners and ethics. One reason for ethical conduct is civility – agreement on ways of operating together that promote one another's interests. In a sense, manners are ethics writ small. As I have mentioned throughout this book, such things have a bearing on the effectiveness of a pastor.

~

Some time back when my wife and I gathered our children and their offspring around the table in our home – on one occasion there were as many as twenty-five of us – a festive mood set in. We savored tasty food, indulged in chatter, punctuated the flow with laughter, and sometimes discussed serious matters. We simply delighted in one another. But all of this went on according to a certain family style, developed over the years. You should not be surprised at this. Every family develops a style for eating together that will lie somewhere on the spectrum from consciously following a plan to what some would see as "every man for himself." Most of us land somewhere in between.

Even yet, we usually begin a family meal by standing behind our chairs and singing a table grace in four-part harmony, followed by a spoken prayer of thanksgiving. The food may be placed on the nearby peninsula, or the dishes may be on the table and the host passes them – always to the right to avoid confusion.

When our granddaughter, Robyn, was twenty-two, she asked us how our family mealtime customs developed. My wife and I rose to the challenge and began tracing the evolution of our way of doing things back across more than sixty years.

My wife was one of seven children raised by a widowed mother. Poverty was real and unrelenting in Kathleen's household, but her mother nevertheless had a feeling for gracious living. As a girl, she had been sent to a finishing school for one year where table manners were part of the curriculum. To add to this influence, my wife was required to take a home economics course in high school. Classes included demonstrating good grooming and practicing table manners over real meals. She brought home to a receptive family what she was learning.

At nearly the same time, her two older brothers went away to the University of Toronto where they ate their meals in a dining room in which meals were treated as a gracious experience. They, too, carried home procedures that they had learned, and the family reenacted them around the table – spiced with wit and banter. By the time I came in to the picture, a fairly established style for serving and eating had formed in my future wife's family. I remember good times around that dining room table, with a sense of conviviality in spite of grinding circumstances.

By contrast, during my childhood in Saskatchewan table manners were fairly basic. I recall that we children had only two rules: no chewing with your mouth open and no smacking of your lips while you eat. My dear English father felt free to bring his newspaper to the table where he read it, folded open to the editorial page. He poured his tea into his saucer to cool it before drinking it, and he smacked his lips in unselfconscious enjoyment of his food. Perhaps these were reflections of the eating style he brought from the mining village in Lancashire, England, where he had grown up. But my mother, meanwhile, said again and again that in all of life we must think about others, and that lesson tended to stick, even disposing us to take a little care in our eating.

Obviously, there's always something new to learn about table manners, but at the core this is what manners are about: thoughtfulness for the feelings of others, civility – the stuff of which civilization is formed! And that's why table manners should matter.

For example, we hold our fork so our elbow isn't in our neighbor's eye; we avoid reaching past another diner so our sleeve doesn't touch their plate; we do not wave our eating utensils in the air to punctuate what we are saying. Really simple stuff.

I reached the threshold of adulthood a bit rough around the edges regarding manners but with a desire to behave well at the table. I found this principle of respect for others a natural basis to support an interest in good table manners. When I married Kathleen, we began developing our own family style.

Since then we've been in widely varied eating situations: sushi bars in Japan, pig roasts in the Philippines, salmon bakes in Alaska. Nearer home there have been lavish banquets where the crystal sparkled under large chandeliers and modest potluck suppers where gifted cooks proudly set forth their finest dishes. Kathleen herself has served hundreds of meals to groups large and small, in some cases to 150 at a time and in others to one or two or three who were guests in our home. All of this has shaped our family style.

After all these years, our practices have become settled. We know that table manners are not intended to make diners uncomfortable. The opposite is the case: they are to provide a gracious conviviality in which diners enjoy one another and think of the needs of others as well as their own. It's true that in this matter of manners we all slip from time to time. Even so, an attempt at good table manners helps to give cordial form to meals. They make dining more than a mere utilitarian experience and separate us as far as possible from the practices of the four-legged animals beneath us.

At the same time, we recognize that in the past sixty years society has changed drastically. Only those who have lived through vastly different eras – the 1940s and 1950s of the twentieth century and the early years of the twenty-first, for example – can fully appreciate the changes. There are growing numbers who appear to view manners with contempt, as if they were an instrument of human oppression. To others, the appropriate response to the subject seems to be, "whatever," with a shrug. Certainly, manners are no longer a part of the curriculum in most schools. And fast-paced family life leaves all too little time for gracious meals together.

Add to all this the fast-food chains with outlets seemingly never far away, which have made eating for many merely a way of satisfying hunger pangs while on the run. It's hard to observe the niceties when you're consuming a double hamburger with mayonnaise, ketchup, tomato slices, and bits of dill pickle oozing onto a paper wrapper spread on the plastic tabletop below. And refinement is not easy to practice when you have only fifteen minutes to soothe hunger pangs before rushing to your next appointment.

No one in our family wishes to see fast-food establishments disappear. We all need them from time to time. Yet, neither are we ready to give up on the gracious family meal. At these times we consciously slow the pace, provide food according to procedures that facilitate order and avoid confusion, and try to eat and converse in such a way as to think as much of the interests and needs of others at the table as we do of our own.

At the same time, we watch our grandchildren with interest and pleasure as they enter the adult world, set up their own homes, and develop for themselves the signature of their eating practices.

CONCLUSION

From a Kitchen Chair to the Pulpit

I close this book with the story of God's call on my life. As you will see – and as may be true of your own calling – this call was and is unspeakably dear to me. Beginning when I was sixteen years old, it has marked, challenged, and sustained my life through the thick and thin, the joys and sorrows, and through it all the great honor and privilege of being a pastor.

~

According to my parents, when I was five years old and our family came home from Sunday worship in our little Free Methodist church on Third Street in Estevan, Saskatchewan, I would climb onto a kitchen chair and preach. With great energy, I declared such certainties as, "The devil is going to be chained for a thousand years." It was a sentence I had probably heard in the sermon earlier that morning. I waved my arms in the air as I declaimed, mimicking the gestures I had likely witnessed.

Back then preachers preached with energy, and although five-year-olds may not have understood the meaning of their words, they nonetheless absorbed the atmosphere of the occasion. It would likely have been no stretch for me to imagine a fire-spewing devil bound in clanking chains.

Estevan was a young prairie town. It was the first third of the twentieth century. The church was a simple structure, built just fifteen years earlier. The Methodist name meant it traced its origins to the great spiritual movement back in eighteenth-century England under the leadership of a clergyman of the Church of England named John Wesley. In that little Estevan church the gospel of Jesus Christ was offered earnestly as evangelical truth.

My parents were immigrants from Lancashire, England. They had been drawn to the church first as an antidote to my mother's searing loneliness and homesickness. This had been brought on by living on the vast prairies, so barren in comparison with her more established Lancashire environment. But once at the church, she had heard a message of salvation that awakened her hunger for forgiveness and assurance of God's favor. They called it "getting saved." Those were the circumstances that, two decades later, put me in the picture.

I was reared in that earnest, spiritual environment. But I don't claim any connection between my five-year-old mimicry on the kitchen chair and the fact that I eventually became a pastor. Then again, who can say? Don't children sometimes show certain proclivities early in their lives? And can't God shape, by his divine providences, a developing life that is responsive to him?

In any event my immature mind did not discern that I would grow up to be a pastor. Nor that I would later be an overseer of pastors, sharing some aspects of my understanding in written form, as I have done in this book.

In this autobiographical sketch I can single out only some of the major influences visited on my wife, Kathleen, and me – and only as our sometimes faulty memories recall.

I had a praying mother. She was under five feet tall, an immigrant from Northern England to Canada in the earliest years of the twentieth century. To the end of her life she spoke English in a broad and delightful accent. My younger sister, Eunice, and I were especially amused by the way she pronounced such words as "cook book." She said them as if they rhymed with "food" or "true." In spite of our prompting she couldn't (or wouldn't) pronounce such words in a Canadian way. But her prayers offered in Lancastrian English were effectual.

Mother was a disciplinarian. She insisted on being obeyed and had just the instrument hanging behind the kitchen door to enforce her rules. She was a devout Christian who carried largely by herself the burden for "the family altar," conducting it after each evening meal. When I went off to high school in the morning, I could hear her voice in her bedroom upstairs as she prayed for each member of the family by name, the three older siblings and my sister and me.

My father was five feet four inches tall and weighed 125 pounds. To me he was not exactly a small man but a compact, well-built, and strong man. He had not attended school except for five weeks when he was five years old. Scarlet fever put him into quarantine, and he was never sent back. But somewhere he had learned to read and write quite well and "to do sums," as he spoke of arithmetic.

Starting at thirteen years of age he worked alongside his father in the coalmines of Lancashire, and then took up that work again when he emigrated to Roche Percée, a coal-mining village in southeastern Saskatchewan. He managed to work his way through several stages – coal miner, market gardener, Watkins products salesman, and sometimes all three together – until he reached his dream of being a merchant in our prairie town.

To this day I'm surprised at the sources my father drew on to teach me the basics of economics. Where did he learn them? In ways I can't trace or understand, the famed Ben Franklin had left his mark on him. When he saw me spending a nickel, carelessly, as he thought, he would say, "Look after the pennies and the dollars will look after themselves." Or, "A penny saved is a penny earned." I didn't understand the point in any depth, but these sayings were seeds that bore fruit much later.

My mother had gone only to the sixth grade in England, but she had her own collection of sayings, which she used judiciously to guide my younger sister and me in the paths of wisdom. She seemed to have a knack for dropping an aphorism and leaving it to do its mighty work. For example, when I stubbornly held to a course that she was sure would cause me trouble, she would say, "If you make your bed you will have to lie in it." Or, "Your chickens will come home to roost." She never explained herself, and I never asked, but that was eighty years ago and the words are still in my head.

My immigrant parents were not agreeable to having children sleep in on Saturday mornings. We were to be up and about, and that expectation was enforced. If I did not respond to the first call given from the bottom of the stairs, my mother stood there again and quoted a proverb. The one I remember was, "Go to the ant, thou sluggard; consider her ways, and be wise." Being likened to something that sounded very bad had a way of bringing me to full consciousness.

My father was not a converted man in the evangelical sense during my formative years, but he had Christian values, and that meant, among other things, that he went to church with the family Sunday after Sunday, both morning and evening. I will never know how much that practice influenced the direction of my life after I entered my teen years.

~

The white clapboard-sided Free Methodist church in Estevan was less than two blocks from our home. As a house of worship it was simple to the extreme, but the congregation had a core of men and women who were both devout and loving. They gave me and about ten other children my age a community of support. They recognized us by name and treated us as though we were important. Regrettably, I and one other, a girl, were perhaps the only two of that number who followed the Lord into adulthood. Most of the others did not have church-going fathers.

It was in the context of this gathering of God's people that I gave my heart to the Lord, in March 1942, three months after I turned sixteen. This event was preceded by a mounting sense of my need of forgiveness for my sins and a desire for inward peace. A desire for inward peace may seem strange for a sixteen-year-old, but I was in great conflict. I knew the Lord was calling me, and, although I resisted, my resistance gave way at the close of a Sunday-night service. At the same time, I was acutely conscious that the Holy Spirit was inwardly pressing me for a decision. I knew then and I know now that I could have gone either way.

I had often responded to spiritual urges, because my heart was tender toward the Lord from early childhood onward. But my previous responses to the gospel suffered from childhood misunderstandings. Somehow as a child – I think from the moral rigor of the times – I had picked up the notion that Christians always behave well, and it didn't seem to be in my DNA to behave well for very long.

At sixteen my response was more fully faith-based, a wholehearted trusting in the Lord for my salvation. Even then, however, it was at the level of my adolescent understanding. From those teenaged years into young adulthood my walk with the Lord was often unsteady and faltering. There were many missteps, but I never turned away from that special moment of conversion.

I had good reason to give my heart to the Lord at sixteen. The pulpit fare in church often emphasized God's holiness. The scroll on the wall above the pulpit read, "Holiness Unto the Lord," words I read countless times as I sat with my parents in church. At first I may have read them to exercise my early reading skills. Later it may have been to deal with boredom when what was going on wasn't interesting. Looking back through the veil of distant memories I can't say that the preaching was always biblically clear or edifying to the saints. But there was enough gospel in it to point a teenaged boy to the way of salvation. Against that backdrop I heard the clear, simple promise of forgiveness and regenerating grace.

At that time the Ten Commandments were still held in the public mind. And they were taught in our home. We memorized them in Sunday school. All of this had been convicting to me. Yet it was at sixteen that I found myself in serious need of forgiveness. And although my offenses were undramatic by today's standards, I knew that to be a true Christian with a clear conscience, even though the Lord had graciously and fully forgiven me, I had to make amends for some of my offenses. From the preaching in that church I learned early the meaning of the word "restitution."

It was fewer than two weeks after that conversion that I said openly that I thought the Lord might be calling me to full-time service. I made this announcement in a small gathering of adult Christians. My understanding of what I was saying was certainly limited, but I testified to this group with these exact words: "Sometimes I think the Lord may have something special for me to do and if he does I'm willing." I remember where I was standing at the time, about four rows back in the church and next to the outside wall.

I had little conception of all that such a commitment would entail, but I remember it as a very serious commitment. That commitment may have faltered or become temporarily vague in the unstable years of adolescence, but it never disappeared, and I never backed away from it.

But what could that "something special" be? To me it was sort of a generic call, asking for a ready response, a general consecration, but lacking in a specific focus.

Then, only months after my conversion, I made an

interesting and to some degree strange decision. Sometime during that summer I decided not to enroll in our high school for grade eleven but to go instead to a small Bible school in Moose Jaw, 145 miles away. I wonder still that my parents allowed me to make that choice.

I cannot say that my motives were exclusively spiritual. I had heard enthusiastic reports of the school from a student from our town who made it sound like a great place to be. The thought of being in a group of young people (though on average several years older than I) held a certain attraction. Perhaps to some degree I was also captured by a spirit of adventure. In any event, as a sixteen-year-old I began a three-year program among a cohort of young adults, most of whom were quite serious about preparing for Christian service.

In a sense I was out of my depth. Those of my classmates still living are quick to tell gleefully of my youthful exuberance and adolescent pranks during those years, and all I can do is blush and plead guilty.

After graduating when I was nineteen I slowly realized that you can't go forward in education or vocation without a high-school diploma. I had not had the wisdom to see this earlier when I decided against completing high school. Now, as a young adult, or nearly so, I had to figure out how I would double back and complete the final two years.

Altogether, Moose Jaw Bible College had been good for me. I had been exposed to the Bible and related subjects in preliminary ways. I had made lifetime friends. Of special significance was the fact that I had gone there with strong interests in music. Earlier, when I was thirteen, I had sung in a boys' trio under the training of a grade-school teacher. We sang three-part harmony. Much earlier than that I had also sung duets in church with my younger sister. I had a passion for singing. Being at MJBC had increased this interest.

At the time it prompted me to think that this generic call

I had given witness to might be fulfilled as a song evangelist. At Bible school I was involved in several music groups – male and mixed quartets, duets, trios, and choir – but I enjoyed singing solos the most. On Sunday afternoons the school provided live gospel music on CHAB, the local radio station, and this motivated us to strive for excellence. I was on occasion put forward to sing a solo.

One experience toward the close of the third year of Bible school deserves the telling. Two years earlier, during the summer after the first year of classes, I had worked in Fred Barber's Men's Store on Hamilton Street in Regina. I was seventeen. During the summer my parents made the 145-mile trip to Regina, I think to look in on me. During their visit the boss apparently told them he was pleased with my work and that I seemed to have a knack for selling men's ties and shirts and even suits.

Then, when I was nineteen, two years later during the winter of my last term of Bible school, my father wrote me that he had bought Louis Reeder's Men's Store in Estevan. His idea was that I would come home to manage it. My older brother, Wilf, who had the grocery store on Main Street, would coach me on the business side. This would be quite an opportunity for a young man not yet twenty years of age.

But I was in conflict. The superintendent of the conference had asked me to travel as a singer with a youth speaker, Douglas Russell, after I graduated. I had considered this a further step in answering what I believed was a call to full-time ministry. Which direction would I go? What would I tell my father? And what would he say?

After a little over a week, and with trepidation, I wrote him that I was answering a call to full-time ministry. To my surprise and relief he was agreeable. He responded with understanding. He showed respect for a professed call to the ministry and would put nothing in my way, which said a great deal about his Christian values.

They would make arrangements, he wrote, to sell the grocery store, and my older brother, Wilf, would take over the men's store. It was during the following summer, when the youth speaker and I were in Estevan holding services, that my father experienced an evangelical conversion, a life-changing placing of his faith fully in Christ. I don't know all that it meant to him, but it was evident to the family. For example, as a result, he was able to break a fifty-year habit of smoking.

~

So, my Bible-school experience was over. Details from the fifteen months following Bible school up to my enrollment for further high-school work remain a bit vague in my memory. I recall that I traveled as a singer, without any promise of remuneration except whatever I might be given along the way for my services. On one occasion after a two-week series of services in Northern Manitoba I had to borrow five dollars to get back to my home in southeastern Saskatchewan. My travel as a song evangelist was sporadic, but it took me to Canada's three prairie provinces, Alberta, Saskatchewan, and Manitoba.

During the second summer, when I was twenty, my geographic range increased. Still traveling with the youth director, Douglas, I sang in family camps in Michigan, Pennsylvania, and New York.

I had talked to Doug from time to time in general terms about my need to finish my high-school courses but apparently was not displaying any strong resolution to get the venture under way. One day when we were together at a camp in Pennsylvania he said with conviction, "If you're going to finish high school you'd better get at it. The months are fading into years." That afternoon I wrote a letter to one of our denomination's schools in Ontario. That letter set the stage for the next chapter in my life.

In Port Credit, Ontario, to the west of Toronto, the Free Methodist Church had a school, Lorne Park College, that offered a high-school program. As I recall, the student body numbered about sixty-five. And in Toronto nearby was the Toronto Conservatory of Music (later the Royal Conservatory of Toronto), where I knew I could take voice lessons under excellent teachers. These two prospects made my decision easy.

Our last stop that summer was at a camp at Hancock, New York, and from New York City we made our way by Canadian Airlines (later Air Canada) to Toronto. From there I found my way out to Lorne Park College in Port Credit to enroll as a high-school student. This was in August 1946. I was twenty years old. I also signed on for voice lessons with Albert Kennedy at the Toronto Conservatory of Music.

Lorne Park College turned out to be an important five-year interval in my life, though I hadn't thought in terms of five years when I enrolled. I could not have guessed the experiences and opportunities that would open up to me during that time.

Coming from a Bible-school background and from a season of ministry as a singer I was beginning to be seen unofficially in our circles as a Christian worker, even though I had not been ordained nor been given any special credentials. I was just a freelance youth singer and song leader.

~

Because of my Bible-school training and the fact that I was older than the average high-school student, LPC began to give me special service opportunities. During five years there, I formed and trained a school choir, taught grade nine music for one year, and for two years was a preceptor over Pinecrest Hall, the boys' dormitory. I was occasionally asked to speak in chapels.

I also became an ambassador for the college. Many

Sundays during the last three years, I was employed to visit churches, taking along a music group and raising offerings for the school. This furthered my experience as a speaker, leader, and organizer. But as to where my trail would lead and what "full-time ministry" would include – I still thought of all this in general terms. Strangely, perhaps because my home conference was in Saskatchewan, no mentor came alongside to give me vocational counsel or to point me toward ordination.

My passion for music remained strong, but more and more, the opportunities that came my way were to speak. In the midst of all this I was working to finish high school, including five courses in what was then called fifth form, or grade thirteen.

Then came my awareness of Kathleen. A schoolmate had told me about her during my first year at LPC. She lived in Niagara Falls and taught school in the Niagara Peninsula back in the days when five years of high school and one year of teachers' college (the two together the equivalent of junior college) were the qualifications needed to teach school. I found my interest curiously piqued, even though I knew her only by name. Besides, my schoolmate was not commending her in any romantic way.

In coming to Ontario I had resolved that I would not date another girl until I met the one I was going to marry. To a present generation of single men who by intention delay marriage often into their thirties, this may seem a strange resolution to be made by a twenty-year-old. Could it be that, because my parents had married in their teens, early marriage was in my DNA? Whatever the factors, I do remember that I thought matter-of-factly as a teenager that I was growing up to get married. I venture that this way of thinking was common among young men at the time.

Also, before I arrived at LPC, I had discussed several times with Doug Russell, who was five years older than I and not married, the topic of "finding the right one." He had come up with a list of qualities that he would be looking for in that special person.

I'm not sure now how I expected to be sure about the outcome of a relationship before even making an attempts to get one under way.

During my first Thanksgiving in Ontario, when school was in recess and students went to their homes, I hitchhiked to Niagara Falls to meet again with Doug, who had come to Ontario from Alberta in his ministry as a youth director. During one afternoon I was one of five young people who got together for a tour of the area. Kathleen was among the five. I noted a quiet beauty about her.

In the winter months following that social outing I thought of her often, and, as she later shared, she thought often of me. But there were several unanswered questions in my mind and perhaps in hers, too. I wanted to know if she was a serious Christian. That was foremost. And since I was intending to make music my life, I wanted to know if she played the piano.

I learned later from a wise older friend that the first question was on target, but the second was well off the mark, even irrelevant. This friend's explicit response was: "You'll have to decide whether you're looking for a pianist or a wife." Those words made instant sense. It was as though I had been given permission to move forward by someone whose judgment I trusted.

This older and wiser friend made his point with me at a province-wide youth weekend in Newmarket, Ontario. He was the speaker, and I was the singer and song leader. It was the first weekend of May 1947. Kathleen was there, and now I felt I had been freed to show guarded interest in her. I got the impression from her participation in the rally and her general attitude toward the good things going on that she was a devout Christian. She appeared to me as comely, mysterious, and quietly appealing.

During that weekend, I arranged through a mutual friend to eat a noon meal in the same home as Kathleen. Also by special third-party arrangement I rode back from the youth weekend in the same car: I to my dorm at LPC and she to her home in Niagara Falls. Though we scarcely spoke to each other, we now say that for both of us it seemed something wonderful was in the offing.

I began seeing her on weekends, and we learned that we were of the same mind on the basic issues of life. Our common roots in the culture of the same denomination, even though our home churches were separated by 1,500 miles, aided our search. It was not love at first sight but very close. We learned that we had each been thinking fondly about the other for many months even though we scarcely saw each other during that time. And we shared that we had remembered each other in our prayers.

The first time we sat together in church in Niagara Falls set the rumor mills to working. Back then, when a boy and girl appeared together in church, it was a big step toward announcing that they were a couple.

Before the morning service began, the pastor saw me in the congregation and came to where we were sitting to ask me to sing a solo in the service. Worship services could be much more impromptu back then than they are now. I had no special music with me so I seized the hymnbook, made a quick selection, and went up and sang "O Love That Will Not Let Me Go." Some in the congregation were more noticeably amused than blessed.

By June 9 of that year our life course together was set. We had agreed that we would marry, though for a couple of months we shared our engagement with no one. Hitchhiking was my usual means of travel, and we saw each other on several weekends. Otherwise we carried on a letter-writing courtship. E-mailing had not yet even been imagined, and phoning long distance was too expensive to contemplate except for very urgent reasons. The mails, however, were swifter then than now and we used them to the full.

Our dates were simple. Money was too scarce for candlelight dining, paid concerts, or even flowers. Until I bought my thirteen-year-old 1934 two-door Ford later that summer, our dates were mostly walks from her house to the Falls and back, a four-mile stroll. Or we walked down to Queen Street to window shop, or crossed the Honeymoon Bridge to the United States to get sugar for her mother. Sugar was not rationed in the United States as it was in Canada. During the long walks we each enjoyed a Revel, caramel-coated ice cream on a stick. The total cost of a date was twenty cents.

Love had overtaken us. Being together was enough, whether we were Falls-gazing or window-shopping. In the early weeks of our courtship, each meeting disclosed to me another aspect of Kathleen's loveliness, discoveries that have remained in my heart ever since.

~

We were married in Kathleen's sister's home on December 20 of that year. How could two twenty-one-year-olds be mature enough to make a lifelong commitment each to the other? What would make our simple but serious public vows lead to an ever-renewing love that spans more than six-and-a-half decades? How could those clear, all-inclusive vows read by a minister in a ritual that had traces of sixteenth-century English in it, and witnessed in reverent silence by family members, create a bond so strong that it would survive life's every vicissitude?

Out of the ancient past comes an answer from a young lover who understood: "For love is as strong as death, its jealousy as unyielding as the grave" (Song of Songs 8:6) and "Many waters cannot quench love; rivers cannot wash it away" (8:7a).

We file the mystery of it all under the wonderful word

"providence," God's gracious endowment in the lives of a young man and woman who had few material resources but who had dreams for their life together and pledges to do the Lord's will as they came to understand it.

During the fall we had begun to talk about being married late in December and going west by train for Christmas so Kathleen could meet my family. By then we would have been engaged for six months. Kathleen's family wanted us to wait until June for a formal wedding, but June seemed to us so far away.

During one weekend visit to Niagara Falls, before I left to return to school, we decided to put out a "fleece." We agreed that if I could find living quarters in the vicinity of the college we would take that as a sign to marry in December.

It was a daring fleece with very little chance of going in our favor. The house-building industry had been arrested for a span of five years during World War II. The war was over, but the economy was just beginning to return to peacetime production. Houses and apartments for rent were scarce.

As we recall, on Sunday night after our agreement I drove my old Ford back to Lorne Park College. On impulse the next morning I drove in to the yard of the house directly across the Queen Elizabeth Way from the campus. It was an upscale two-story house set among the trees in a large stand of woods. There was nothing in its appearance to suggest that it would contain rental facilities – no commercial aspect to attract me, no sign at the entrance announcing Vacancies or For Rent. And the people living in the fine dwelling were total strangers.

As I recall, Mr. Adams was standing in the yard. I introduced myself as a student from across the way. I then explained that my fiancée and I were considering getting married at Christmas time and were looking for an apartment to rent. I wondered if he knew of any such facilities in the area. At that point, as I recall, his wife appeared.

To my surprise, and without fanfare, they explained that they were putting the finishing touches on a one-room apartment above the two-car garage and were going to put it up for rent on the first of January. They offered that they could easily have it ready a few days earlier, at the end of December, if we needed it then.

We struck an agreement then and there. The room would be furnished except for a stove; we would have a space in their refrigerator for milk and butter; and we would use their washing machine for washing our clothes.

That Monday evening I phoned Kathleen to tell her of my success. She was amazed by the news because she knew that we were searching in an overcrowded market. Plans for a simple December 20 wedding began to take form.

After a Saturday wedding and a day in Toronto, we boarded the train to Estevan, Saskatchewan, for Christmas. Kathleen would meet my parents, my younger sister, and my older brother and his wife. She had had no contact with any members of my family. It would be as though I were bringing home a war bride from overseas.

On reflection, the thought of making this journey in December and calling it a honeymoon does not conjure up romantic visions. And taking a bride in this manner to meet her new in-laws was not the most creative way to forge the new family bond. Options were fewer and times less sophisticated then, and besides, ours was the audacity of youth.

A surprise awaited us in Saskatchewan: two older sisters with husbands and children had driven all the way from British Columbia to get in on the introductions along with the others.

Kathleen was a bit overwhelmed at first (which she acknowledged only to me), but she was a brave soul through it all. The newness and curiosity wore off quickly, and the family was delighted with her. A bonding began, and the whole venture ended well. As the train pulled out of the station to take us back to Ontario, we knew we had my family's blessing.

Back at Lorne Park College we took up residence in our one-room apartment. We were the first occupants, and the landlord had furnished it tastily. Once there, I resumed my studies and other duties at the college.

Usually in the forties teachers did not continue to teach after marriage, so Kathleen had time to settle and care for our loft, put delicious meals on the table, and from time to time entertain our friends from the college. She also accompanied me sometimes when I went out for weekend ministries. During our six months in that place we struggled each month to patch together $45 to pay our rent; we always succeeded, but sometimes barely.

Kathleen, a superb financial manager, set herself the limit of seven dollars a week for groceries from the start and never went beyond.

Now that we were married, however, was some kind of full-time ministry still my goal? And would Kathleen agree to that goal or would some compromises be required? People who believe they are called to a life of ministry sometimes find that marriage changes the roadmap.

During our courtship we had compared notes to discover that during the same March 1942, and at the same age of sixteen, we each had given our hearts fully to the Lord, I in Saskatchewan and she in Ontario. Both of us had grown up in a church environment where the gospel appeal was sounded and responses were expected. We had been responsive during those years of our childhood, but the 1942 date was the life-directing occasion for both of us.

At the beginning of our relationship Kathleen had not neglected to ponder the prospect of being married to a minister. She did not know the specifics, but she did not draw back. She was in full agreement that to marry me was to marry my calling. In fact, from the start she shared the calling. We were "one" in that respect, too, as the Lord Jesus had affirmed (Matthew 19:4-5).

And she did not draw back when she realized that I would have several years ahead of me to complete training for that vocation, which turned out to be eight years of schooling – during five of which I would be a full-time student.

Her support was fully in keeping with her family's story and culture. Kathleen's mother, Norma Swallow, was widowed when her farmer husband died unexpectedly after a surgery. She was left with seven children to raise, the oldest thirteen and the youngest four months from birth. I remember her as a noble woman, a person of keen intellect, steadfast principle, and tested faith. Her quiet endurance was admirable.

Although she raised the children on a widow's pension, and income was always barely enough (as I learned much later), when I came in to the family there was no sense of poverty. The house was small and crowded but always neat and clean and tastefully arranged. The family members carried themselves with dignity. Whatever burdens they bore, of mind or body, were not open to the public. The family was poor, but the word "poor" did not describe their minds or outlooks.

In spite of restricted resources Kathleen's mother expected the children to get an education and prepare themselves for a useful life. They responded early in their teens by working away from home, scrubbing floors, babysitting, and working on production lines in local factories. Some managed to earn scholarships, and they even worked to lend money to one another to aid them in reaching their educational goals. The result: by early adulthood five were certified teachers, one a registered nurse, and one a chartered accountant.

All this helps to explain why Kathleen stood with me without complaint through our first three and a half years at Lorne Park College, then through two years while I was finishing a college degree, followed by three years of seminary. She brought to our marriage not only a devout faith but also a family-bequeathed conviction that education was worth the sacrifice.

Our time at Lorne Park College was not yet over. I continued to work off academic subjects and to carry out the duties assigned me by the college. Though we are only two months apart in age Kathleen still enjoys telling people – with a twinkle in her eye – that when she married me she was a teacher and I was in high school.

By summer, seven months after we married, the college presented us with a fresh challenge. They asked us to occupy a main-floor apartment at Pinecrest Hall, the boys' dorm, to give supervision to the boys. That meant enforcing study hall discipline each weeknight, making sure the boys kept their rooms clean, providing food for any who were ill, and otherwise giving general oversight. On Sundays, taking a singing group with me, I often traveled out to supporting churches within driving distance of the college.

On December 10, at the end of our first year of marriage, Carolyn was born. Our dorm apartment was her first home. She brought great delight to us, and the interest the students showed in her, both the boys and girls, and the pleasure she gave them was quite remarkable. She was received as though a member of a large family.

At the end of Carolyn's first year, Kathleen was invited to teach for half a year at the nearby public school. We made arrangements at the college for Carolyn to be cared for. However, by spring we could see that the busy environment and her overexposure to the students were not good for her. We decided to forego the extra income, even though the public-school principal offered strong inducements for Kathleen to stay on staff for the second year.

~

By the summer of 1951, three and a half years after our marriage, we were becoming increasingly aware that I must move on to complete a college degree. I had accumulated enough credits from grade thirteen subjects of high school, three years of Bible school, and from the conservatory to count for two of the four years needed. But where would we go?

During that summer we drove our little gray English Austin to Roberts Wesleyan College located across Lake Ontario, and then to Houghton College, about sixty miles south of Buffalo, to check out the possibilities. Nothing materialized on either of the two campuses that could make college possible for us.

About that time, a businessman in Toronto, a member of the board of trustees of Greenville College in Illinois, told me he would pay half my tuition at Greenville if, after graduating, I would return to Canada and work in the Free Methodist Church for at least five years. He did not specify the exact work he expected, though I'm sure he had in mind that I would serve as a pastor.

Half tuition for a semester at the time, as I recall, was $350. I had already been assured of a half-tuition scholarship by the college itself. Thus, my full tuition would be covered.

In mid-August another clear providence presented itself. The businessman's son, a former LPC schoolmate of mine, notified me that he was taking his girlfriend back to her home in Greenville. It would be a lightning-fast trip, he explained, and I was welcome to go with them. Driven by my sense of urgency I seized the opportunity. It was a trip of 750 miles before the interstate highway system existed, which meant that part of the journey took us through one town after another. It was a long day's drive.

I spent only one complete day on the Greenville College campus, but the college personnel I met, the conversations I shared, and even the quiet setting of the campus during August caused me to fall in love with the place. Before leaving campus I engaged the least expensive apartment on the college's list in full expectation of returning in a few weeks with the family. How I was going to make that happen was unclear to me.

I returned to Ontario to tell Kathleen that we were going to Greenville. I confess it was a command decision. We were twenty-five, Carolyn was nearly three, and we were expecting our second child. A less urgent person might have decided to delay the opportunity for a year. But I was aware that doing so might make the delay permanent. I could see that time was running out.

Kathleen was startled by my announcement. That was no surprise. But she could see that my urgency was well founded and fell in with the plan. In little more than two weeks we had sold our few household possessions and our car. We packed what remained in a second-hand steamer trunk and shipped it on ahead by rail. An American immigration officer proved helpful and permitted us to travel to the United States on visitor permits, which meant I could be in the U.S. for three or four months at a time.

The three of us set off in a Greyhound bus 200 miles west, to Detroit, where we hoped to buy a used car, the prices being lower in the United States. Everything we carried with us fit one suitcase and a bulging briefcase.

Unfortunately, the steamer trunk went astray and would not reach us in Greenville until December. It contained our wardrobes, especially our winter attire; a baby bassinet; towels and bed sheets; along with cooking utensils and a few other miscellaneous items. It turned out that the trunk had been incorrectly sent to Pennsylvania and had been sidetracked there awaiting further orders. We learned from our search for it that there are actually thirty-three Greenvilles in the United States. We lived out of that one suitcase until the trunk arrived.

I had known that I would not be allowed to work for pay during the first period, but had asked the immigration officer if it was permissible to receive honoraria for singing and speaking in churches He said it was, so long as payment was offered, not contracted for. We knew this avenue was my only hope of support until we returned to Canada at Christmas to get better papers.

I had become known in churches in Ontario and beyond, and was kept busy as a singer or speaker for special occasions. However, when I got to Greenville I learned, to my surprise, that because I was not known in Illinois churches the income we had hoped for would be dangerously sparse.

Our funds were limited from the start, though we had kept aside enough money to pay the doctor and hospital for the birth of our second child. That child, Donald, was born five weeks after our arrival in Greenville.

By Thanksgiving we had no food in our cupboards and no money in our pockets. We had two children to feed. But a few days before that weekend, R. R. Thompson, a Free Methodist pastor from Springfield, about sixty-five miles away, came to our upstairs apartment like an angel of hope and invited me to come, with my family, and speak at his church for the weekend. We breathed easier and seized the invitation with warm thanks. He had no idea of our dire circumstances. By then I had ceased driving the car, but fortunately we had enough gas in the tank to make the round trip, and at the end of the weekend we returned to our apartment carrying the gift of a bag of groceries and a ten dollar bill.

I write about these close scrapes during our first four months in Greenville with composure. They are ancient history to us. But I was not composed then. I had the fatherly instinct that I was to provide for my children, yet I seemed blocked on every side. My prayers were urgent, even desperate. I fought frustration even while I prayed. Kathleen felt the same way. Since we were there to prepare for a life of ministry, why didn't some miracle take place, say, a sealed envelope of money left outside our door?

We were seeking to do the Lord's will, and he had allowed

us the urgent, youthful choice to be there. Today I would chalk such a situation up to the fact that decisions have consequences, even when made with serious spiritual intentions. Back then I expected miracles, and they just weren't happening. The Lord let us live with our decisions, but he didn't forsake us. He knew our motives. Sparse resources came from somewhere. We don't remember how we survived.

It seems strange now that the thought never occurred to us to go to a bank and try to borrow or to seek a student loan of some sort. But to my knowledge, students didn't do that back then. And we never thought of seeking out a soup kitchen or charitable agency. If there were any such places, they were not on our radar. We never thought of announcing our dire situation to the college or church. We considered our problem to be our problem.

We survived the first semester at Greenville College living hand-to-mouth. At Christmas, we were back in Canada. Money given by the two students we took with us to their homes in New York paid for the gas. Before returning we got better immigration clearance. And in the spring I began to get invitations for weekend meetings and youth camps during the summer. I was invited to California for one month of engagements, as well as to Pennsylvania and Kentucky. Kathleen, without complaint, endured the lot of staying home with the children in an upstairs apartment neither air conditioned nor insulated from the oppressive heat. She knew we were on a mission. When it was time to start my second year, we had been able to put aside $750 from the summer's activities.

Two years later – a few weeks after I graduated – our son Robert was born. We say that Donald and Robert are the parentheses bracketing our Greenville adventure. And what parentheses – one now a publisher and one a doctor and both strong churchmen.

Kathleen anchored the two-year undertaking at Greenville, freeing me to give as much time as needed to the courses I was taking for a major in English literature. And she released me to fill invitations off campus that provided me with opportunities to exercise my gifts and subsistence funds for our survival. Scheduling made every moment count. One Friday and Saturday I studied every minute until 5:00 p.m., caught a quick meal, then drove fifty miles to a church for a service in a weekend series.

~

The life we were developing together was busy, venturesome, even daring at times, with lots of ups and downs and ins and outs. We could have exercised other options, which would have taken us in other directions, perhaps even out of ministry. Yet we could trace a line of action back to my conversion and commitment to a life of ministry, both of which responses I had made at sixteen years of age, and, in Kathleen's case, back to the serious intent that prompted her, at the same age, to serve the Lord.

Back in the 1950s, Greenville College sponsored a Spiritual Emphasis Week once a semester, bringing in an off-campus guest to speak in five morning chapels and five evening services. The object was to focus on the spiritual realities of life and bring to bear on them the gospel of our Lord Jesus Christ.

To my surprise, when I was beginning my senior year, the college administration, in an unprecedented action, invited me, a member of the student body, to be the speaker. The officers of the student council had requested it, they told me. It was an honor I will never forget. Student interest was strong and the services were well supported with good responses.

During the final six months at Greenville College two fresh paths opened up before us. During those two years I had flirted, as good students often do, with the possibility of trying to go on for a doctorate, in my case in English literature. I probably assumed I could give a lifetime of ministry in teaching at a Christian college. Or that a doctorate would be a good credential in any other branch of Christian ministry.

A few weeks before I graduated, the superintendent of the Wabash Conference, which was headquartered in Indiana, visited me. If I would accept an appointment to the Urbana, Illinois, Free Methodist Church, he said, the congregation would give me time to work off a doctorate, at the University of Illinois, which was located nearby. The pay would be $65 a week along with a comfortable parsonage.

But at about the same time, the Director of the John Wesley Seminary Foundation at Asbury Theological Seminary, Dr. W.C. Mavis, told me, when he was visiting the Greenville campus, that a student pastorate would be open for me at a small church on the north end of Lexington, Kentucky, while I attended the seminary nearby. He had talked to the superintendent of the Kentucky Conference. The pay would be $31 a week, and, as the practice was then, the denomination would pay my tuition.

Urbana and Lexington were both enticing, but in different ways.

Kathleen and I discussed this decision back and forth, seeking guidance on the matter. One day during this time I met Dr. Mary Alice Tenney crossing the Greenville campus. She was one of the college's most respected professors and the head of the English department. I told her of the options before us, thinking she would be delighted at the Urbana challenge. She had spent her own career teaching English on a Christian campus, which she must have considered a ministry.

"Oh, Don, you should go to seminary," she said with great earnestness. She added nothing more, but her response was forceful. I heard in it what I thought was wise counsel from the Lord. From that day on we set our sights on seminary.

The summer after my graduation, in 1953, I again traveled in ministry. By then I was invited more for speaking than singing and song leading. My travel at the time took me to camps in Illinois and Wisconsin. I was to be sure to be back in Greenville for baby Robert's arrival the second week in July. Meanwhile, Kathleen stayed home through early July awaiting the day. In the early morning of July 5, 1953, Robert arrived at the Highland St. Joseph Hospital with a great, lusty cry, which I heard ringing through the corridors of the hospital's maternity ward.

~

To commit ourselves to the seminary track meant that we would devote another three years to pursuing adequate educational credentials for full-time ministry. This time, at least, a weekly income was assured. It was modest for a family of five, and the church increased it before our time with them was over.

By deciding on seminary we increased the likelihood that a lifetime of ministry for me would involve serving a church as a pastor. But, even so, the picture still lacked clear focus. Preparing to serve a congregation and begin my seminary studies, I could not have anticipated how the picture would sharpen over the next three years.

First, though, we had to move 325 miles southeast from Greenville to Lexington, Kentucky, where the church I was to serve was located. Asbury seminary was just under twenty miles to the southwest, in Wilmore.

We made the move in three stages. First, in the spring of my senior year, 1953, I was invited to visit this potential student pastorate for a weekend of meetings. This was apparently to give the local congregation the opportunity to meet me and gather their impressions. To keep this invitation, I left Greenville classes in the morning on a Friday and drove the 325 miles (before the days of interstates) to speak four times – Friday evening, Saturday evening, and Sunday morning and evening. After the Sunday-evening service I drove back to Greenville, arriving at our dwelling as dawn was breaking and the birds were beginning to chirp. I slept for an hour and a half and then got up and went to classes.

The second stage, later in the summer, involved loading up our Ford with nearly everything we had to transport to Lexington: wardrobes, kitchen utensils, and other miscellany we had accumulated for use in our semi-furnished apartment. I drove this load to Wilmore, where I deposited it in a kind seminarian's garage until we had located a place to live in Lexington.

The third stage involved closing out our connections in Greenville and getting on the road with a wife and three little children, the youngest only five weeks old. (Imagine: There were no car seats or seat belts in 1953.) This we did, as I recall, toward the end of August. When we got to Wilmore, all five of us slept in a bedroom of the John Wesley Seminary Foundation House for the first night. Then a seminarian and his wife offered us the use of their apartment while they were away.

Our objective was to locate more permanently in Lexington within reach of the little church on Locust Street. This was expected of us, but finding those lodgings turned out to be something of an adventure, if not a challenge, to our endurance.

The congregation had no parsonage. Their plan all along was that we would apply for residence in the low-rent public housing project, a section of the city where row houses were built and divided into small apartments. There were acres of them – red brick buildings row-on-row, with about six dwellings to each row.

But to be eligible, we first had to occupy facilities somewhere in Lexington that city officials would judge as "substandard." One rule was that to be deemed substandard a lodging had to have a bathroom that was shared by at least nine people.

And so our search for that substandard dwelling was

launched. Another seminarian's wife offered to take care of the three children at their place in Wilmore while we went back and forth to Lexington running down leads. We spent several hot, steamy late-August days scanning ads or walking the streets in our search. Sometimes we saw an Apartment-for-Rent sign in a window and applied. This proved fruitless, for one reason. We were never asked, "Do you have pets?" or "Do you drink?" It was always, "Do you have children?" At our answer, the door was closed.

One day we came upon a big vacant house, where a man in shirtsleeves and work clothes was standing in the somewhat overgrown front yard. At some time in the distant past the house had been a splendid dwelling. Now it looked neglected. On a whim I parked the car and went to speak to the man. As we chatted he identified himself as a Church of God minister who was in the process of refurbishing the house to make it suitable for at least five apartments. It was to generate income for him and his wife when they retired.

We told him who we were, and what our mission was, and he warmed to us. He thought perhaps he could make two rooms available right away, although he made it clear that the rest of the building would be vacant while he completed his repairs and upgrades. He also said he couldn't promise us a date when heat would be available in the building. It was August and heating didn't seem a priority so we happily accepted his offer as a last hope.

The two rooms were on the second floor, across a wide hall from each other. One room was spacious and the other of a moderate size. The bathroom was at the end of a long dark hallway. The oak floors and baseboard trim bore hints of better days. We made the larger of the two rooms a bedroom for five. The smaller room, furnished with an outdated kitchen gas stove and a tall, sturdy, old-fashioned cupboard, became our kitchen. There was no sink or running water. We had to carry water from and to the bathroom at the end of the hall, the same routine we had followed in our Greenville apartment.

Once the deal was struck and the rooms were ready to be occupied, I hustled about, scanning newspaper ads and running down other leads and very soon had acquired a clean, acceptable second-hand bed, a folding canvas cot for Carolyn, and a crib for Don. The bassinet for Bobby we had brought with us from Greenville. I had found a table and chairs for the make-do kitchen and a used wringer washing machine, which we set up in the basement.

We hereby bear witness that cash-strapped seminarians, pursuing an urgent need, can find very adequate furnishings at low cost – and fast.

What we didn't know was that we would be in that apartment until November, and would be without heat for most of that time. During the increasingly cold days of fall, at bedtime we warmed ourselves in the kitchen by the open oven and then hurried across the cold hall to get under the covers as quickly as possible. Kathleen and our oldest, Carolyn, five, were stricken with tonsillitis, and both were quite sick for what seemed like a long time.

Caring for a family while nursing a fever days on end is not a desirable state of being. It was stressful and debilitating, but I don't recall that we fretted.

Maybe we were too busy to fret. At least we were young and eager. And we were approaching an educational opportunity that we could scarcely claim to deserve. The ordeal seemed long and demanding, but, in another sense, in spite of the hot sticky August days and the cooler days to follow, it was an adventure.

Eventually, by November there was heat in our rooms, and the two adjoining apartments were occupied. City officials visited us for an inspection. By then, the bathroom at the end of the hall was shared by eleven people from three families. The officials judged that we needed a two-bedroom apartment in the housing project. We moved, and after Kathleen had won a determined battle against the cockroach population that was there to welcome us to our new dwelling, we settled in to home and community.

Months later, because of the number of children in our family, the authorities reassigned us to a three-bedroom unit without our asking. This time it was a new unit. Rooms were small but adequate. There we spent the remainder of our three years while we pastored that Lexington church and attended seminary.

~

It was at least daring if not audacious of me to take the pastoral assignment in Lexington. I knew that some worshipers in the Sunday congregations would be second- and third-year seminarians and at least one professor and his wife would attend. Over against that worthy number, I was the freshman, just entering the seminary program, and taking up a new and untried pastoral assignment at the same time.

I sensed the peril on the first Sunday or two when it appeared to me that some of my fellow seminarians were viewing the morning service as something of a clinic. They were not taking notes but their knowing glances were apparent. I solved that problem by going to the empty church early on two successive Saturday and Sunday mornings and walking the center aisle, hands raised, asking the Lord to make this place a genuine house of worship for all. Answers to that petition came quickly. We had many great services of worship there together.

We approached the pastoral assignment with energy. Kathleen did what she could to show herself a part of the team. She had the three children in attendance at services twice on Sundays as well as on Wednesday nights. No one had suggested this regimen; she followed it in response to her good instincts. Her faithfulness spoke silently of her commitment to the congregation and endeared her to them.

Also on some Sundays she fed several seminarians a noon

meal in our apartment so that in the afternoon I could engage them in canvassing communities around the church. On two or three occasions when seminary wives gave birth to babies Kathleen brought mother and baby from the hospital to our home for a few days to help the young mother get her bearings and establish new routines. She saw all this as pastoral.

It was strenuous serving a church, raising a family, and attending seminary full time. In the ups-and-downs and ebb-and-flow of daily life there were times of special stress. But neither of us remembers that such stresses created hurtful tensions between us. We were on a mission together. We each had our role to play.

~

Sometime during our first year at the Lexington church Dr. Mavis raised the subject of ordination with me, something I had never really thought about. I had been a singer and youth speaker, for which special credentials were not required. And what track I would eventually be on was not yet clear.

My home base would have been the Saskatchewan annual conference, but I had lived in Ontario and Illinois for seven years, though apparently the Saskatchewan conference had me on their records as a potential ministerial candidate or the equivalent. With me it was not a matter of resistance or indifference; it was more a matter of ignorance about procedures, and perhaps some immaturity of understanding about the importance of credentials.

I have since written in detail about the meaning of ordination and the denomination's procedures, including what is written in this book (chapter 2). I learned during my later years in the bishopric that many beginning candidates also do not have a clear idea of what ordination is, why it matters, the qualifications required, and the church's procedures.

While at the outset ordination was not an issue with me, it apparently was with denominational leaders who faithfully tended to denominational concerns. Dr. Mavis had apparently been in touch with the bishop assigned to the Saskatchewan conference and perhaps the conference itself. My Bible-school training and my extensive experience in ministry must have met requirements for the first level of ordination.

Approval for ordination was sent. Services of ordination are normally conducted at annual conferences, which in my circumstances was not possible. It was sometime during the first year that Bishop C.V. Fairbairn came to Lexington for a weekend. During that weekend he ordained me to deacon's orders during a church service.

My appointment to the Lexington church was good for me, but in certain ways it was also good for the congregation. During the 1950s most seminarians went directly from college to seminary – I calculate that the average age upon arrival was twenty-two or twenty-three. At least that's how I remember it. By contrast, Kathleen and I were both twenty-seven when we arrived and were married with three little children. This must have given the local congregation some sense that we were mature and could be trusted. Although I was not experienced as a pastor, I did have a wealth of experience in visiting churches as a speaker and singer, carrying out various duties at Lorne Park College, and before that even of dealing with customers in my brother's grocery store.

The congregation in Lexington accepted us warmly. Their delight in the children helped us in this respect. And Kathleen endeared herself to them by identifying with the congregation from the start. She is not one to promote herself, but her readiness to reach out to the people in quiet ways and include herself and the children regularly in the services and other activities was very affirming to the people. People know when they are liked and appreciated.

Average attendance was in the sixty-five range, topping one hundred for a special event a couple of times in the year. This latter number filled the little church. Usually twenty to twenty-five percent or so of those in attendance were from the seminary.

It was a large task: responsibility for three services a week plus visitation in the homes of the congregation, and hospital calling as needed. But I was in Kentucky to attend seminary; at the beginning of our time there, we had three activities on the go: finding a dwelling and getting our little family settled with a roof over their heads, becoming acquainted with a new congregation and the pastoral duties expected of me, and enrolling for a full academic load and getting classes under way.

Those seminary years, though valuable, were hard years. During our second year I developed health issues that made it difficult for me to keep up my demanding schedule. In my search for help I visited two or three doctors. One of them, noting my fatigue and night sweats, suspected tuberculosis and sent me for x-rays.

At that time, TB was more common in that area, and treatment involved staying in a sanitarium. Over a weekend as I awaited the x-ray results I reflected nervously on what it would mean for me to be separated from my family. But the x-rays came back negative, and I was finally referred to an allergist who traced several strange and debilitating symptoms to allergies. Once he put me under treatment, the symptoms settled down.

Raising children in a housing project presented interesting challenges. A neighbor in the unit across the walk from our back door had alcohol problems, and we saw the ravages of his drunken bouts close up. In the other direction across from our front door was a woman who lived alone until her husband came home to "renew their marriage." To celebrate he bought her some new furniture – on her credit. Later he flew into a rage, smashed the new furniture, and left.

Our five-year-old daughter saw two women get into a fistfight that landed one of them on the ground overpowered by the other. Ambulances came to the project often. Our children's trikes went missing and repeatedly had to be located and retrieved. But other neighbors, though poor, were stable people and like us were there for a temporary stay. We formed some passing friendships.

On April 2 of our final year of seminary our fourth child, John David, was born. From the start he made unusually great demands on our time and energies, especially during the night. His high-pitched and inconsolable crying until 3 a.m during most nights was wearing on us. Only after we left Kentucky did we learn of his profound retardation, which explained the night crying and other troubling symptoms.

We learned the full extent of his problem later, after we arrived at our appointment in Western Canada. Kathleen devoted much of her life for three years to caring for him until we found it necessary to place him in an institution that could give him the special care he needed. To the present he lives in a group home in Surrey, British Columbia.

Yet neither of us can recall that the heavy and demanding three-year load at seminary critically damaged the harmony of our home. There were the usual stresses, anxieties, children's squabbles and fevers, and hard decisions. But these were in the range of the normal. And later we bore together the pain of our loss of John David from our family.

During our seminary days, Kathleen, in her methodical way, kept the home orderly, the children well cared for, and meals on schedule so that domestic life remained basically predictable. And despite all that, she took an active part in the programs of the church.

Four days a week I left the apartment at seven in the morning to carpool the twenty miles to the seminary with two or three other seminarians. I did what studying I could while there. When I was home with the family I worked at a makeshift desk in our bedroom.

By my third year, we had to instruct our two little boys

that if the bedroom door was closed they were not to bother me. But on occasion when little pudgy hands tapped weakly at the door I opened it, sat on the floor, and gathered them into my arms to hear a recitation of their troubles. I could call it a study break and it was good for all three of us.

Three years of seminary was a priceless gift to our lives, and especially to mine. Courses piled one upon another let light in on areas of thought that were new to me. Old Testament books were opened up to my wonder and understanding. Classes gave me tools for Bible study, methods for theological reflection, lessons on how to communicate the gospel, an introduction to philosophy, and tips for administrating a church. What I was learning in Wilmore I could put into practice in a real living, breathing church not far away.

I learned things about myself during those three years that helped me to be a more effective servant of the Lord. There were painful times and joyful moments and there were occasions when I felt I had taken a step forward in keener self-understanding.

Kathleen and I had developed daily prayer and Bible-reading habits before arriving there, but the spiritual tone of the seminary enhanced those habits. As well, I found myself being taught by professors who were easy to look up to. They were role models whose excellence in their fields gave them strong credentials.

In a nutshell, three years in seminary sealed my sense that my life's calling was to be a pastor of God's people. This had crept up on me month by month. Each week I took what I was learning back to my congregational assignment. By using these lessons I tended to fix them in my mind.

I remember setting myself the goal of developing a "concept" for every aspect of pastoral life. Perhaps that goal was too sweeping. In any case, when I left the seminary in the summer of 1956 I did so with no other dream than to spend the rest of my life as a pastor in the service of the Lord.

Although Kathleen had not attended classes with me, she and I had discussed ongoing academic issues together often – doctrinal, psychological, and otherwise. She added her own insights. In fact, from the beginning of those discussions she held high ideals about the standards a pastor should meet both in conduct, performance, and appearance. She gently shared these insights with me and others as opportunities presented themselves. I continue to be their beneficiary.

Was this sense that I had been called to the pastoral office just a notion? In bearing witness to it openly had I simply talked myself into it? Was it in any sense an escape from some other more pressing duty? I recall that, during eighteen of our twenty-one years assigned to pastoral duties at the local level, we were invited repeatedly to consider several other positions in the Christian enterprise – inside the denomination but away from the local church. Several involved invitations to consider a college or seminary opportunity.

For example, during our thirteen years at the college church, there were thirteen such invitations. Though each had its special appeal, we steadfastly though graciously refused to leave a pastoral assignment for larger fields. We have no regrets.

~

Thus I have met the main purpose of this review: I have touched on certain highlights of two lives graciously reached by the saving grace of God as teenagers, called in the one case directly and in the other indirectly to a life of ministry in the pastoral office, and allowed by the grace of God to fulfill that commitment to full-time service together for a long string of decades.

I'll add here just a sketch of our ministries after seminary.

Upon my graduation, we packed our four children into our car. Then, towing all our earthly possessions behind us in a springless trailer, we joggled across the continent diagonally to New Westminster, British Columbia.

Visualize three little children without seat belts or car seats sharing the back seat, defending their territories, and enduring the long, tedious days across such large states as Kansas without the benefit of air conditioning. The front seat contained two adults and a little infant between us. For the three in the back we brought along distractions and applied our strategies to keep them occupied, but they had to be little soldiers to survive the long journey.

The journey lasted fourteen days, including one stop of ten days at Wabash Camp in Indiana. This took ingenuity.

For example, traveling with an infant on board before the days of Pampers, how do you keep a fresh supply of clean cloth diapers on hand day after day? Inventiveness came to our aid. Kathleen washed diapers thoroughly each night at our motel, wrung them out, and placed them in a basin. As we began the new day's travels, we each held a diaper out the window by one corner. The diapers dried quickly, and soon they were folded and fluffy white and we had a fresh supply for the new day. Oncoming drivers must have thought we were flying flags of surrender as we barreled toward them.

When we arrived at New Westminster, we found there a Free Methodist congregation eager for leadership. During five years of strenuous but fruitful pastoral labors in that city, 40,000 strong at the time, we saw significant growth in attendance, membership, giving, and especially in Sunday-school development. We carried out our labors with great joy.

After five years we were invited by a conference superintendent to lead the college church, my alma mater, in Greenville. The invitation had great appeal. At the same time it created conflict because of our deep commitments to the church we were serving. At the depth of our conflict I walked the streets of our city praying and wrestling with the decision.

I remember where I was when I finally decided. I was kneeling at a green platform chair in a vacant sanctuary. Even after making the decision to go, which I believed was in the will of the Lord, I was conflicted in my humanity, and by long distance telephone I sought the superintendent's release. At the same time we had determined that if not released, I would stand by the word I had given. The human element was strong and perplexing and the pull in both directions powerful.

When the decision was final and irreversible, we said our farewells with lumps in our throats, sold our car, and started eastward across Canada by train so we could take three children through the majestic mountains of British Columbia and across the vast Canadian prairies. We stopped in Ontario to visit Kathleen's mother and brother, Harold. Then we crossed the American border at Detroit, bought a used car, and traveled the final distance to Greenville.

I grieved for several months over the separation from our previous appointment. I'm not sure now whether leave-taking could have been less painful. I didn't know how to make it so. Even as I grieved privately, I was becoming more deeply involved in our new appointment.

One factor that contributed to the grieving was the significant cultural shift from Western Canada to the Midwest of the United States. But the Lord sustained us, held us steady, and helped us to sink our roots into the life of a new community. We served a wonderful congregation at the college church from 1961 to 1974. We were immersed in college life at all levels, but also had a growing ministry in the city and surrounding county. The service required of us was in some respects different from our previous appointment, but it continued in every sense to be pastoral.

In 1964, when I was thirty-eight years of age, the Free Methodist General Conference, meeting in Winona Lake, Indiana, elected me to the office of bishop. By that time I had been out of seminary for only eight years. I appreciated the honor very deeply but resigned the next day, declaring my action to be a matter of conscience and deep conviction. The passion for pastoral ministry continued with me. My resignation was a first in our denomination's history, and I was sure that my action would end any further useful ministry that I might be invited to give in the denomination. But the denomination was gracious and honored my conviction as expressed.

In 1974 I was elected again. By then I was forty-eight, and the Canadian delegates to General Conference had been urging me for some months to come and lead their branch of the denomination to General Conference status. At first I rejected the overtures, graciously but firmly. I asked myself, what about my call to pastoral ministry to which I was adhering so diligently?

But gradually I yielded to their entreaties. The church in Canada needed me, they said. I was a native son. I began to see that this might be an assignment I could carry out while keeping at its core a strong pastoral element. I was elected and served in that office for nineteen years – the first sixteen as a member of the five-person board of bishops over the North American general conference, while living in Canada, and for the last three years as the elected bishop of the newly formed Canadian conference.

Nineteen years is a long time to stay on course with so heavy and constant an assignment. In fact, mine was the longest tenure of any of our bishops since Bishop Leslie R. Marston's tenure had ended in his retirement in 1964. But his twenty-nine years of service in the office and the forty-nine years of Bishop William Pierce's term before him make my tenure seem relatively brief. During my tenure we enjoyed the blessing of serving in a pastoral mode both in Canada and the United States as well as in several overseas conferences.

By the grace of God, on August 2012, Kathleen and I completed twenty years of a very active retirement. It has been a very active retirement; by that same matchless grace, I continue to find opportunities to give pastoral service on both sides of the border, preaching, teaching, blogging, and writing for publication.

On December 20, 2012, also by the grace of God, Kathleen and I celebrated sixty-five years of marriage. Our prayer times together each morning after breakfast are wide-ranging and grow increasingly rich and renewing. In them we pray often for pastors who carry out the ministries of the pastoral office. Our prayers are that their love for Jesus Christ will continue to be their first love, undergirding all their strivings for excellence in their ministry for him.

www.ingramcontent.com/pod-product-compliance
Lightning Source LLC
Chambersburg PA
CBHW060515170426
43199CB00011B/1455

9781927483466